THE RUSSIAN CINEMA READER

Volume One

1908 to the Stalin Era

CULTURAL SYLLABUS

Series Editor:
MARK LIPOVETSKY (University of Colorado Boulder)

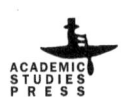

THE RUSSIAN CINEMA READER

Volume One

1908 to the Stalin Era

EDITED BY RIMGAILA SALYS

BOSTON / 2013

Library of Congress Cataloging-in-Publication Data:
A catalog record for this book is available from the Library of Congress.

ISBN 978-1-61811-212-5 (paperback)
ISBN 978-1-61811-213-2 (electronic)

Cover design by Ivan Grave
On the cover: Lion, *Battleship Potemkin*

Published by Academic Studies Press in 2013
28 Montfern Avenue
Brighton, MA 02135, USA

press@academicstudiespress.com
www.academicstudiespress.com

CONTENTS

LIST OF ILLUSTRATIONS

PREFACE

The *Russian Cinema Reader* is intended both for History of Russian Cinema and Russian Culture courses which emphasize film. The two volumes consist of period surveys and individual chapters on widely taught films (plus a few that I think *should* be taught), all of which are available with English subtitles. The period surveys provide historical context, outline genres, themes and emblematic aesthetic markers for each era, and give brief information on important films and directors not included in the reader. The chapters on individual films consist of general information on directors' careers, followed by commissioned essays and published criticism (both excerpts and complete essays) intended as starting points for class discussion, with suggested further readings appropriate to undergraduates. All film introductions without an author attribution were written by me. Except for Tengiz Abuladze's *Repentance*, a Georgian film which influenced the direction of Russian cinema, films of the former Soviet republics have not been included in the collection.

Readers will notice an unavoidable discrepancy in transliteration and formatting between newly commissioned and previously published material. Apart from accepted western spellings such as Tolstoy, Yeltsin, Meyerhold, Tarkovsky and Mosfilm, Russian names and terms in new essays have been transliterated according to the simplified Library of Congress system. To facilitate searching, bibliographic entries are cited in the same system. By necessity, the original editing, citation format and transliteration have mostly been retained for previously published essays.

For students who have not taken an introductory film studies course, Timothy Corrigan's *A Short Guide to Writing about Film* (Longman, 2012; also Kindle edition) is a useful text which covers film terminology, different approaches to writing about cinema, sources for research and guidelines for writing and formatting papers. The Yale Film Studies Film Analysis website 2.0 (http://

classes.yale.edu/film-analysis/) is an excellent resource for basic terms relating to mise-en-scène, cinematography, editing, sound and analysis, accompanied by illustrations and short clips. The most recent, comprehensive studies of Russian cinema are Birgit Beumers, *A History of Russian Cinema* (Oxford and New York: Berg, 2009) and N.M. Zorkaia, *Istoriia sovetskogo kino* (St. Petersburg: Aleteiia, 2005). A recent reference work is Peter Rollberg, *Historical Dictionary of Russian and Soviet Cinema* (Lanham, MD: The Scarecrow Press, Inc., 2009). All the films included in the reader are available from Russian or American distributors.

This reader would not have been possible without the expertise and generosity of the authors of the period introductions and newly commissioned essays, as well as the good will of authors who gave permission to include their published essays. I have learned from and been inspired by their work; this reader is intended to share their insights with students interested in Russian culture and film. I owe special thanks to Philip Rogers and Mark Leiderman for their unwavering support and advice, to Tim Riggs of the University of Colorado at Boulder who produced images for the reader, as well as to Kira Nemirovsky and her staff.

Rimgaila Salys
Boulder, 2013

ACKNOWLEDGMENTS

Beumers, Birgit, ed. *Directory of World Cinema. Russia*. Bristol, UK and Chicago: Intellect, 2011, pp. 37-41. Reprinted by permission of Intellect Press.

Bordwell, David. *The Cinema of Eisenstein*. New York and London: Routledge, 2005, pp. 43, 61-66, 68-74, 76-9. Reprinted with permission of Taylor and Francis Group, LLC-Books; permission conveyed through Copyright Clearance Center, Inc.

Bulgakova, Oksana. *Fabrika zhestov*. Moscow: NLO, 2005, pp. 71-2, 248-50, 252. Translated text published by permission of the author. Translated by Rimgaila Salys.

Graffy, Julian. *Bed and Sofa*. London and New York: I.B. Tauris, 2001, pp. 16-21, 25-9. Reprinted by permission of the author.

Hutchings, Stephen. "Chapaev." In *The Cinema of Russia and the Former Soviet Union*. Ed. Birgit Beumers, pp. 69-70, 72, 74-77. © Columbia University Press. Reprinted with permission of the publisher.

Kepley, Jr., Vance. "Mr. Kuleshov in the Land of the Modernists." In *The Red Screen. Politics, Society, Art in Soviet Cinema*. Ed. Anna Lawton. London and NY: Routledge, pp. 134, 136-37, 139, 140-42. © 1992 Routledge. Reproduced by permission of Taylor & Francis Books UK.

Kepley, Jr., Vance. *In the Service of the State. The Cinema of Alexander Dovzhenko*. Madison, WI: The University of Wisconsin Press, pp. 76-84. ©1986 by the Board of Regents of the University of Wisconsin System. Reprinted by permission of The University of Wisconsin Press.

Petrić, Vlada. "A Subtextual Reading of Kuleshov's Satire *The Extraordinary Adventures of Mr. West in the Land of the Bolsheviks (1924)*." In *Inside Soviet Film Satire: Laughter with a Lash*. Ed. Andrew Horton. Cambridge: Cambridge University Press, pp. 68-72. © Cambridge University Press 1993. Reprinted with the permission of Cambridge University Press.

Salys, Rimgaila. "Life into Art: Laying Bare the Theme in *Bed and Sofa*." *Russian Language Journal*, Vol. 52, Nos. 171-73 (1998): 291-303. Reprinted by permission of the *Russian Language Journal*.

Acknowledgments

Salys, Rimgaila. *The Musical Comedy Films of Grigorii Aleksandrov.* Bristol, UK and Chicago: Intellect Press, 2009, pp. 168-69, 171-73, 177-78, 180-82. Reprinted by permission of Intellect Press.

Tsivian, Yuri. "New Notes on Russian Film Culture between 1908 and 1919." In *The Silent Cinema Reader.* Eds. Lee Grieveson and Peter Krämer. London and New York: Routledge, 2004. Reprinted by permission of the author.

IMAGE CREDITS

PART
ONE

EARLY RUSSIAN CINEMA 1908-1919

Denise J. Youngblood

The history of pre-revolutionary Russian cinema was little known outside Russia until the 1990s, with most scholarship on Russian films focusing on Soviet cinema in the 1920s. As a result of the 1989 Pordenone Film Festival, an annotated catalogue of surviving early Russian films, Yuri Tsivian's *Silent Witnesses: Russian Films 1908-1919* appeared.[1] In 1992 the British Film Institute, in conjunction with the Library of Congress, preserved a number of these films, which were also released on videotape by Milestone Films. As a result, there is now a small but important body of research available in English on this subject, and work continues. The purpose of this essay is to provide an overview, starting with a brief history of early Russian cinema, followed by a survey of some of the major films.

History

The final decade of imperial Russia was a time of social tumult and political discord that led to war in 1914 and two revolutions in 1917. This was the era in which Russian cinema was born. Although films were first shown in Russia five months after they appeared in France, on May 4, 1896, this momentous date did not mark the beginnings of a truly *Russian* cinema. For the next twelve years, foreign movies were the only ones shown on Russian screens, a good example of the west's cultural imperialism. In 1908, a Russian photographer, Aleksandr Drankov, released the first Russian film, *Sten'ka Razin,* based on the legendary seventeenth-century cossack rebel. Although *Sten'ka Razin* was primitive compared to French

---

[1]   Yuri Tsivian, *Silent Witnesses,* in Further Reading.

production, and to our eyes, more than a bit comical, Drankov's production spurred the development of a native film industry.

Filmmaking took off, with 19 films made in 1909, quickly rising to 102 in 1912.[2] Only about one-third of these films were acted; the vast majority were newsreels or other films based on factual material. Of the acted films, most were short literary adaptations of well-known stories, plays, or poems; audiences were expected to know the plot before they came to the movies. By 1912, Russian cinema had its first full-length hit: Vasilii Goncharov's *The Defense of Sevastopol'* (*Oborona Sevastopolia*), which ran one and one-half hours, a length that critics believed Russian audiences would not tolerate. By 1913, when the box office sensation, Iakov Protazanov and Vladimir Gardin's *The Keys to Happiness* (*Kliuchi schast'ia*) appeared, clocking in at over three hours and shown in two parts, more and more Russian films were feature films that lasted at least an hour. Although historical movies and adaptations from literary classics remained popular, after 1913 most blockbusters came from the pages of best-selling contemporary prose writers.

Despite these successes, it is important to remember that on the eve of World War I in 1914, foreign films, especially from Italy, Germany and France, continued to dominate the Russian market. One might think that the advent of war would be calamitous for a fledgling art form deemed frivolous by many critics. Fortunately for Russian cinema, the opposite was true.

The closing of Russia's borders made trade exceedingly difficult, even with its allies. In one sense the new trade barriers were harmful to the industry, which had relied on German equipment and film stock. The American company Kodak took up part of the slack, and despite occasional shortages that increased as the war went on, native film production boomed. In 1914, production nearly doubled from 1913, to 230 films. By 1916, the country was producing 500 films a year.[3] These films were shown in 4,000 movie theaters nationwide,

---

[2]   N.A. Lebedev, *Ocherk istorii kino SSSR*, vol. 1, *Nemoe kino* (Moscow: Goskinoizdat, 1947), 15.

[3]   Lebedev, 35; S.S. Ginzburg, *Kinematografiia dorevoliutsionnoi Rossii* (Moscow:

to 2 million viewers per day.[4] One must remember, however, that the movies in Russia were primarily an urban phenomenon; cinema had yet to become a mass art as it would be in the 1920s.

This dramatic increase in production created new opportunities for Russian actors, and Russian stars began to compete with their European counterparts for the affections of Russian audiences. The kings of early Russian cinema were Vladimir Maksimov, Vitol'd Polonskii, and especially the fabled Ivan Mozzhukhin. The ranks of the queens included Natal'ia Lisenko, Vera Karalli, Ol'ga Gzovskaia and the eternal favorite, Vera Kholodnaia.[5]

The boom in business masked some serious difficulties. The shortages in film stock were a real problem, and a black market in supplies developed, with black market prices. This allowed only the major studios to survive: most of the smaller ones were driven out of business in 1916, when the majors snapped up a shipment of Kodak film.[6]

Genre development was uneven. The historical films that had been so popular prior to World War I lost their cachet during the war, being seen as too sedate. Film adaptations from literature remained popular, but more and more often were adapted from contemporary, rather than classical, literature, as noted above. This reflected the tastes of the audiences, as we can see by comparing film with the other arts. Just as serialized novels drew large readerships in the penny press, serialized adventure films like *Son'ka the "Golden Hand"* (*Son'ka zolotaia ruchka*) drew spectators in droves. Erotic melodramas with mystical or even satanic flourishes also were as popular with movie viewers as they were with readers. (These were common motifs in Silver Age culture as a whole.)

Native comedy continued to lag behind the popularity of French films, especially those of the French comedic star Max Linder. However, comedians who modeled themselves after

---

Iskusstvo, 1963), 157.

[4]   Ginzburg, 158.

[5]   Lebedev, 46.

[6]   Ginzburg, 170-71.

popular western stars came to the forefront during the war. "Antosha" (Anton Fertner) reputedly modeled Charlie Chaplin while "Arkasha" (Arkadii Boitler) imitated the antics of John Bunny, known in Russia as "Fat Man Pokson."[7]

The most curious feature of Russian wartime filmmaking was the absence of war films. From August through December 1914, 50 of 103 pictures were war pictures that celebrated patriotism. After that, interest in war films quickly evaporated, undoubtedly a reflection of declining public support for the tsarist regime. In 1915, only 21 feature films were on war-related themes; in 1916, 13; in 1917, none, unless one counts Evgenii Bauer's *The Revolutionary* (*Revoliutsioner*).

The newfound strength of Russian films during the war notwithstanding, European filmmaking continued to exert a profound influence on Russian filmmakers and audiences. French films, like Max Linder's comedies or the *Fantomas* detective-adventure series, were preeminent, spawning Russian imitators. Extremely popular but impossible for Russian directors to copy were Italian costume dramas from the life of ancient Rome, which were considered to be the height of good taste and elegance by more discerning movie-goers. In addition, the "psychologism" of Danish cinema made a significant impact on Russian cinematic style, particularly in the contemporary melodramas.[8]

American influence became strong late in the war. The eminent Russian director Iakov Protazanov had seen some of D. W. Griffith's work, and Russian directors generally admired American editing styles.[9] The Khokhlovkin distribution company brought the films of the well-known comic actors such as Charlie Chaplin and Fatty Arbuckle to the attention of Russian moviegoers.[10] Other wartime

---

[7]   R. Sobolev, *Liudi i fil'my russkogo dorevoliutsionnogo kino* (Moscow: Iskusstvo, 1961), 154, 159.

[8]   Ginzburg, 137-38.

[9]   Ibid., 140.

[10]   Ibid., 213, 261.

American hits included Tom Mix westerns and Pearl White adventure serials.[11]

By 1917, Russian cinema, like everything else in Russia, was in deep crisis, and if anything, the February Revolution exacerbated that crisis. Shortages had plagued the industry since 1915, but now the shortage of electricity and film stock became acute. Studios began to fail; only nine survived, most important among them Khanzhonkov, Ermol'ev, and Rus'.[12] American pictures began to take over, especially escapist movies to divert people's attention from their problems. Studio heads organized a union to protect their interests. Unions for film crews, publishers, theater owners, and distributors followed. Despite this grassroots movement toward collectivism, the Bolsheviks, upon coming to power in October 1917, moved to shut the film unions down, labeling them "reactionary" and "counterrevolutionary."[13]

The Bolsheviks, who would later use cinema to their political advantage, were extremely hostile to early Russian commercial cinema, seeing it as decadent. They temporarily closed movie theaters in November and December 1917, citing a lack of electricity. Studio heads sensed trouble, and the exodus of film companies to the Crimea, where the counterrevolutionary White armies were gathering, began in spring 1918. Despite all this disruption, the 1917 box office broke previous records. Taking the skyrocketing inflation into account, which had caused a 50 percent increase in ticket prices in 1917, the box office was 33 percent higher in 1917 than in 1916, which was also a banner year.[14]

It is commonly supposed that only Bolshevik-sponsored organizations made films after October 1917. In fact, private studios continued producing, making 352 films in the period of 1917-1921,

---

[11]   B.S. Likhachev, "Materialy k istorii kino v Rossii (1914-1916)," in *Iz istorii kino*, vol. 3 (Moscow: Iskusstvo, 1960), 65-67.

[12]   Ginzburg, 320.

[13]   Ibid., 323-31.

[14]   Ibid., 322.

with most appearing in 1918-1919.[15] This was far from the 500 films produced in 1916 alone, but considering the political and economic tumult, the number is impressive. The Bolsheviks were concerned enough to restore film censorship in June 1918.[16]

Most of the films that were banned were prohibited for moral, not political, reasons, particularly as pornography. Only 6 of the 32 banned films were prohibited for political content.[17] The problem was not, therefore, that the studios were making explicitly anti-Bolshevik films. In fact, they continued to produce sensational melodramas of four basic kinds: the Satan genre, the "God Seekers" genre (about the occult, mysticism, and the sexual shenanigans of monks and nuns), historical pictures, and the sex-and-suicide melodrama.[18]

The Film Repertory

It is difficult to be certain which films were authentic hits. Most movie reviews of the time appeared in studio journals, where almost every picture was labeled a *chef d'oeuvre*. Advertising was hyperbolic in the extreme, as this example from 1915 shows:

> "Sensation! Sensation! Sensation!
> Attention! Attention! Attention!
> Hit! Hit! Hit!
> Monopoly! Monopoly! Monopoly!"[19]

---

[15] *Sovetskie khudozhestvennye fil'my: Annotirovannyi katalog*, vol. 3 (Moscow: Iskusstvo, 1966), 248-306; 42 of these are extant either in whole or in part.

[16] Kate Betz, "As Tycoons Die: Class Struggle and Censorship in the Russian Cinema, 1917-1921," in Nils Ake Nilsson, ed., *Art, Society and Revolution: Russia:1917-1921* (Stockholm: Almqvist and Wiksell, 1979), 217. Richard Taylor notes that some censorship existed in Moscow as early as March 1918, "Agitation, Propaganda, and the Cinema," in Nilsson, 242.

[17] Betz, 221-22.

[18] Ibid., 212-13.

[19] V.D., "Mutnaia voda—iz sluchainogo khlama," *Proektor* 1., no. 3 (1 November 1915): 7.

Based on the advertisements that appeared in the film journals of the time, audiences appear to have selected which films to see based on directors (Evgenii Bauer, Petr Chardynin, Vladimir Gardin and Iakov Protazanov were the names most often advertised), stars (like Ivan Mozzhukhin or Vera Kholodnaia), and especially writers. If popular writers like Leonid Andreev, Mikhail Artsybashev, or Anastasiia Verbitskaia had their works adapted to the screen, then their names were always featured much more prominently than even the actors' or director's.[20]

As already mentioned, the indisputable blockbuster of pre-revolutionary cinema was Protazanov and Gardin's *The Keys to Happiness*, a two-part adaptation of Anastasiia Verbitskaia's best-selling novel. The film follows the sexual and romantic adventures of Mania, a young and bold example of the "new woman." Her attempts at navigating this unsettled world proving unsuccessful, she commits suicide.

Unfortunately, no print of this famous film has survived, but its role in the development of Russian cinema cannot be overestimated. It showed that Russian audiences had the attention span necessary to sit through a full-length film and would pay handsomely for the privilege. It showed theater owners that one solid full-length film (albeit one with an "insane" box office) could earn more than the traditional four-to-five short film program.[21] Finally, it forced theater owners to advertise the times the film would be showing, rather than merely when they opened. This suggested to viewers that they needed to come "on time," rather than walking in whenever the fancy struck them, as had been the practice previously.[22]

The Thiemann & Reinhardt studio's advertising campaign was extensive, but relatively restrained. One four-page spread contained

---

[20] For example, the advertisements for *Vavochka* and *Muzh* in *Sine-fono* 8, nos. 1/2 (25 October 1914).

[21] See the advertisement in *Sine-fono* 14 (15 April 1912): 37 and Ivan Perestiani's recollections of the film in his *75 let v iskusstve* (Moscow, 1960), 248.

[22] Yuri Tsivian, *Early Cinema in Russia and Its Cultural Reception*, ed. Richard Taylor, trans. Alan Bodger (London, 1994), 39-40.

only the studio's name on the first and last pages, with the centerfold pages giving only the studio's name and Verbitskaia's.[23] (The names of the co-directors were conspicuous by their absence; Protazanov told Gardin that Thiemann feared another studio's poaching them.)[24]

The studio was clearly anticipating a big hit. The film was printed in 27 copies and sold for 35,000 rubles, with the studio also getting a cut from the box office.[25] Gardin reported that the studio earned a net profit of 200,000 rubles, a "colossal" sum that enabled it to embark on a major renovation.[26] The cinema press was unanimously enthusiastic in its praise, and theater owners declared it a film up to European standards.[27] One Soviet film historian labeled it a "mega-hit" that led to the new practice of advance ticket sales, with tickets even being sold for standing room.[28] Thereafter every film's box office success was compared to that of *The Keys to Happiness.*

By looking at which films were most widely distributed for longer durations, it is possible to infer other hits. Naturally, *The Keys to Happiness* led to other adaptations of best-selling "sensational" fiction, like Artsybashev's *Jealousy* (*Revnost'*) and *The Husband* (*Muzh*), both of which played multiple venues.[29] The father of Russian cinema, Aleksandr Drankov, produced a series of adventure films based on the legends of the "famous Russian adventuress" and thief Sonia Bliuvshtein, called *Son'ka the "Golden Hand."* Drankov advertised extensively in the respectable Russian daily newspaper *The Russian Word* (*Russkoe slovo*); apparently this campaign was successful. Theater advertisements show that the

[23]　See *Kine-zhurnal* 19 (5 September 1913): 57-60.

[24]　V. R. Gardin and T.D. Bulakh, *Zhizn' i trud artista* (Moscow: Iskusstvo, 1960), 121.

[25]　V.R. Gardin and T.D. Bulakh, *Vospominaniia* (Moscow: Goskinoizdat, 1949), 59.

[26]　Ibid., 60; Gardin and Bulakh, *Zhizn' i trud artista*, 115, 121.

[27]　"Khronika," *Kine-zhurnal* 4, no. 21 (2 November 1913), 38.

[28]　Likhachev, 121-23.

[29]　Advertisements in *Russkoe slovo* (19 January 1914) and (8 March 1915).

film's first installment played in *eleven* of Moscow's finest movie palaces simultaneously.[30] The success of the *Son'ka* series was followed in quick order by the Ermol'ev adventure serial, *Sashka the Seminary Student (Sashka seminarist)*. Although it, too, was screened in multiple theaters, a segment of the *Son'ka* series quickly ousted *Sashka*.[31]

The best way to present the variety of ways a Russian film could become a hit is to take a more in-depth look at some of the works of its two greatest directors, Iakov Protazanov and Evgenii Bauer. Protazanov (1881-1945) was the grandson of a wealthy Moscow merchant and as such was expected to join the family business. Instead, he went abroad to Paris in 1905, where he became acquainted with the Pathé studio.[32] In 1908, he began working as an interpreter for the Russian Gloria studio, translating for the cameraman. He acted in a few films and wrote screenplays before becoming a director in 1912 for the Thiemann & Reinhardt studio. He co-directed *The Passing of the Great Old Man (Ukhod velikogo startsa, 1912)*, a story of Lev Tolstoy's last days, with Elizaveta Thiemann. The film, which cost the extraordinary amount of 40,000 rubles, became embroiled in a lawsuit brought by the Tolstoy family.[33] Because of the publicity this generated, Protazanov immediately became a big name director. Until 1915, he frequently co-directed with Vladimir Gardin.

We have already discussed Protazanov and Gardin's biggest hit, *The Keys to Happiness*. After this Protazanov could have continued to churn out potboilers, but he chose a different path, becoming perhaps the most versatile of Russian directors. He

30   *Russkoe slovo* (10 January 1915).

31   *Kine-zhurnal* 10 (17 May 1914): 114; no. 23/24 (23 December 1914): 4; *Russkoe slovo* (3 January 1915).

32   For more on Protazanov's early life see Denise J. Youngblood, *Movies for the Masses: Popular Cinema and Soviet Society in the 1920s* (Cambridge: Cambridge University Press, 1992), 106-08.

33   "Khronika," *Kine-zhurnal* 3, no. 20 (23 October 1912): 20, and Likhachev, 104-06.

directed adaptations from Russian literary classics as often as from contemporary Russian literature.

Alexander Pushkin was a favorite author for studios looking for "prestige" productions. Pushkin's literary reputation was unsurpassed, and unlike living writers, he could not sue for infringement of author's rights. His story *The Queen of Spades* (*Pikovaia dama*) was produced by the powerful Ermol'ev studio, which became known for its artistic and technical quality. Ermol'ev chose Protazanov to direct this big-budget picture, and Protazanov cast the brightest male star of the Russian screen, Ivan Mozzhukhin, as the story's anti-hero, Herman. The film was probably the Ermol'ev studio's biggest hit (Fig. 1).[34]

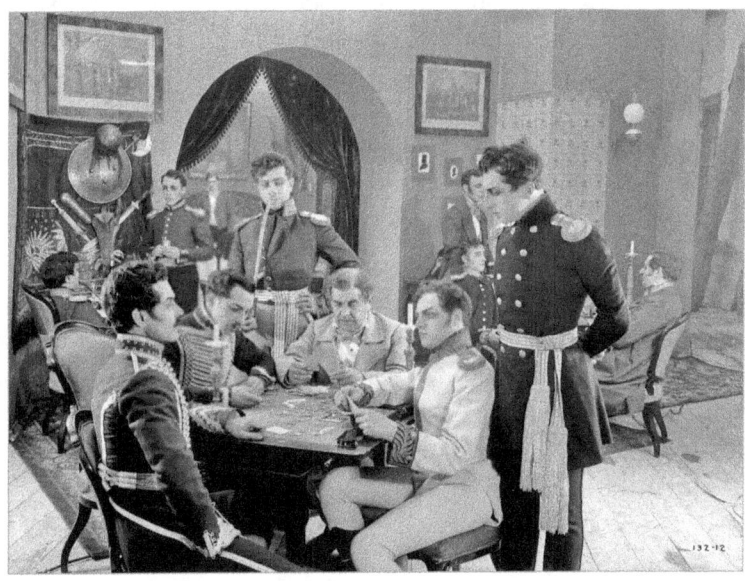

Fig. 1. Herman Watches the Card Game

This tale of an officer who is willing to seduce an innocent girl in order to learn from her guardian, an elderly countess, the sequence of three cards guaranteed to win the card game *chemin de fer* has two

---

[34]   G., *"Pikovaia dama,"* *Kine-zhurnal* 7, no. 7/8 (30 April 1916): 52.

tragedies: the death of the countess from fright as Herman steals into her bedroom and Herman's descent into madness after he lost all his money by playing the queen of spades. Protazanov used all the cinematic tricks available to relate Pushkin's compelling story. There are two important flashbacks. When a fellow officer recounts to Herman the countess's story, we see it as a story within a story. The second is a flashback as a dream: while the countess remembers herself as a beautiful young woman with many lovers, Protazanov utilizes the split screen to show Herman in the present, along with Herman's fevered imagination of his winnings. The use of cross-cutting, as in the scene where Herman waits for the countess to return from a ball, is unusually sophisticated for the times. The fade shot and superimposition are also used, the first to represent the countess's ghost, the second, to replace the queen of spades' face with the countess's on the losing card.

Another example of Protazanov's finest work is *Father Sergius* (*Otets Sergii*). Made in 1917, it was not, however, released until 1918 due to the temporary closure of movie theaters after the October Revolution. Protazanov had long wanted to adapt Tolstoy's story of a naïve, self-centered young officer who becomes a monk and faith healer, but could not until the censorship lifted. (The story had been considered too incendiary to film because of the highly negative portrayal of Tsar Nicholas I and the Russian Orthodox Church as well as Father Sergius's inability to control his sexual desires.) The picture earned its place in film history primarily due to Ivan Mozzhukhin's brilliant portrayal of the title character, whose sexual obsession ultimately proves to be his salvation. Despite Sergius's ambitious, narcissistic attempts to become the holiest of all monks, he cannot escape his sexual impulses and memories of his beautiful fiancée, who had been the tsar's mistress, which Protazanov renders in flashbacks. The film's most famous scene, in which the glamorous and frivolous Madame Makovkina (played by Mozzhukhin's real life wife, Natal'ia Lisenko) attempts to seduce Sergius, is deeply erotic. Although she fails, Sergius's battle with fleshly desires is not over. Twenty years later, his reputation as a faith healer brings him into contact with a merchant's lascivious, mentally unbalanced daughter. Sergius rapes her—or in a more charitable interpretation, is seduced by her. As he is looking for an ax to murder her for "luring" him to sin, he is stopped by a fellow monk who offers to chop wood for him. This is Sergius's epiphany. He leaves the monastery to become a pilgrim. Eventually he is arrested and deported to Siberia, where he lives out his days as a truly humble man.

Protazanov also made films that for Soviet film historians epitomized the "decadence" of bourgeois cinema. His full-scale, two-part blockbuster, *Satan Triumphant* (*Satana likuiushchii*, 1917), was in a class by itself and exemplified the marked turn toward apocalypticism in revolutionary Russian society. It also reflected late imperial Russia's fascination with Satanism.[35] In this film, the great Ivan Mozzhukhin plays both a fire-and-brimstone pastor and his son Sandro. A lost traveler arrives, and it quickly becomes clear that he is Satan. Sexual strife threatens to destroy the household, as the pastor sleeps with his married sister-in-law. The child that is born from this unholy union, Sandro, becomes a famous pianist, eventually selling his soul to the devil. Much shocking behavior results, including sexual misadventures. Although critics were divided on the merits of this film, Mozzhukhin received kudos for his acting, one critic describing him as "virtually the most exciting screen actor in the Moscow pléiade."[36]

However, the best of Protazanov's post-revolution films made for the Ermol'ev studio is *Little Ellie* (*Maliutka Elli*), arguably the greatest film of his "bourgeois" period. A psychological melodrama about a child rapist-murderer, the film stars Ivan Mozzhukhin as the predator. *Little Ellie* takes the preoccupation of Russian cinema with sexual degradation to a new extreme, but was also an intricate work, constructed with multiple flashbacks. Mozzhukhin plays Norton, the unnamed town's mayor, who in the opening scene is examining his bruised arm and torn shirtsleeve.

---

35 Kristi A. Groberg, "The Shade of Lucifer's Dark Wing: Satanism in Silver Age Russia," in Bernice Glatzer Rosenthal, ed., *The Occult in Russian and Soviet Culture* (Ithaca, NY: Cornell University Press, 1997), 99-133.

36 Tsivian, *Silent Witnesses*, 422-26.

Next we learn that a young girl has been found murdered in the woods. This is Ellie, the little sister of Clara, soon to become Norton's fiancée. Her murder remains unsolved, but Norton, stricken with panic attacks, starts acting very strangely. He is disturbed enough to decide to commit suicide, but as he sits down to write the note, he writes a confession to the murder instead. Surprised by Clara as he is writing, he manages to hide the incriminating letter.

After that his psychological condition enters a downward spiral. Here Protazanov inserts flashbacks, first of the history of his relationship with Clara and Ellie, second the image of the dead child lying on the path disturbs his sleep, and third, the chilling recreation of the crime. Here Protazanov and Mozzhukhin penetrate the mind of a pedophile. He had, after all, turned to Ellie for "love," when he believed that Clara was not responding to his affections. The little girl was flattered by his grown-up attentions and in Norton's twisted mind, she flirted with him at a party he escorted her to. On the day of the murder, Norton had been drinking heavily. He meets Ellie on her way home from school and persuades her to take a path through the woods. He begins kissing and caressing her; she bites his arm and breaks away. As he chases the terrified child, he is caught in blurred close-up, the camera tracking him as he runs. Norton tells Clara that Ellie's death was an accident: she tripped and fell while running away from him. Clara goes to the police station with the confession, but changes her mind and burns it. Norton commits suicide.

This is quite a stunning film. Rather than focusing on the victim, *Little Ellie* provides a chilling psychological portrait of the perpetrator. It is sensational, but not exploitative and still has the power to shock nearly a century later. As one *Cinema Gazette* (*Kinogazeta*) reviewer noted, the final flashback produces an "unpleasant sensation" of "excessive tension and intensity."[37]

Although Protazanov was a highly talented director who made some remarkable films, Evgenii Bauer (1865-1917) was certainly the most original talent of early Russian cinema. He was the acknowl-

---

[37]   Tsivian, *Silent Witnesses*, 466-70.

edged master of the contemporary melodrama. A painter, photographer and set designer before he became a film director, Bauer came from an artistic family of Czech origin. Bauer worked briefly for the French firm Pathé before joining the eminent Khanzhonkov studio in 1913. His salary was reputedly the princely sum of 40,000 rubles a year, which (if true) made him Russia's highest paid director. He was Khanzhonkov's star director, and his untimely death after an accident in summer 1917 was a serious blow to the artistic aspirations of the Russian film industry. Bauer's visual style was so distinctive that his contemporaries used the term "Bauer film" to describe it. He was praised as being not only one of the best Russian directors, but also one of the best European directors of the time.[38]

Many of Bauer's films fit into the "sex and suicide" category that was so popular after *The Keys to Happiness*. A brilliant early example is *Twilight of a Woman's Soul* (*Sumerki zhenskoi dushi*, 1913), a full-length feature co-produced by Khanzhonkov and Pathé. The picture has a sensational plot. Vera, a beautiful young noblewoman, is raped by a working-class ruffian whom she encounters on a charity mission. She finally decides to reveal her terrible secret to her handsome fiancé, Prince Dol'skii. But the letter she writes goes astray, and so the prince does not learn about the rape until after the wedding. His disgust is palpable, and she leaves him. Years pass, during which Dol'skii has become a dissolute playboy, while Vera has transformed herself into "Ellen Kay," a famous actress. When they meet at the opera, he realizes that he still loves her, but she rejects him. He returns home and shoots himself in the heart.

This quintessential "Bauer film" transcends its clichés. It is a remarkable combination of Bauer's aestheticism, with its elaborate mise-en-scène, and realism, with its vivid depiction of urban poverty. It is characterized by long takes and painterly compositions that may make the film seem too slow to the twenty-first-century viewer; indeed, even some of his contemporaries found his pacing

---

[38] "E.F. Bauer," *Kine-zhurnal*, nos. 11/16 (30 August 1917): 104.

too slow. Nevertheless, Bauer was an innovator. Camera and lighting techniques in the film are quite modern, with light and shadow employed for psychological effect. Bauer eschewed the static long shots that many of his peers used, favoring the close-up and the tracking camera. One scene was even shot in deep focus.

Bauer continued to develop his favorite motif of strong woman/weak man in his 1914 film *Child of the Big City* (*Ditia bol'shogo goroda*). Here he deals with the corrupting influences of urban life more directly than he did in the *Twilight of a Woman's Soul*. Again the plot sounds clichéd. Mania, a poor orphan girl who has come to the city to find work, becomes the mistress of a rich young man, Viktor. Viktor transforms sweet and innocent Mania into "Mary," a cold and heartless spendthrift who cares only about his money. When he loses it, Mary abandons him and takes up with his friends. The degraded and obsessed Viktor tries to see her one last time, but she refuses. He shoots himself.

In 1915, Bauer made one of the stranger films in early Russian cinema, *Daydreams* (*Grezy*). Viktor, a well-to-do gentleman, is obsessed with his late wife Elena, keeping her clothes and other mementoes, including her luxurious long tresses, which he keeps in a glass box. Out on a walk, Viktor spies a woman who looks remarkably like Elena and follows her. She turns out to be an actress, Tina, whom Viktor is convinced is the reincarnation of his dead wife. Tina, a calculating soubrette, is determined to take whatever advantage she can of the besotted Viktor. Although Viktor will not give Tina Elena's clothing and jewelry, he does allow her to dress up in them so that her portrait can be painted. Eventually, Tina is exhausted by Viktor's compulsions. When she urges him to lie down with his dead wife, Viktor beats her, which provokes Tina to grab the sacred hair and to dance around the room mockingly, the hair wrapped around her neck like a boa. Enraged, Viktor strangles her with it.

During World War I, hints of necrophilia in the movies became common enough to concern some critics, who feared a societal backlash as directors and producers continued to push the limits of what was acceptable. The mysticism and interest in the supernatural that characterized Russian society at this time

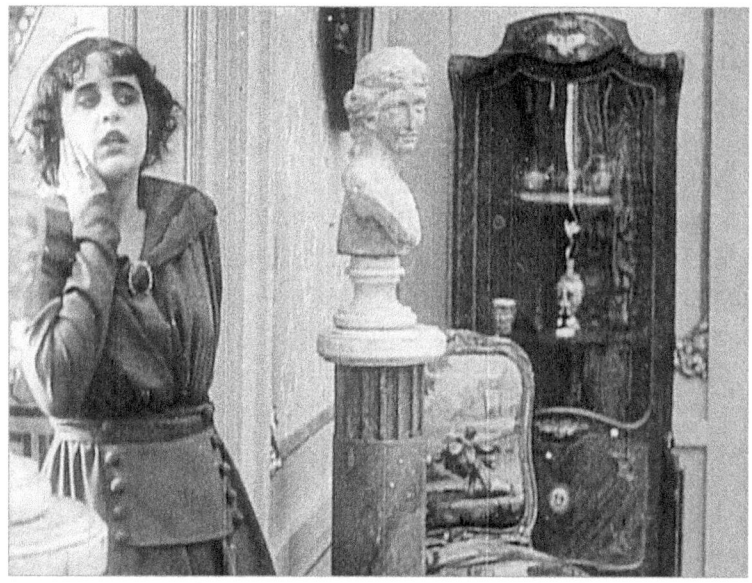

Fig. 2. Nata Learns that the Prince is to Marry

also figured prominently in the film;[39] Elena's ghost appears to Viktor on two occasions. The murder of the bold and vivacious Tina, who represents a danger to the social order, seems justified: she has driven the inherently decent Viktor to a crime born of madness.

A Life for a Life (*Zhizn' za zhizn'*, 1916) is arguably Bauer's greatest picture (Fig. 2). Based on the novel by the French writer Georges Ohnet, *A Life for a Life* featured an all-star cast: Vera Kholodnaia as Nata, the adopted daughter of a wealthy businesswoman; Vitol'd Polonskii as her lover Prince Bartinskii; Ivan Perestiani as her husband Zhurov, a rich merchant; Lidiia Koreneva as Musia; and Ol'ga Rakhmanova as Mme Khromova, Musia's mother and woman of affairs. Two young women, Nata and Musia, have grown up like sisters in the Khromov household, but both love the same man, the dissolute Prince Bartinskii. Nata becomes his lover; Musia becomes his wife. The prince's behavior as a married man confirms

---

[39]   Groberg, 115-16.

Mme Khromova's worst fears. Soon after his wedding, Bartinskii and Nata resume their affair, even though Nata has married the merchant Zhurov.

The film comes to a climax when Nata's husband Zhurov discovers that Bartinskii has forged Zhurov's signature to cover one of his gambling debts. A trap is laid to capture the lovers in Nata's bedroom. Zhurov had planned to kill them both but decided instead to have Bartinskii arrested for fraud. As police surround the house, Mme Khromova gives her son-in-law his pistol and tells him to "be a man." He refuses, so Khromova takes the gun and kills him, putting the weapon in his hand to make it look like a suicide.

Although Kholodnaia, perhaps feeling ill at ease in the unsympathetic role of Nata, did not command the screen with her usual panache, the acting of the other principals is outstanding, especially that of Lidiia Koreneva as Musia. The framing and staging of individual scenes represent some of Bauer's finest work as is his use of cross-cutting and parallel structures. As always in a Bauer film, set design and decoration are elaborate. One critic remarked, only half jokingly, "Columns, columns, columns...columns in the parlor, in the office and on the fireplace, columns here, there, and everywhere."[40] The reviews of the film were so good that the Khanzhonkov studio compiled excerpts that were then published in *The Cinematographic Herald* (*Vestnik kinematografii*).[41] Even the arch-rival Ermol'ev studio praised it in its journal *Projector* (*Proektor*), but could not refrain from alleging that the film was "too western."[42]

By the end of 1919, it was clear to many Russian filmmakers that the Whites would likely lose the Civil War, and that the Bolsheviks, with their very different ideas about cinema, were in Russia to stay. Filmmakers began to emigrate, to Paris, Berlin, Prague, San Francisco, among other places. Most were unsuccess-

---

40   "Sredi novinok," *Kine-zhurnal*, no 9/10 (29 May 1916): 52. An excerpt from this review appears in Tsivian, *Silent Witnesses*, 326-28.

41   "*Zhizn' za zhizn'*," *Vestnik kinematografii* 118 (June 1916): 19-21.

42   Tsivian, *Silent Witnesses*, 328.

ful in reestablishing their film careers, although there were a few exceptions.[43] This emigration marked the end of a flourishing early film industry. The traditions were, however, carried on by the filmmakers who stayed in Soviet Russia, like Petr Chardynin, Vladimir Gardin, Lev Kuleshov and Ivan Perestiani, and those who returned, most notably Iakov Protazanov.

Further Reading

Ivanova, V., et al., eds. *Velikii Kinemo: Katalog sokhranivshikhsia igrovykh fil'mov Rossii (1908-1919)*. Moscow: Novoe literaturnoe obozrenie, 2003.

Taylor, Richard, and Ian Christie, eds. *The Film Factory: Russian and Soviet Cinema in Documents, 1896-1939*. Translated by Richard Taylor. Cambridge, MA: Harvard University Press, 1988.

Tsivian, Yuri. *Early Cinema in Russia and Its Cultural Reception*. Edited by Richard Taylor. Translated by Alan Bodger. London: Routledge, 1994.

------. *Silent Witnesses: Russian Films, 1908-1919*. Edited by Paolo Cherchi Usai, Lorenzo Codelli, Carlos Montanaro, and David Robinson. London: British Film Institute/Pordenone: Edizioni Biblioteca dell'Immagine, 1989.

Youngblood, Denise J. *The Magic Mirror: Moviemaking in Russia, 1908-1918*. Madison: University of Wisconsin Press, 1999.

Further Viewing

Early Russian Cinema. 10 vols. DVD format. Milestone Films, 2010.

Mad Love: The Films of Evgeni Bauer. Image Entertainment, 2003.

---

43 The Ermol'ev studio reemerged in France as "Albatross"; Protazanov continued to work for it before he returned to Soviet Russia in 1924. Mozzhukhin acted in French silent cinema but did not transition to sound.

NEW NOTES ON RUSSIAN FILM CULTURE BETWEEN 1908 AND 1919

Yuri Tsivian

A first encounter with Russian films of the 1910s can be puzzling: their stories seem to be moving at a wrong pace and in the wrong direction. Was this cinema out of tune with what was going on elsewhere at that time? Has this something to do with Russian culture at large? Such are the questions I will be looking at in the following notes—not to provide a detailed portrayal of "Russian style," but to highlight those of its features that set it apart from the general practice of the teens.

I call these notes new for the following reason. My first attempt at an essay like this took place thirteen years ago in an introduction to *Silent Witnesses*, the catalogue of surviving Russian films prepared for a retrospective at the Silent Film Festival in Pordenone[1]; it was that essay (or, rather, its extended version of 1991[2]) that I was asked to contribute to the present anthology. As I reread what I wrote I was pleased to discover how far away our field—the field of early film studies—has got from the level of knowledge we had then. Here was my chance not to revise or rewrite, but to overwrite that old essay, correcting its mistakes and challenging my own assumptions. The result is not simply a mixture of old and new. I kept the facts and quotes I found worth repeating from the first version, but on the whole the new picture is different and, I hope, more accurate than before.

---

[1]   *Silent Witnesses: Russian Films, 1908-1919* (Pordenone/London: British Film Institute & Edizioni dell' Immagine, 1989). For the full version of "New Notes," see Yuri Tsivian, "New Notes on Russian Film Culture Between 1908 and 1919," in *The Silent Cinema Reader*, ed. Lee Grieveson and Peter Krämer, 339-48 (London and NY: Routledge, 2007).

[2]   "Some Preparatory Remarks on Russian Cinema," in *Inside the Film Factory*, ed. Ian Christie and Richard Taylor (London: Routledge, 1991).

Yuri Tsivian

Russian Endings (Thirteen Years Later)

[...] In 1918 two film press organs, one Russian and one American, made—independently of one another—an identical observation. *The Moving Picture World*, after reviewing a batch of Russian pictures that had just arrived in the USA, thus summarized the general impression of its reviewers:

> As was pointed out in the first and favorable review of these films in *The Moving Picture World*, the tragic note is frequently sounded; this is in marked contrast to prevailing American methods. The Russian films, in other words, incline to what has been termed "the inevitable ending" rather than an idealized or happy ending. That was the thing that gave the reviewers some slight shivers of apprehension as to the reception that might be accorded these films by our public.[3]

At the same time but on the Russian side the Moscow *Kino-gazeta* was informing its readers:

> "All's well that ends well!" This is the guiding principle of foreign cinema. But Russian cinema stubbornly refuses to accept this and goes its own way. Here it's "All's well that ends badly"—we need tragic endings.[4]

It is a fact that only a handful of Russian movies ended well, but what agency was the "we" that needed tragic endings—the nation, the audiences, the filmmakers—is still unclear. Would Russian filmgoers leave the theatre disappointed if the hero and heroine they liked stayed alive, or, worse, ended up marrying each other? No evidence (other than films) exists to blame them for that; if critical reviews can pass as factual testimony, some facts even point to the contrary. Take the case of *Jenny the Maid* reviewed in *Kino-gazeta* (the same weekly in which, a few issues later, the above credo appeared).

---

3   *The Moving Picture World*, vol. 35, no. 5 (1918): 640. I thank Kristin Thompson for pointing out this source.

4   *Kino-gazeta*, no. 15 (1918): 5.

Unlike most Russian melodramas, *Jenny the Maid* (*Gornichnaya Dzhenny*, 1918, written and directed by Yakov Protazanov) ended in a marriage; to support his approval, the reviewer appeals to the voice of the people:

> It was curious to observe how passionately the public desired a happy resolution, how watchful it grew as soon as it began to scent melodrama somewhere about the middle of the film—and to hear the sigh of relief when it transpired that the hero is recovering from his wound, and that the film, after all, would not end with the harmonium huskily wailing.[5]

This could be truly what the viewing-hall mood was, for it is impossible to imagine anyone watching their touching love story (a print survives) to wish anything less than a marriage for Jenny and Georges Engère; but it is also true that cautious Protazanov set his film abroad. In a Russian setting such turn of events might have seemed forced.

Whether or not audiences were happy about tragic endings, the industry thought they were. Some time in 1912 those film companies in Russia which had a market abroad, and, reciprocally, foreign companies with an eye to Russian markets got into a practice of supplementing their films with an export ending. No print of a Russian movie with such extra tail has been identified archivally—we only know about their existence from memoir sources. Thus, a recollection left by Sofia Giatsintova, the actress that starred in *By Her Mother's Hand*, a 1913 movie shot by Protazanov (the same director who would, five years later, venture a happy end in *Jenny the Maid*) tells us she was asked to do two such scenes in a row, in the same interior and in the same white dress: "One ending, the happy ending, was 'for export': Lidochka recalls. The other, more dramatic, was 'for Russia': Lidochka in her coffin."[6]

---

[5]   A. Ostroumov, "Jenny the Maid," *Kino-gazeta*, no. 8 (1918): 3.

[6]   Giatsintova's interview with Tatyana Ponomareva (preserved at Ponomareva's personal archive in Moscow).

[...] There was a time in film history when (to repeat Nabokov's *mot à propos* literary dénouements) "harm was the norm." In the first dozen years or so endings of the kind to be later labeled as "Russian" were much in current internationally. "Happy end" as a program, as Richard Abel has recently shown, began to crystallize around 1908 as part of the American film industry's effort to win its home market from the Pathé Frères. It was then that American trade papers launched a campaign to promote what they called "clean, wholesome" subjects, in the American tradition of "ethical melodrama" and its "bright, happy dénouements," contrasting those to the thumb-down ends habitual to *Grand-guignol* melodramas then fashionable on stage as in films.[7] It is not cultures, as I initially thought, that give shape to film history; it is the other way round: when in need for a tool, film history resorts to culture.

The period (roughly, 1912–1914) during which the Hollywood endings became what they are, and the Russian endings became geographically Russian was linked to another film-historical process: the passage from shorts to features. This was the time when the issue of how to end the film was back on the table: having to choose only one story that would thus define the mood of your show meant that prudent film exhibitors could not any more, as many had done, balance the morbid with the wholesome. There are, I am sure, a number of ways in which the American choice can be accounted for—by linking it to general regulatory concerns, for instance (at any rate, much of the rhetoric around it was regulatory[8]), though straightforward societal explanations may be as insidious as cultural ones; as to the Russian choice, I think it was influenced—in

---

[7] Richard Abel, *The Red Rooster Scare: Making Cinema American, 1900–1910* (Berkeley, CA.: University of California Press, 1999), 99; see also p. 122.

[8] "There simply must be a moral ending," wrote Henry Albert Phillips in his screenwriting manual in 1914; "stories in which the good element is overcome by the bad, thus placing the premium on the bad, are unmoral." *Photodrama* by Henry Albert Phillips (New York, 1914), 89. Compare this phrase in a review of the Russian film *The Cloven Tongue*: "there is little trace of what an American producer would regard as a safe picture to offer the tender public which he is careful to shield from unhappy thoughts" ("*The Cloven Tongue*," *Photoplay* (April, 1918): 109).

a strange negative way—by its American counterpart. I will try to explain how in the next section.

The Pace of the Action

> These films are amazing. They appear to have only two speeds, "slow" and "stop."
>
> *Kevin Brownlow, 1989*[9]

> The essential condition of life is movement; the essential condition of thinking is pause.
>
> *Sergei Volkonsky, 1912*[10]

We now turn to that other oddity of Russian film culture that amazed Kevin Brownlow (and many others who saw a selection of early Russian films shown at the Silent Film Festival in Pordenone in 1989)—the defiant immobility of their figures. But before looking into this, let me specify what I mean by Russian film culture and by film culture in general. National film culture is not (as the term may misleadingly suggest) a cinema's place on the map of its national culture, but an arsenal of cultural tools deployed by a national cinema to stake a claim on the map of international filmmaking. The Russian way of doing this was to rely on pre-existing cultural difference. "The Three Schools of Cinematography: 1. Movements: the American School; 2. Forms: the European School; 3. The Psychological: the Russian School," wrote Fyodor Otsep (not yet the screenwriter and the filmmaker he would soon become, but already a young trade press journalist) in an outline for a film theory book conceived in 1913.[11] The book was never written, but if it were, Otsep's attempt to make use of "psychology" in order to dissociate Russian cinema from either of its western sisters would

---

9   Kevin Brownlow in an intervention at the round table on early Russian cinema in Pordenone, October, 1989.

10   Sergei Volkonskii, *Vyrazitel'nyi chelovek. Stsenicheskoe vospitanie zhesta po Delsartu* (*The Expressive Man. Education of Stage Gesture According to Delsarte*) (St. Petersburg: Apollon, 1912), 69.

11   F. Otsep, *Kinematograf* (*Cinema*) (Plan for a book), Russian State Archive for Literature and Art, 2734/1/72.

look something like this: we need psychology for our films to be recognized as Russian; for what, if not "psychology," had brought recognition to the Russian novel; and was it not "psychology" which marked Chekhov's drama and Moscow Art Theatre acting as unique?

This line of reasoning may look neat on paper, but there remained a practical problem Russian film culture kept trying to resolve. Tolstoy enjoyed the advantage of using verbal descriptions for his readers to access the hero's mental life; likewise, the playwright and the actor can use speech and voice to bring those matters home; but how about cinema? Is silent film—that voiceless and linguistically impaired medium—a vehicle capable of carrying characters' psychology across? The "immobility" doctrine popular among Russian trade paper theorists round about 1914–1916 was the Russian answer to this question. Here filmic "psychology" was defined by contraries: while others invested in action and movement, immobility and inaction were declared to be native assets: "The [Russian] film story breaks decisively with all the established views on the essence of the cinematographic picture: it repudiates *movement*,"[12] wrote a *Proektor* theorist early in 1916; and looking at film reviews that this trade magazine published that year we see how easy this immobility doctrine metamorphoses into an appreciative category, as in a review of Aleksander Volkov's *His Eyes* (*Ego glaza*): "[Particularly] the scenes that are devoid of traditional cinematic movement produce a great impression."[13]

Another connection we can observe looking at the period's film literature is one between the immobility doctrine and the image of the film star. Whenever this or that critic would broach the subject of tempo, the review was likely to slip into a discussion of acting. When the notion of national style began to gain ground in film criticism and filmmaking (most energetically, around 1913[14]), it

---

[12] I. Petrovskii, "Kinodrama ili kinopovest'?" ("Film Drama or Film Story?"), *Proektor*, no. 20 (1916): 3 (italics in the original).

[13] *Proektor*, no. 19 (1916): 11.

[14] See a good overview of the process in Tom Gunning's "Notes and Queries

was the manner of acting—more so than the tempo of editing, or scenery and sets—that beckoned people anxious to identify movies by nationality. National cinemas crystallized around national acting schools, each with its own agenda for "good acting." American actors relied on little movements, like quick facial reactions and byplay with props; one could tell an Italian diva by her exquisite gestures of arms and hands; Russians valued pensive moods and introvert psychology; needless to say, all this had to do with the pace, not only with the character of acting. Much as it was done in the case of sad endings, Russian trade-paper pundits held up slow acting—that other programmatic characteristic of Russian films—as an example for American movies frequently slighted as slapdash. Note this, for instance, in a smugly condescending review of the American movie *Business is Business* (1915, dir. Otis Turner) distributed in Russian under a more loaded title *The Slave of Profit* (*Raba nazhivy*):

> As far as the whole pace of the action is concerned, neither the director nor the cast have managed to capture that slow tempo that is so common in the Russian feature-film play. The actors are still too fidgety, as the Americans are wont to be; their acting still derives largely from the superficial, from objects and facts rather than from experiences and emotions.[15]

The actor, indeed, was seen as cinema's ultimate metronome. Much as the Russian public may have enjoyed snappy American acting (and I am sure they did), no busybody (other than in a comedy) had much of a chance to get ahead in a Russian film of the teens. The Russian idea of good acting spelt feet and feet of stillness. To quote again from the essay that "repudiated movement":

> In the world of the screen, where everything is counted in metres, the actor's struggle for the freedom to act has led to

---

about the Year 1913 and Film Style: National Styles and Deep Staging," *1895*, October 1993: "L'Année 1913 en France," ed. Thierry Lefebre and Laurent Mannoni, 195-204.

15 *Proektor*, no. 9 (1916): 15.

a battle for long (in terms of metres) scenes or, more accurately, for "full" scenes, to use Olga Gzovskaya's marvelous expression. A "full" scene is one in which the actor is given the opportunity to depict in stage terms a specific spiritual experience, no matter how many metres it takes. The "full" scene involves a complete rejection of the usual hurried tempo of the film drama. Instead of a rapidly changing kaleidoscope of images, it aspires to *rivet* the attention of the audience on to a single image. . . . This may sound like a paradox for the art of cinema (which derives its name from the Greek word for "movement") but the involvement of our best actors in cinema will lead to the slowest possible tempo. . . . Each and every one of our best film actors has his or her own *style* of mime: Mosjoukine has his steely hypnotized look; Gzovskaya has a gentle, endlessly varying lyrical "face"; Maximov has his nervous tension and Polonsky his refined grace. But with all of them, given their unusual economy of gesture, their entire acting process is subjugated to a rhythm that rises and falls particularly *slowly*. . . . It is true that this kind of portrayal is conventional, but convention is the sign of any true art.[16]

Such was Russian film culture viewed from the side of its theory. To get a glimpse of the practical side let us look, once again, at Protazanov's 1918 *Jenny the Maid*. This film, we recall, was made in Russia and set in France; its ending was happy, its tempo Russian. As it happened, many years after the film had been released two of its principal players—the former Moscow Art Theatre actress Olga Gzovskaya that did Jenny (the same Gzovskaya whom the excerpt above credits with inventing the "marvelous" concept of "full scenes"), and her partner Vladimir Gaidarov who played Georges—remembered the making of *Jenny the Maid* in their memoirs written, respectively, in 1948 and 1966—so strong must have been the impress of Protazanov's voice behind the camera telling them what to do next or, to be more to the point, how long to wait before doing it. Writes Gzovskaya:

---

[16] Petrovskii, 3.

Protazanov was keen on the actor's eyes and liked to work
with the glance of a character. Among all the directors only
he could catch in an expression of the eyes a transition to
the next step in the action, for he felt the exact duration of
a glance. His famous signals during rehearsal: "pause—
looks closely—looks closely—pause—remembers—pause—
pause—pause—lowers eyelids" were not prompts or dictates
as to what the actress or actor must carry out but rather
a perfect merger with the internal life of the performer.[17]

And this—the following quote—is from Gaidarov; his report dwells
on a specific scene in which he, as convalescing Georges, is shown
sitting in the armchair while Gzovskaya (Jenny the maid) is reading
to him. The "inner" action that underpins the "outer" business of
this scene was to be revealed through this by-play of glances:

Protazanov insisted on this scene being acted at a reduced
pace as he dictated his famous pauses—for example, when
Georges's glance lingers for a while on Jenny. There we were,
face to face, and . . . pause, pause, pause . . . Jenny lowers
her eyes . . . pause . . . she gets up quickly, turns and goes to
leave. . . . Georges calls to her. . . . She lingers in the doorway
without turning round . . . pause, pause . . . and then she turns
and says, "I must get your medicine. It's time for you to take
it!" Pause . . . she turns and leaves . . . Georges is left alone.
He looks after her . . . again pause, pause, pause. . . . Then we
see his elbow resting on the arm of the chair, his head bowed
towards his hand, and Georges thinking to himself, "What
a strange girl she is!" Pause, pause . . . and . . . iris.[18]

[...] Projectionists—that fifth column within the Russian film
industry—were another group of people impatient with the slow
Russian style. All over the world projectionists were known for

---

[17]   Olga Gzovskaia, "Rezhisser—drug aktera" ("The Director, the Actor's
Friend"), in *Iakov Protazanov. Sbornik statei i materialov* (Moscow: Iskusstvo,
1948), 259.

[18]   V. Gaidarov, *V teatre i kino* (*In Theatre and Cinema*) (Leningrad-Moscow:
Iskusstvo, 1966), 101-02.

their tendency (particularly strong during the last picture show) to project films faster than they had been shot, but I wonder how many actors other than those in Russia would stand up and act as Ivan Mosjoukine (aka Mozzhukhin, the star remembered for his long steady gaze), whose open letter published in *Teatral'naya gazeta* in 1915 called on filmgoers "to make their protest known by banging their sticks and stamping their feet, etc.":

> The poor innocent actors jump and jerk about like cardboard clowns and the audience, which is unfamiliar with the secrets of the projection booth, stigmatises them for their lack of talent and experience. I cannot convey the feeling you experience when you watch your own scene transformed at the whim of a mere boy from normal movements into a wild dance. You feel as if you were being slandered in front of everyone and you have no way of proving your innocence.[19]

Hard to tell on whose side audiences were in this debate; however, a phrase ostensibly used in the teens to yell at hasty projectionists — *Nie goni kartinu*! (Don't speed the picture!) — still exists in colloquial Russian, now meaning simply "Not so fast!"

[...] Yes, immobility looks like a strange program for the medium of motion pictures, particularly if viewed from 1925, for by this year (after the first feature-long pictures by Kuleshov, Vertov and Eisenstein) the cutting rate and acting speed of Russian films had swung to the opposite extreme, beating the fastest American movies on their own racing track, as it were. This turnabout was not an isolated phenomenon — it dovetails with an overarching makeover of taste that began to sweep Russia around 1900 when, to use John E. Bowlt's felicitous phrase, "Russian culture moves from slow to fast lane."[20] But, tempting though it may seem to connect film and culture causally, it is exactly at this threshold that

---

19   I. Mozzhukhin [Mosjoukine], "V chem defekt?" ("Where Lies the Defect?"), *Teatral'naia gazeta*, no. 30 (1915): 13.

20   John E. Bowlt, "Velocity" (work-in-progress pathway for the distance learning project "Russia: A Modernist Perspective," sponsored by the Annenberg Foundation and University of Southern California).

41

we must watch our step. Causal explanations—vague at their best, essentialist at their worst—will creep in each time the junction is left unattended, be it between the slow pace of Russian films and Russian imperial culture, or between the cult of speed peculiar to Russian modernism and the fast-cutting craze that set in around 1924. I wish I could offer a neat workable theory of how it happens between film and culture, but at least I have a picture of how it does not. We—myself included—are often trapped into picturing a particular cinema vis-à-vis the particular culture in which it is nested as a passive, derivative, filial agency; we either picture national cinemas as "sponging up" their respective cultures, or look for some sort of cultural genus.

[…] Cinema is not a culture's compass needle, nor is it a cultural symptom, psychological or otherwise, but rather, an active, aggressive, manipulative agency, which may, when needed, use a culture as a means to an end. Likewise, the film historian is not a geologist interested in deeper layers of culture. Culture is useful insofar as it helps us to understand films, not the other way round. In the back-and-forth between film and culture it is film that has the first serve.

In other words, there is no such thing as "grass-root" cinema, American, Russian or Fredonian. Cinema is architecture; culture is its wallpaper. Early Russian film culture was not a blotter that absorbed the ink of Russian theatre and literature to eventually become their pale likeness; a better term to describe the workings of film cultures is not "absorption," but "annexation"—cinema works forcibly and aggressively to annex culture's traditional territories, to capture and enslave its innermost topoi, and does so with an eye to an international "slave market"; a better image to understand cinema's cultural policy is to think of it as one of those science fiction aliens endowed with a gift to take the shape of terrestrial creatures not with the aim to be like them, but in order to rip them off.

STEN'KA RAZIN

1908

224 meters

Director: **Vladimir Romashkov**

Screenplay: **Vasilii Goncharov**

Cinematography: **Aleksandr Drankov** and **Nikolai Kozlovskii**

Production Company: **Aleksandr Drankov Company**

Cast: **Evgenii Petrov-Kraevskii (Sten'ka Razin) and the actors of the St. Petersburg People's House (Narodnyi Dom) Theatre**

Beginning in 1896, with the demonstration of the Lumière Brothers' first films in St. Petersburg and Moscow, foreign entrepreneurs dominated the Russian cinema market. In 1907 Pathé Brothers released the three-minute documentary film *Cossacks of the Don* (*Donskie kazaki*), which sold 219 copies in less than two weeks, a record for pre-revolutionary Russian cinema.[1] This audience demand for Russian subjects was not lost on Aleksandr Drankov (1886-1949), a Duma photographer and enterprising businessman, who established the first Russian "cinematographic atelier" in 1907. Drankov turned out documentary films on native subjects, such as the Moscow racetrack, celebrity funerals, views of Moscow and St. Petersburg, and the comings and goings of royals and other prominent figures, achieving national prominence with his August 1908 short film on Lev Tolstoy's eightieth birthday at Iasnaia Poliana.

On October 15, 1908 he released *Sten'ka Razin: Freemen from the Lower Reaches of the Volga* (*Ponizovaia vol'nitsa*), the first Russian feature film. *Sten'ka Razin* was shot on location in Sestroretsk, near

---

[1]   Moisei Ginzburg, *Kinematografiia dorevoliutsionnoi Rossii* (Moscow: Agraf, 2007), 50. More typically, in 1913 no film sold more than twenty copies.

St. Petersburg, with Lake Razliv standing in for the Volga river. Razin was played by the tragedian Petrov-Kraevskii, the identity of the actress portraying the Persian princess is unknown (Fig. 3) and Razin's band of brigands was played by the semiprofessional actors of the St. Petersburg People's House Theatre. Seeking to elevate the cultural importance of the event, Drankov commissioned Mikhail

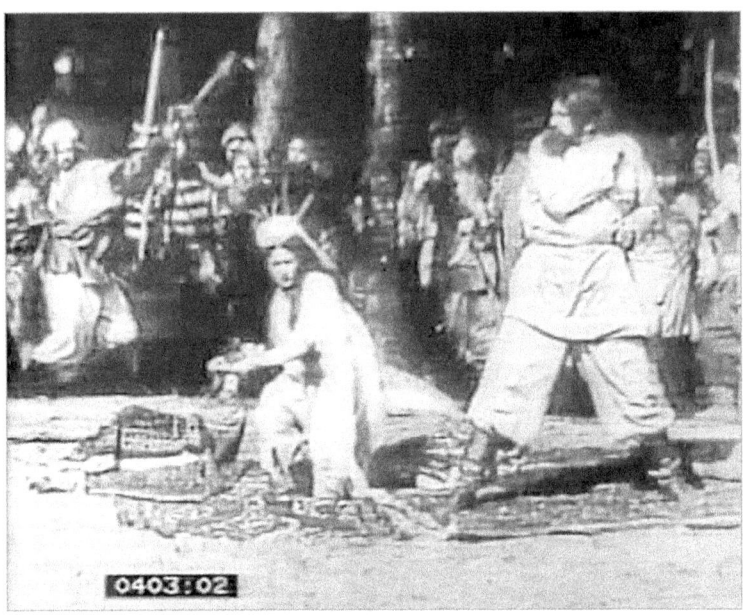

Fig. 3. Razin Accuses the Princess of Betrayal

Ippolitov-Ivanov, the director of the Moscow Conservatory, to compose a score for the silent film, with the overture played by a symphonic orchestra at the premiere. Drankov even sutured spectators into the cinematic experience by encouraging the audience to sing "Down the Mother Volga" ("Vniz po matushke po Volge"), known on the street as the "drunkard's ballad," during the screening.[2]

---

[2]   Jay Leyda, *Kino: A History of the Russian and Soviet Film*, 3rd ed. (Princeton: Princeton University Press, 1983), 35.

Once attractions ceased to impress Russian audiences, filmmakers began to develop narratives adapted from the Bible, historical events, novels, plays, poems, songs and operas. Based on the well-known song, "Iz-za ostrova na strezhen'" ("From Behind the Island to the Midstream"), *Sten'ka Razin* recounts an episode from the seventeenth-century robber, rebel and folk hero's life—his ill-fated infatuation with a princess he had captured during his Persian campaign. His men resent his preoccupation with the "Muslim princess," and his pausing to party with her on the banks of the Volga, while the brigands are being pursued by the tsar's troops. During their forest revels they even attempt to compete with her, opposing manly Russian steps to her seductive oriental dancing. The men devise a scheme to prove the princess unfaithful via a counterfeited letter to her supposed lover, Prince Hassan. The plot succeeds: inflamed by drink, the jealous Razin throws the princess overboard as a gift to the Volga river. Although Drankov may have chosen his subject with an eye toward the continuing popular unrest after the 1905 revolution (at one point the men urge Razin to drink to the "honest people"), the film itself presents a politically conservative, if sensational, treatment of Razin: he is portrayed as a violent and abusive drunkard, not a freedom-loving folk hero.

Sten'ka Razin consists of six separate tableaux scenes (Revels on the Volga, Revels in the Forest, The Brigands' Plot against the Princess, Jealousy Awakened, The Plot Succeeds, The Death of the Princess), a characteristic mode of construction borrowed from French and American film, that preceded the development of continuous, coherent narration. Although the tableau structure in early films derived from theatre and painting—the new medium's aspirational association with high culture—the legend of Sten'ka Razin, embedded as it was in folk culture, was also a popular subject in the *lubok* (woodcut engravings accompanied by explanatory titles or short texts), a parallel model for the static pictorial structure of the film. *Sten'ka Razin* was also influenced by the folk play "The Boat" ("*Lodka*"), popular at *balagany* (folk spectacles), which, like the film, both culminated and concluded with the pitching of the princess into the Volga.[3] The subject was well chosen for silent film in that the Sten'ka Razin-princess story had long been familiar to Russian audiences through folklore and song, obviating the need for extended explanation. It was only the conspiracy and fictional Prince Hassan narrative that required lengthy intertitles.

Although tracking and panning were familiar techniques by 1908, the camera remains stationary for the entire film, shooting in a long shot either from the shore or from a distance into the forest. Composition within the frame is haphazard: in the first scene on the boat it is difficult to locate Razin and the princess in the crowd; other boats float by in random fashion and, at the climax of the film, just as the princess is about to be thrown overboard, a second boat floats into the foreground and the actors must row furiously to get out of the way of the action. Acting is primitive, consisting mostly of frantic arm-waving. Editing is timed poorly for psychological effect: the princess hits the water just barely before the film ends. (Note the quick cut that replaces the actress with a dummy to be thrown overboard.) To modern eyes, *Sten'ka Razin* gives the impression of hasty work, but the film was nonetheless a hit, and Russian cinema was established.

ИЗ-ЗА ОСТРОВА НА СТРЕЖЕНЬ	FROM BEHIND THE ISLAND TO THE MIDSTREAM
Из-за острова на стрежень,	From behind the island to the midstream deeps,
На простор речной волны Выбегают расписные, Острогрудые челны.	Into the broad river's waves Sail out the ornamented, Arrow-breasted barks.
На переднем Стенька Разин, Обнявшись, сидит с княжной, Свадьбу новую справляет— И веселый и хмельной.	In the first in Sten'ka Razin. Hugging the princess, he sits. Merry and drunk, He celebrates a new wedding.

---

[3]   Neia Zorkaia, *Kino. Teatr. Literatura. Opyt sistemnogo analiza* (Moscow: Agraf, 2010), 20.

А княжна, склонивши очи,
Ни жива и ни мертва,
Робко слушает хмельные,
Неразумные слова.

«Ничего не пожалею!
Буйну голову отдам!»—
Раздается по окрестным
Берегам и островам.

«Ишь ты, братцы, атаман-то
Нас на бабу променял!
Ночку с нею провозился—
Сам наутро бабой стал...»

Ошалел... Насмешки, шепот
Слышит пьяный атаман.
Персиянки полоненной
Крепче обнял полный стан.

Гневно кровью налилися
Атамановы глаза,
Брови черные нависли,
Собирается гроза...

Эх, кормилица родная,
Волга, матушка-река!
Не видала ты подарков
От донского казака!...

...Мощным взмахом поднимает
Полоненную княжну
И, не глядя, прочь кидает
В набежавшую волну...

«Что затихли, удалые?
Эй ты, Фролка-черт, пляши!
Грянь, ребята, хоровую
За помин ее души!»[4]

But the princess, lowering her eyes,
Seeming neither alive nor dead,
Timidly listens to his drunken,
Foolish words.

"I'll begrudge you nothing!
I'll lay down my wild head!"
Resounds along the nearby
Shores and islands.

"How do you like it, brothers,
The ataman has traded us for a wench.
He had a romp with her one night—
Became a wench himself the next morning."

He went crazy, the drunken ataman,
Hearing jibes and whispers,
He holds the captive Persian's
Buxom body tighter.

The ataman's eyes welled
Wrathfully with blood.
His black brows furrowed,
A storm is gathering.

"Oh, my dear wetnurse,
Volga, mother-river!
You have never seen gifts
From a cossack of the Don!"

With a powerful sweep, he lifts
The captive princess and,
Without looking, throws her overboard
Into the cresting wave.

"Why have you fallen silent, bold ones?
Hey you—Frolka, you devil, dance!
Raise your choral voices, boys
In memory of her soul!"

---

[4]   D. N. Sadovnikov, *Pesni Volgi* (St. Petersburg: Izd. V. Ternovskogo, 1909), 164.

THE CAMERAMAN'S REVENGE
Mest' kinematograficheskogo operatora

1912

285 meters

Director, Screenplay, Cinematography, Artistic Director:

Władysław Starewicz

Production Company:

Aleksandr Khanzhonkov Company

The Polish animator, director, cinematographer, scriptwriter and actor Władysław Starewicz (1882-1965) was the founder of Russian animation and was responsible for turning stop-motion photography, previously a novelty special effect, into a story-telling art for cinema. Starewicz grew up in Kaunas, Lithuania, where he developed interests in drawing, photography, acting and, from an early age, butterfly collecting. With a camera bought from producer Aleksandr Khanzhonkov and a gift of film, Starewicz shot his first ethnographic work, *Nad Niemanom* (*Beyond the River Nemunas*) in 1909. The next year, following Khanzhonkov's plan to produce popular science films and his own love of entomology, Starewicz attempted to film the battle of two stag beetles, but the frightened creatures refused to fight under the bright lights. Inspired by Emile Cohl's *Les allumettes animées* (*The Animated Matches*, 1908), he decided to recreate the fight through stop-motion, using articulated insect puppets constructed of actual carapaces with legs reinforced by fine wire and attached by wax to the thorax. By 1912 Starewicz was installed in his own Moscow studio making highly successful films for Khanzhonkov. Stop-motion techniques were not well known at the time, and audiences and critics sometimes assumed Starewicz had managed to film his own trained beetle-performers.

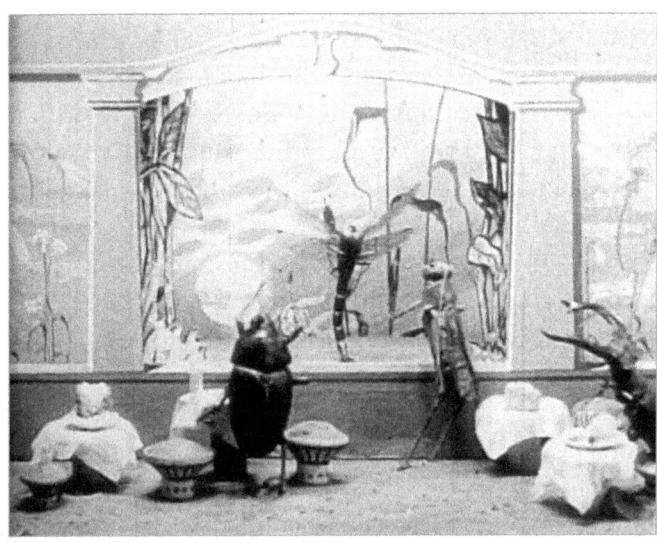

Fig. 4
At the Cabaret

The animator, who enjoyed jokes and mystifications, and kept his working methods secret, maintained the deception as good publicity.[1]

In 1917 Starewicz and his family moved to Yalta to work in Khanzhonkov's studio, and then emigrated to France via Italy in 1920. Unlike most émigrés in the industry, Starewicz continued to work successfully abroad. Always insisting on his independence and complete creative control, he established his own home-studio, reaching the height of his career during the late 1920s-early 30s. In France, Starewicz's animals became more anthropomorphic and he often combined human and puppet characters in a single film. Among his most accomplished works in emigration were *Le Roman de Renard* (*The Tale of the Fox*, 1930) and *Fétiche Mascotte* (*Fétiche the Mascot*,1933).

The Cameraman's Revenge, Starewicz's most famous Russian film, charms and provokes laughter even today. *Revenge* follows the amours of a well-to-do, but bored insect couple, which are disrupted by the public, cinematic exposure of Mr. Beetle's tryst

---

[1]   See Yuri Tsivian, "The Case of the Bioscope Beetle: Starewicz's Answer to Genetics," *Discourse* 17, no. 3 (1995): 119-25.

with a dragonfly cabaret dancer (Fig. 4), engineered by an angry grasshopper-cameraman who has lost the girl to Mr. Beetle, and Mr. Beetle's discovery of his wife's simultaneous affair with a grasshopper artist. The plot parodies the popular salon or high society melodrama, which dealt with the moral-psychological struggles of the upper classes and bohemian artists. In reviews and advertising for the film, the cabaret performer is described as "the famous barefoot dancer Dragonfly," adding that "the role of Isadora Duncan will be played by a dragonfly."[2] As dragonfly, the cabaret performer also derives from the figuration of the female dancer in nineteenth-century romantic ballets as a butterfly or other graceful insect, in costumes adorned with wings.[3]

The Cameraman's Revenge lampoons period melodramas through comic devices rooted in incongruity. Influenced by J. I. Grandville's drawings, Starewicz figures the idle rich as insects, with the difference that their biological naturalism and lack of facial mimicry, joined to anthropomorphized movements and attire (a beetle servant wearing shoes; the artist wearing the emblematic large, floppy hat; kissing insects; expressing anger and threats with insect legs; riding a bike; turning a camera crank) produce a comic albeit disconcerting effect. While the bugs inhabit miniature human establishments, the incongruity of their tiny figures in full-size nature scenes is also humorous. Finally, the high emotion of melodrama is dispelled by the introduction of farcical motifs, such as unexpected discovery, physical humor, including pratfalls, fights, gags (escape through a burning fireplace, breaking down a door, diving through a movie screen), and physical violence with an umbrella and a painting.

---

2   *Vestnik kinematografii* (Moscow) 2 (13 October 1912), and French advertising, cited in Władysław Jewsiewicki, *Ezop XX wieku. Władysław Starewicz pionier filmu lalkowego i sztuki filmowej* (Warsaw: Wydawnictwa Radia i Telewizji, 1989), 44-5. Modern dancer Duncan danced barefoot and was notorious for her scandalous (for the era) love life.

3   M.B. Iampol'skii, "Starevich: Mimika nasekomykh i kul'turnaia traditsiia," *Kinovedcheskie zapiski* 1 (1988): 84-90. See images of Maria Taglioni in *Zephyr and Flora* (1831) and *La Sylphide* (1832), http://en.wikipedia.org/wiki/Marie_Taglioni and http://en.wikipedia.org/wiki/La_Sylphide (accessed 17 June 2013).

The two professionally creative characters in the film, the cameraman and the artist Usachini (from "usy"—moustache), are large and strong grasshoppers—more attractive than the clumsy bourgeois beetle, and Starewicz heroicizes the cameraman, who exposes hypocrisy by secretly filming and then screening Mr. Beetle's tryst as a Khanzhonkov film, *The Unfaithful Husband*. In the end the cameraman knows the pleasure of revenge, the audience experiences the voyeuristic pleasure of observed eroticism, and the beetle couple are shamed, then punished by imprisonment for disorderly conduct. Starewicz further elevates the profession by demonstrating the skills, attributes and risks of the medium: the physical exertion of filming, the edited and titled final product, the movie theatre and screen, the projection process and the dangers of flammable nitrate film.

Further Reading

Béatrice, Léona, and François Martin. *Ladislas Starewitch. 1882-1965. Le cinema rend visibles les rêves de l'imaginations*. Paris: L'Harmattan, 2003. The appendix provides several extant versions of the intertitles to the film, including the British version which substitutes, for the adulterous beetle couple, a brother and sister, Bill and Sal, who are hiding secret marriages.

Belodubrovskaya, Maria. "Understanding the Magic: Special Effects in Ladislas Starewitch's *L'Horloge magique*." *KinoKultura* 23 (2009). http://www.kinokultura.com/2009/23-belodubrovskaya.shtml (accessed 17 June 2013).

Krivulia, N.G. *Ozhivshie teni volshebnogo fonaria.* Krasnodar: Ametist, 2006, 405-69.

Ladislas Starewitch. http://ls.pagesperso-orange.fr./ladislas.htm (accessed 17 June 2013). This informative Starewicz website is maintained by family members.

Further Viewing

The Bug Trainer (*Vabzdžių Dresuotojas*), Lithuania/Poland/Japan/The Netherlands/Finland, 2008. Directors: Linas Augutis, Donatas Ulvydas, Rasa Miškinytė, Era Film. Chronicles Starewicz's life and work.

THE MERCHANT BASHKIROV'S DAUGHTER

Doch' kuptsa Bashkirova

1913
1610 meters: 5 reels (3 preserved, without intertitles)
Director: **Nikolai Larin**
Screenplay: **Nikolai Larin**
Cinematography: **Jan Dored**
Production Company: **Volga Company, G. Libken**
Cast: **unknown**

The Merchant Bashkirov's Daughter exemplifies the sensationalism of early Russian cinema. Rural melodramas tended to be less psychological than their urban counterparts, with more emphasis on physical violence and brutality. Although Nadia, the young daughter of the prosperous merchant Bashkirov, loves the steward Egorushka, her father decides to marry her to an aged business associate. When the father returns home unexpectedly, Nadia hides Egorushka under a heavy quilt, where he suffocates. Nadia's mother then bribes the caretaker to dispose of the body, which he takes to the Volga in a barrel and dumps into the river. Fishermen retrieve the body in their nets, precipitating a police investigation. The drunken caretaker begins blackmailing the mother and daughter, and forces Nadia into sex. When he calls Nadia to a tavern to brag about his conquest before friends, she waits until the men are asleep in a drunken stupor, considers killing the caretaker with an axe, but then decides to set fire to the tavern. The ending shows her running from the scene laughing and then watching the conflagration from her window, still laughing dementedly.

The Merchant Bashkirov's Daughter was directed by Nikolai Larin, who had finished co-directing *The Tercentenary of the Romanov*

Dynasty's Accession (*Trekhsotletie Tsarstvovaniia Doma Romanovykh*) earlier in 1913. Larin emigrated around 1920 to Bulgaria, where he founded the local film industry and also directed films in Germany and Czechoslovakia. The film was the first production of the Iaroslavl' film studio owned by sausage maker Grigorii Libken, who was notorious for his unscrupulous business practices. It is unclear whether the film was based on an actual murder case in the Bashkirov merchant family, wealthy owners of a steamship company, or a nineteenth-century literary source but, in any case, the title generated scandalous publicity for the film. M. E. Bashkirov successfully petitioned the government press censor to forbid the screening of a film that besmirched the family name, known all over the Volga region. The film was then advertised as *Drama on the Volga* and *The Merchant's Daughter*.

The Merchant Bashkirov's Daughter depicts a patriarchal provincial society in which the father commands and abuses almost everyone—his wife, his steward, his caretaker—and views his daughter as a commodity, selecting an associate for her husband, clearly for business reasons. Moreover, the prospective husband is an almost exact copy of the father himself in hair, beard and clothing.

Nadia hides her beloved Egorushka under her bed, a welcoming into intimacy. However Egorushka's asphyxiation under a mattress, quilt and pillows—a version of the farcical under-the-bed hiding place turned tragic—also metaphorically realizes the smothering oppression of merchant society, forcing the mother and daughter into a secrecy which also suffocates Egorushka. Unlike the women in many urban melodramas, neither mother nor daughter is a passive victim, but rather victims who resist the dominant social order. The mother approves the daughter's lover, allowing her to be alone with Egorushka, and then works to save her daughter from a murder charge and scandal. Blackmailed and raped by the caretaker, Nadia is ultimately vindicated by her murder of the villain and his cronies.

By this time Russian directors had learned to tell a story through continuity editing. Although *The Merchant Bashkirov's Daughter* employs traditional gestures—the mother's servile bowing, the suitor's lascivious beard-stroking, the caretaker's intoxication conveyed by a carelessly buttoned coat—the acting is not overly melodramatic. Shots are composed carefully: in one scene the mother and daughter are placed together on the right, united against the father and aged suitor on the left; Egorushka and Nadia kiss in silhouette, effectively framed by an arch with a view of the Volga and the town in the distance (Fig. 5). The lovers meet twice outside, surrounded and outlined by tall greenery that fills the screen (their love is natural)—a visual trope that later cinema puts to good use, as in Tarkovsky's *Stalker*.

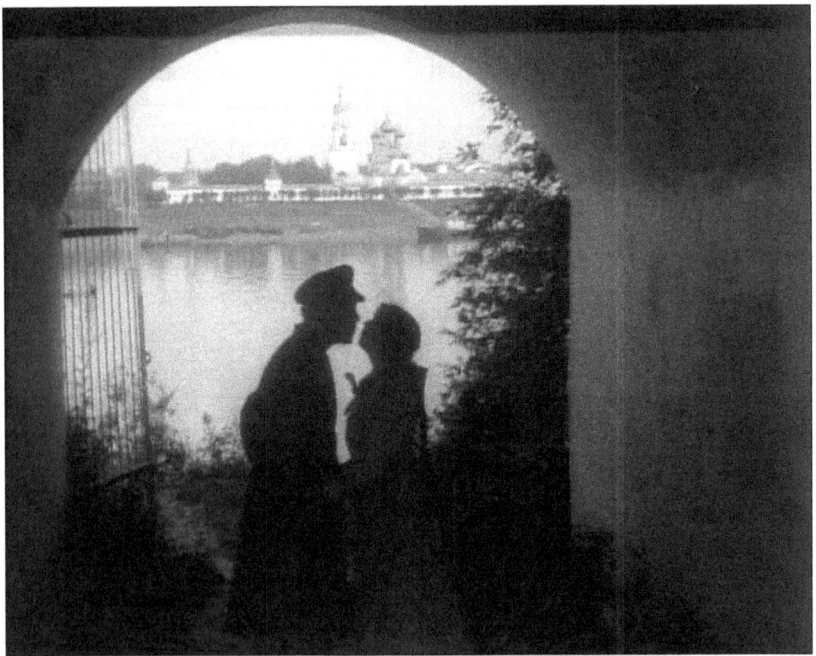

Fig. 5. The Lovers by the Volga

CHILD OF THE BIG CITY

Ditia bol'shogo goroda

Alternate title:

The Girl from the Street (Devushka s ulitsy)

1914

**1135 meters (4 reels with prologue); preserved without opening
scenes and intertitles**

Director, Art Director: **Evgenii Bauer**

Screenplay: **unknown author**

Cinematography: **Boris Zavelev**

Production Company: **A. Khanzhonkov Company**

Cast: **Elena Smirnova (Manechka-Mary), Nina Kozlianinova
(Manechka as a child), Mikhail Salarov (Viktor Kravtsov),
Leonid Iost (Victor's valet), Lidiia Tridenskaia
(Masha, a laundress), Emma Bauer (the "Indian dancer")**

During his brief career spanning the years 1913-1917, Evgenii
Bauer made more than 75 films, becoming Russia's most popular
and highly paid director. Post-revolutionary filmmakers rejected
his work as decadent, reactionary and stylistically retrograde, and
he fell into obscurity during the Soviet era. With perestroika his
26 surviving films were retrieved from the archives and the 1989
Pordenone Silent Film Festival introduced his work to international
audiences.

Bauer studied at the Moscow School of Painting, Architecture
and Sculpture from 1882 to 1887, after which he tried different
careers—actor, cartoonist, satirical journalist, photographer, theatre
impresario—but found success as a stage designer and later worked
as art director for the Drankov and Khanzhonkov studios. Bauer's
career spanned the difficult years of the Great War leading up to the
1917 revolution. Although he directed a number of comedies, his

most popular films were urban melodramas made for Khanzhonkov, of which the opulent *A Life for a Life* (*Zhizn' za zhizn'*, 1916) is the most famous. Bauer was an innovator in making women the central subjects of many of his melodramas. His female characters often embody the tension between the Symbolist ideal of the eternal feminine and the new woman of late imperial society, and his films insist on the futility of finding stability in heterosexual relations. His work testifies to the rise of consumer culture and the importance of women as both consumers of manufactured goods and as cinema-goers. Bauer's Silver Age aestheticism, his psychological treatment of gender relations and his innovations to mise-en-scène make him the outstanding auteur of pre-revolutionary Russian cinema.

Child of the Big City

Orphaned in childhood, Manechka works as a seamstress and dreams of a better life. Wealthy man about town Viktor Kravtsov has lost interest in the society women of his circle and dreams of a "pure love." Viktor and his friend Kramskoi, as idle urban flâneurs, meet Mania on the street and invite her to dinner. By protecting her from Kramskoi's advances, Viktor is able to seduce Mania and she becomes his mistress. Mania—now the cigarette-smoking, emancipated and westernized "Mary"—gradually ruins Viktor financially and leaves him when he suggests a more modest way of life. In the meantime Mary has seduced Viktor's valet and sets herself up as a high-class prostitute. The impoverished Viktor continues to love her, but when he tries to see her, Mary gets rid of him by sending the maid out to give him three rubles. As Mary dances the tango with the former valet, Viktor shoots himself on her front steps. With an expression of disgust and an offhand proverb, Mary steps over his body, leading the partygoers to a fashionable restaurant. The film ends with a close-up of the dead Viktor.

Bauer's *Silent Witnesses*, released a few months after *Child of the Big City*, employs a conventional melodramatic plot: a girl of the lower classes is seduced and abandoned by a self-indulgent aristocrat. *Child of the Big City* reverses the clichés of the traditional model as Bauer turns to the depiction of the vamp, the sexually predatory heroine and phallic woman of late nineteenth-early twentieth-century culture who ruined men by "sucking their blood," depleting their life force, not to mention their material resources.[1] Consequently, at the level of genre motifs it is the feminized Viktor who acts out the fate of earlier heroines of melodrama: he is hopelessly infatuated with Mary, but is abandoned by his bored, flighty lover and reduced to poverty and a cold garret existence. He writes the usual letter to his former lover, but Mary has found other male friends and rejects him with a humiliating handout. Unable to see his former lover, in despair with nowhere to turn, he makes a final, futile attempt to attract her attention by shooting himself in her vicinity. The ending of the film reprises its beginning, the death of a parallel female victim, Manechka's mother.

Bauer's melodramas are concerned with the tensions of a destabilized patriarchy in late imperial Russia. The genre was an effective medium for pre-revolutionary audiences trapped in an anachronistic political system yet struggling to adapt to the social and cultural pressures that followed in the wake of rapid industrialization and early capitalism. In a patriarchal system the male was ruined by losing his ethical honor; the woman was ruined by losing her physical honor, her virginity. In a Bauer film the "honor" of both male and female derives solely from material wealth. Although Manechka has transformed herself into the elegant Mary, she ultimately reverts to her lower class identity (the vamp often comes from a "degenerate" social stratum) in choosing a man of her own kind, Viktor's valet, as her lover. When Viktor discovers them together, he attempts to shoot Mary, but only succeeds in shooting his reflection in the mirror. Bauer avoids moralizing but depicts gender relations without idealizing either sex: Viktor and Mary simply use each other for their own ends. The New Woman is gaining agency but does so by appropriating traditional male predation. Mary's tango, the dance of sex and death, is intercut with

---

[1]   See Bram Dykstra, *Evil Sisters: The Threat of Female Sexuality and the Cult of Manhood* (NY: Alfred A. Knopf, 1996). Kramskoi, Victor's pragmatic friend, is named for the artist Ivan Kramskoi, whose famous *Neizvestnaia* (*Unknown Woman*, 1883) depicts a haughty and challenging vamp.

Viktor's suicide, thereby underscoring her murderous role in the relationship.[2] The luxurious, idle life of the upper classes encourages sexual fantasies and self-indulgence. However, the patriarchal male can no longer control woman: he either fetishizes her as spectacle, or constructs an ideal of his own creation, or dies because he is unable to adapt to her new reality. But Viktor is denied sympathy because he is implicated in his own fate: he has made Mary into what she is.

Bauer's artistic background and design experience sensitized him to the potentialities of mise-en-scène.[3] In *Child of the Big City* the mise-en-scène functions in three ways: as always in Bauer, the treatment of space works to combat the flatness of the cinema screen; composition draws attention to characters, while emblematic props—what Kuleshov called Bauer's *dikovinki*—serve to support the narrative. Space is constructed so as to create a sense of depth through architecture. Although Bauer's signature columns are missing from this film, Manechka sits by a window with a deep focus view of the city; doorways open onto deep focus views of streets; a staircase extends space upward, and when Manechka stands in front of a flower shop, Bauer shoots from the inside, layering the interior, the glass window, Viktor and Kramskoi and the street scene outside.[4] Although interiors are crowded with objects replicating the prestige of the department store in a private

---

[2] Both Mary (Elena Smirnova) and the valet (Leonid Iost) worked as nightclub tango dancers. On the tango's 1913 arrival in Russia, see Yuri Tsivian, "The Tango in Russia," *Experiment* 2 (1996): 307-35.

[3] According to Ivan Perestiani, who starred in several Bauer films, the director's motto was "First of all beauty, then truth" ("Prezhde vsego krasota, potom Pravda," I. Perestiani, *75 let zhizni v iskusstve* [Moscow: Iskusstvo, 1962], 258) and he is known to have halted filming for the greater part of a day while the right candelabra was found for an interior (E. Gromov, "Dekorativnoe masterstvo Evgeniia Bauera," *Voprosy kinoiskusstva* 18 [1976]: 301). The mise-en-scène sometimes assumed such prominence that Bauer preferred to place the actor at the edge of the frame.

[4] Architecture also carries its traditional symbolic functions: initially Manechka is reluctant to cross the threshold to the restaurant in which she is seduced; before the nightclub episode, she crosses a threshold and climbs a staircase,

home, these same objects (screens, statuettes, furniture) are placed so as to extend interior space. In the nightclub episode, space is extended through three bands—Mary and Viktor at a table in the foreground, the revelers dancing in the middle area, and the stage with the Indian dancer in the background. Bauer also uses curtains, a theatrical device, to extend space during Mary's party and decenter the frame into dark and light areas that highlight action. In the first party scene, a semi-opaque gauze curtain divides the frame, but its transparent side on the right focuses attention on Mary. Viktor's room has a dark wall with a bright window on the left. In the subsequent formal parallel, a dark curtain in Mary's apartment fills the screen, but it is open to the light on the left, highlighting Mary and the valet's tango dancing.

Viktor's study is full of classical statues of women and he keeps the images of his female acquaintances in a photo album—a controlling objectification of the women with whom he ultimately cannot cope. Analogously, Viktor continues to venerate first his dream image of Manechka (superimpositions) and later, her photograph, neither of which corresponds to her reality. Less obviously, an Art Nouveau bust of a woman with flowing hair and an intricate decorative grille support the narrative in two episodes: in the breakfast scene the bust stands behind Viktor, denoting his control of woman's image, while Mary sits in front of the grille, perhaps implying a more complex personality than Viktor acknowledges. When Mary writes her note rejecting Viktor's offer to live modestly and for each other, both the bust and grille are placed behind her as she assumes possession of her own subjectivity.

The static camera and longshot were conventions of early Russian cinema. Consequently, the one long track-in (popularized by Bauer) and two inserts (close-ups depicting objects or parts of the body) are marked, and all figure Mary as vamp. Through intercutting, the track-in connects Mary in the foreground to the "Indian dancer" on stage, played by Bauer's wife. As a sexually aggressive woman,

---

as she moves up in the world. Before his suicide, Victor crosses a bridge on the Moscow River.

the literary and iconographic vamp was often associated with a sinuous and sinister phallic serpent.[5] It is the dancer's undulating hands, a talismanic part of woman's body, that first appear from behind the curtain, and the rest of her then emerges to perform a snake dance. Meanwhile Mary flirts with various men who come up to kiss her hand and forearm. The first insert in *Child of the Big City* signals Mary's ultimate empowerment: her hands have placed a three-ruble note into the maid's hands to buy off Viktor, and she pushes the maid to accomplish the task quickly. In the second insert Mary's elegant tango shoe steps over Viktor's body, highlighting the triumph of murderous sexuality. The discovery of Viktor's body is not the film's climax; rather it is Mary's reaction: her initial shock turns to indifference, and then impatience.[6] Reverting to type, she trots out a folk saying about meeting a dead man as good luck.[7] The film then concludes with a close-up of Viktor's face, a relatively common ending in early Russian films.

---

[5] See description of Rider Haggard's: "She who moved with 'a certain snake-like grace'" and Franz von Stuck's paintings (H. Rider. *She*. Facsimile copy of first edition [1887]. [NY: Hart Publishing, 1976], 149; *Dykstra* 135, 436).

[6] Rachel Morley, "'Crime Without Punishment': Reworkings of Nineteenth-century Russian Literary Sources in Evgenii Bauer's *Child of the Big City*," in *Russian and Soviet Film Adaptations of Literature, 1900-2001: Screening the Word,* ed. Stephen Hutchings and Anat Vernitski (London: Routledge Curzon, 2005), 39.

[7] "Pokoinik—dobraia vstrecha na vyezdakh." Chichikov makes the same remark when meeting a funeral procession in *Dead Souls.*

THE SCHEHEREZADE
OF THE BOULEVARD NOVEL

A PIQUANT MIX OF THE VULGAR AND THE PROPER

Oksana Bulgakova

The actress plays two bodies. Mania the milliner makes many small, fussy motions. Even when her hands are occupied with a large hatbox, she manages to fling up one hand and wipe away tears with it, wave away the men, touch her dress and face. Finding herself in a private room of the restaurant and having rid herself of the box, she now flings up both hands, wrings them, defends herself, and stretches her hands out in front of her. Playing up her low social origins, the director shows her way of eating greedily with both hands while grabbing food from various plates. The bored aristocrat, tired of mannered society girls, perceives all this as "an unspoiled nature."

In the bourgeois salons of 1914, the bodily behavior of young Mayakovsky, who was defined by Livshitz as "a walking grand guignol," "a character from a puppet theatre of horrors," had the same shocking-attracting effect. At table in the dining room of Petersburg arts patrons, "he provocatively broke off pieces of cake with hands that were red from the cold, and when D., who had lost patience, made some sort of comment about his dirty nails, he responded with a horribly rude remark."[1]

[George Bernard] Shaw, who in 1912 transferred the Pygmalion plot from mythological to social space, mainly stressed pronunciation and language, changes which also engendered the transformation of Eliza Doolittle's inner world and body techniques. In silent film this plot takes shape (and is palpable) through gesture alone. When Mania becomes Mary and assumes the position of cocotte, she stops eating onscreen and only sips coffee or champagne, holding the

---

[1]   Benedikt Livshitz, *Polutoraglazyi strelets* (Moscow: Khudozhestvennaia literatura, 1991), 102-3.

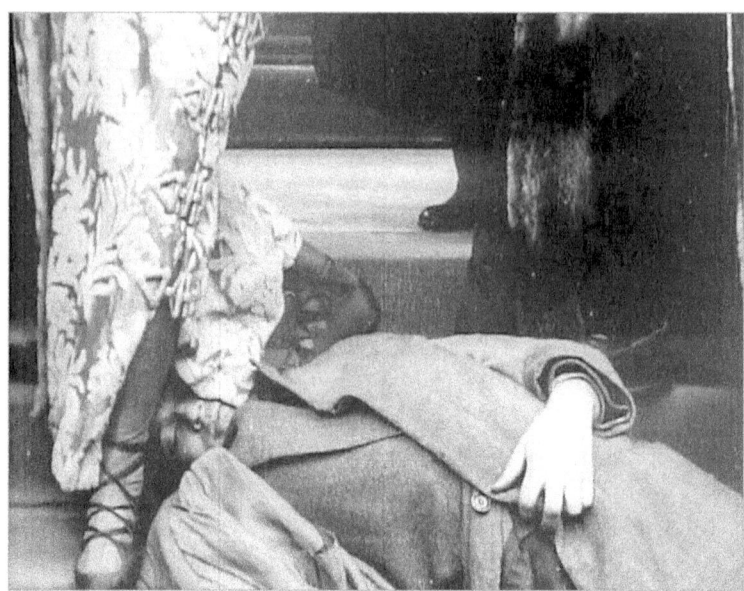

Fig. 6. Stepping over Viktor

goblet, not with two hands, like Nastia the maid,[2] but carelessly, with the fingers of one hand. Her contact with conversation partners observes the accepted forms of bodily communication of a higher social stratum: she doesn't fall on her knees before her lover (as does Nastia before the master), but extends her hand to him for a kiss, which gives her an opportunity to highlight the nakedness of her shoulders and demonstrate a balletic suppleness of the elbow — like the aristocratic lady, as played by Elsa Krüger. In her seductive poses — arching her torso, leaning back, toying coquettishly with her hand, Mary imitates the models of early (soft) porn postcards. In the finale of the film, performing the tango completes the eroticization of her body.

However, the director and actress consciously retain recurrences of her plebeian origins in the heroine's body language. During her first screen appearance in her new status and in a different dress,

---

[2]   A character in Bauer's *Silent Witnesses* (*Nemye svideteli*, 1916). Elsa Krüger plays an aristocratic lady in the film.

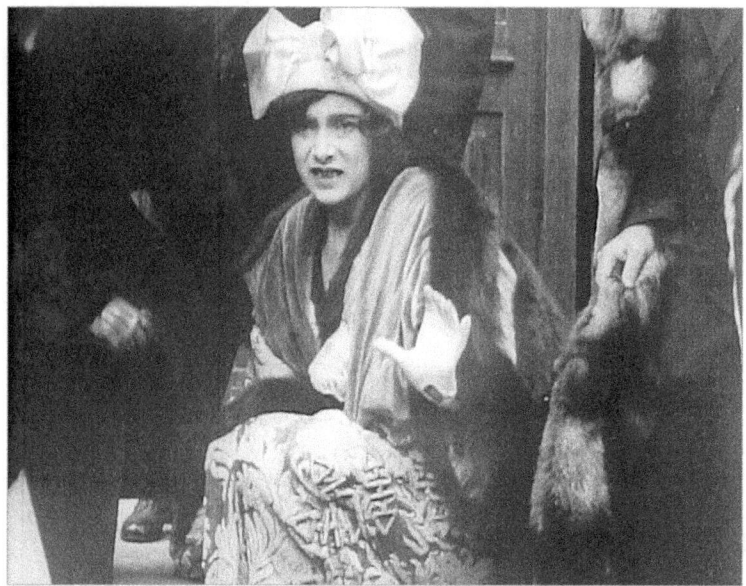

Fig. 7. Warding Off Evil

during her visit to the café-concert with her lover, she fusses about, giggles and constantly straightens her clothing. Later these gestures disappear in "society," but in private space Mania remains a vulgar daughter of the masses. Sitting in her boudoir, she "doesn't hold her back straight," yawns, stretches and leans her head on her hands, as she did in the workshop. In the stormy jealousy scene, she twitches, and with a "spreading of the extremities," as Gogol' would say, jumps to one side, abandoning the fluid, slowly gliding and graceful languor that distinguished her plasticity before the "affect."

The ending of the film is especially interesting: through montage the director separates her body into an eroticized leg and an archaicized-vulgarized hand. When Mary steps across the corpse of the aristocrat who has committed suicide (her ruined lover), Bauer inserts a close-up of her elegant foot in a transparent stocking and tango shoes (Fig. 6). Contrasted to this shot is her expressive gesture of disgust (palm extended forward with spread fingers), which returns the heroine not to etiquette-related gesture, but to the sphere of the incantational-folkloric (Fig. 7). This is an accepted magical gesture to ward off an evil power or a bad omen.

FURTHER READING

DeBlasio, Alyssa. "Choreographing Space, Time, and *Dikovinki* in the Films of Evgenii Bauer." *The Russian Review* 66 (October 2007): 671-92.

McReynolds, Louise. "Demanding Men, Desiring Women and Social Collapse in the Films of Evgenii Bauer, 1913-17." *Studies in Russian and Soviet Cinema* 3, no. 2 (2009): 145-56.

------. "Home Was Never Where the Heart Was: Domestic Dystopias in Russia's Silent Movie Melodramas." In *Imitations of Life. Two Centuries of Melodrama in Russia*, edited by L. McReynolds and J. Neuberger, 127-51. Durham, NC: Duke University Press, 2002.

------. "The Silent Movie Melodrama: Evgenii Bauer Fashions the Heroine's Self." In *Self and Story in Russian History*, edited and with an introduction by Laura Engelstein and Stephanie Sandler, 120-40. Ithaca: Cornell University Press, 2000.

Morley, Rachel. "Gender Relations in the Films of Evgenii Bauer." *Slavonic and East European Review* 81, no. 1 (2003): 32-69.

Torre, Michele L. "Filtering Culture: Symbolism, Modernity and Gender Construction in Evgenii Bauer's Films." In *Screen Culture: History and Textuality*, edited by John Fullerton, 99-112. Eastleigh, England: John Libbey, 2004.

PART
TWO

SOVIET SILENT CINEMA 1918-1930

Denise J. Youngblood

The silent film era is the best-known period in Soviet film history. Many books and articles have been written about this "Golden Age," usually focusing on the great avant-garde film artists— Sergei Eisenstein, Lev Kuleshov, Alexander Dovzhenko, Vsevolod Pudovkin and Dziga Vertov. This essay shall provide a more inclusive picture by also discussing some of the films and directors that most moviegoers wanted to see, like Iakov Protazanov, Boris Barnet, Fridrikh Ermler and Abram Room.

1918-1921

From the beginning of Soviet power, cinema occupied a central place among the arts and was deeply politicized.[1] As the bourgeois film industry continued to churn out the lurid but sophisticated melodramas noted in the previous chapters, the Bolsheviks began making their first films, called agit-films. The difference between the quality and topics of Soviet cinema and pre-revolutionary cinema was, not surprisingly, striking. Agit-films were short, simple agitational movies designed to propagandize Bolshevik programs and policies, primarily during the period of the Russian Civil War, 1918-1921, when the agit-film was the dominant cinema form.

The length of the typical agit-film was less than 30 minutes. It was feared that longer propaganda films would bore and thereby alienate audiences, which consisted of city-dwellers, peasants, soldiers and especially children. Another reason for the short

---

[1]   Lenin supposedly said that "for us, cinema is the most important of the arts," in recognition of the propaganda potential of this very new art form. The slogan was emblazoned in all Soviet movie theaters.

running time of the films was the shortage of film stock.[2] Although the Bolsheviks immediately seized control of the studios of the Skobelev Committee (which had produced tsarist World War I propaganda films), the amount of film stock available legally through an agreement with Kodak, and illegally through the black market, fell far below the demand. The Bolsheviks were so desperate for film stock that they sought to reuse it through a re-emulsification process, which produced film of very low quality.

Because most movie theaters were closed for much of the Civil War, agit-films were shown at agit-points, stationary exhibition centers usually set up at train stations, special political houses, agit-trains[3] and even agit-steamboats. Given the shortage of film copies, agit-trains and agit-steamers were extremely important; sometimes only one or two copies were made, which made the traveling shows all the more necessary. All exhibition sites were colorfully decorated with political slogans and political paintings (often by avant-garde artists like Mayakovsky and Lissitsky, although realist paintings came later).

The agit-films were always the major draw at political meetings, especially in the countryside, which had been poorly served by the pre-revolutionary film industry. The films were the first item of business at meetings, followed by propaganda and other activities for the literacy and agricultural campaigns. People who enjoyed the films—and the little evidence available indicated that many did— would stay for the rest of the program and become involved with the other activities.[4]

Over the course of the Civil War, 69 agit-films were made, comprising 66 percent of Soviet film production.[5] Often the directors

---

2   Richard Taylor, "Agitation, Propaganda, and the Cinema," in Nils Ake Nilsson, ed., *Art, Society and Revolution, 1917-1921* (Stockholm: Almqvist and Wiksell, 1979), 245.

3   See Taylor, "Agitation, Propaganda, and the Cinema," 248-53, for a detailed discussion of the agit-trains.

4   Richard Taylor, *The Politics of the Soviet Cinema*, 58-59, in Further Reading.

5   *Sovetskie khudozhestvennye fil'my: Annotirovannyi katalog*, vol. 1, *Nemye fil'my (1918-1935)* (Moscow: Iskusstvo, 1961).

were well-known figures from the tsarist cinema or soon to become well-known in Soviet cinema. Agit-film directors included famous names such as Vladimir Gardin, Lev Kuleshov, Aleksandr Ivanovskii, Aleksandr Panteleev, Ivan Perestiani, Aleksandr Razumnyi and Iurii Zheliabuzhskii.

Despite the fact that only ten agit-films have survived, the annotated catalogue *Soviet Fiction Films* (*Sovetskie khudozhestvennye fil'my*), provides brief plot descriptions for most of them, based on archival materials.[6] The agit-films can be divided into two major genres. A few were comedies, like *The Frightened Bourgeois* (*Ispugannyi burzhui*), in which an insomniac capitalist finds his condition cured by hard labor. Most, however, were melodramas, such as *Father and Son* (*Otets i syn*), in which a captured Red Army soldier is guarded by his father, whom the Whites had drafted; the son persuades his father of the rightness of the Red cause and induces him to free all the Red prisoners and join the Red Army. (Agit-films on civil war themes were particularly prominent.)

The popularity of military agit-films notwithstanding, *Overcrowding* (*Uplotnenie*, 1918)[7] is the most famous of the agit-films, a true prestige project. The film script was written by the Commissar of Enlightenment, Anatolii Lunacharskii; the movie begins with a shot of Lunacharskii grinning boyishly at the camera. It is the story of a pampered professor who is forced to give up some rooms in his large house to workers. After a rough start, all turns out well. The professor begins teaching science at a workers' club, and his son falls in love with a proletarian girl who has moved in with them.

Overcrowding is a perfect example of an agit-film: it has a rudimentary plot, a simple message supporting a regime goal and limited character development. Its poster shows the professor standing beside a worker, their arms draped over each other's shoulders, with the slogan "Workers of the World Unite!" above them. The

---

6   See also Nikolai Iezuitov, "Agitki epokhi grazhdanskoi voiny," *Iskusstvo kino* 5 (May 1940): 47-51.

7   "Uplotnenie" actually translates to "consolidation," but *Overcrowding* is a more apt translation in this case and is the title the film is known by in the West.

cinematic style can be charitably described as primitive; despite the simplicity of the plot and the limited cast of characters, the actions and relationships of the characters are often confusing. A political instructor or agitator really would have been necessary to explain the film.

The primitiveness of the production distinguishes agit-films from the fiction films of the rest of the 1920s—and from the Russian bourgeois cinema that preceded it. As Richard Taylor has noted, however, the filmic style of the agit-films nonetheless became the foundation for important filmmakers like Sergei Eisenstein, Lev Kuleshov (who taught at the film school), Vsevolod Pudovkin, Esfir' Shub, and Dziga Vertov. Especially important to the success of the agit-films was their concise and dynamic style, achieved by skillful editing. "Without the challenge of the Civil War it is unlikely that the Soviet cinema would have developed the forceful, distinctive and revolutionary visual style of the 1920s."[8]

1922-1928

The Civil War was over in most parts of the country by 1921. Late that year, Lenin decided to end the draconian economic system known as War Communism in favor of a mixed economy, called the New Economic Policy (NEP). The NEP had a very beneficial effect on the fledgling Soviet film industry. In 1922, the first state film trust, Goskino, was organized, to be renamed Sovkino in 1924. Another key event was the opening of the semi-private studio Mezhrabpom-Rus', which combined capital from a German communist organization, the International Workers' Aid, with the facilities of the pre-revolutionary studio Rus'. Mezhrabpom soon became famous as the leading producer of entertainment films. Movie theaters, some badly damaged by neglect or war, gradually began to reopen.

Because of the still dire shortage of film stock, young artists who were intrigued by the revolutionary potential of the movies became

---

[8] Taylor, *The Politics of the Soviet Cinema*, 63.

theorists first and directors second. The "old man" of the young guard, Lev Kuleshov (only 23 in 1922), had worked in early Russian cinema as a set designer and actor for Evgenii Bauer. His collective became a center for new talent. Kuleshov laid the foundations for Soviet revolutionary film theory. He was the first to declare that revolutionary style demanded quick, rhythmic cutting, which he called "American montage" in recognition of the quick cutting of American action films. (Ironically, this style of editing is known in film histories as "Russian montage.") Kuleshov also sought a new kind of actor that he labeled the "actor-model," who needed to undertake a special program of exercise to develop body language.

His most famous experiment was the "Kuleshov effect." The basis for relational montage, this experiment alternated shots of the pre-revolutionary star Ivan Mozzhukhin with neutral shots like a bowl of soup or a coffin. Although it was always the same shot of Mozzhukhin, viewers reported that his expression was changing in relation to the object, that he looked hungry when cut with the soup, sad with the coffin, etc.[9]

Important as Kuleshov's ideas about film were, those of Sergei Eisenstein and Dziga Vertov had even greater international impact. In terms of their theoretical positions, the two directors were sworn enemies who engaged in many public debates that roiled the avant-garde filmmaking community. Eisenstein argued in favor of acted cinema, that is, fiction films with actors. This does not sound particularly revolutionary until we understand that Eisenstein disdained the glamorous stars who had dominated early Russian cinema in favor of non-professional actors or those whose physiognomy fit certain "types": worker, peasant, bourgeois, etc. He also believed that in a socialist cinema, the hero should be the collective (the masses) as opposed to the individuals who populated pre-revolutionary filmmaking.[10]

[9]   Lev Kuleshov, *Kuleshov on Film: Writings of Lev Kuleshov*, trans. and ed. Ronald Levaco (Berkeley: University of California Press, 1974).

[10]   Sergei Eisenstein, *Selected Works*, vol. 1, *1922-1934*, ed. and trans. Richard Taylor (London: BFI and Bloomington: Indiana University Press, 1988); *Selected Works*, vol. 2, *Toward a Theory of Montage*, ed. Michael Glenny and

In marked contrast, Vertov supported non-acted (documentary) films because he believed that the real image, not the actor, should be the focal point of any movie. Indeed, Vertov labeled the movie camera the "cinema eye" and his production collective became popularly known as the Cinema Eyes. He proclaimed that the purpose of cinema was to capture "life off-guard" or "unaware." Yet despite his allegiance to unvarnished reality (if there can ever be such a thing), Vertov frequently manipulated time and space in his films, with the assistance of his wife, film editor Elizaveta Svilova. Vertov also forcefully opposed the narrative film and especially the drama. He argued that a well-edited kaleidoscope of shots best represented revolutionary reality.[11]

Other young directors contributed significantly to early Soviet film theory. Seventeen year old Grigorii Kozintsev and his "senior" partner Leonid Trauberg, age 20, published a futurist manifesto in 1922, titled "Eccentrism" ("Ekstsentrizm"). This zany collection of fragmentary thoughts about pop culture, technology and "Americanism" captured the attention of futurist critics and writers, most notably the "poet of the revolution" Vladimir Maya-kovsky.[12]

Vsevolod Pudovkin occupies a transitional space in revolutionary cinema, between the avant-garde and the realist styles that eventually would come to dominate Soviet cinema. Like Eisenstein, he believed in "typage," the actor as type, but unlike Eisenstein, he placed individuals at the center of his revolution-themed films. Pudovkin also believed that quick-cutting (Kuleshov's "American" montage) was essential to a truly revolutionary filmmaking style, but he argued that ideas should determine the action, rather than the other way around. Pudovkin's editing style, which he dubbed

Richard Taylor, trans. Michael Glenny (London: BFI, 1991).

[11] Dziga Vertov, *Kino-Eye: The Writings of Dziga Vertov*, ed. Annette Michelson, trans. Kevin O'Brien (Berkeley: University of California Press, 1984).

[12] Ian Christie and John Gillett, eds., *Futurism/Formalism/FEKS: Eccentrism and Soviet Cinema, 1918-1936* (London: British Film Institute, 1987).

"associational montage," worked to reinforce the socialist content of his films.[13]

Few of these young filmmakers had the opportunity to put their ideas into practice before 1925. They were discouraged to see that leading directors from the old regime, like Petr Chardynin, Vladimir Gardin and Iakov Protazanov, were reinventing themselves as "Soviet" directors by making films that were superficially revolutionary in content. Protazanov's first Soviet feature, *Aelita* (1924), is a case in point. Based on Aleksei Tolstoi's popular science fiction novel about a workers' revolt on Mars, *Aelita* featured the beautiful Iuliia Solntseva in the title role, phantasmagoric sets and constructivist costumes by the noted avant-garde artist Aleksandra Ekster (Fig. 8). This was contrasted with the bleakness of NEP Russia, a world filled with speculators. The film's undeniably communist

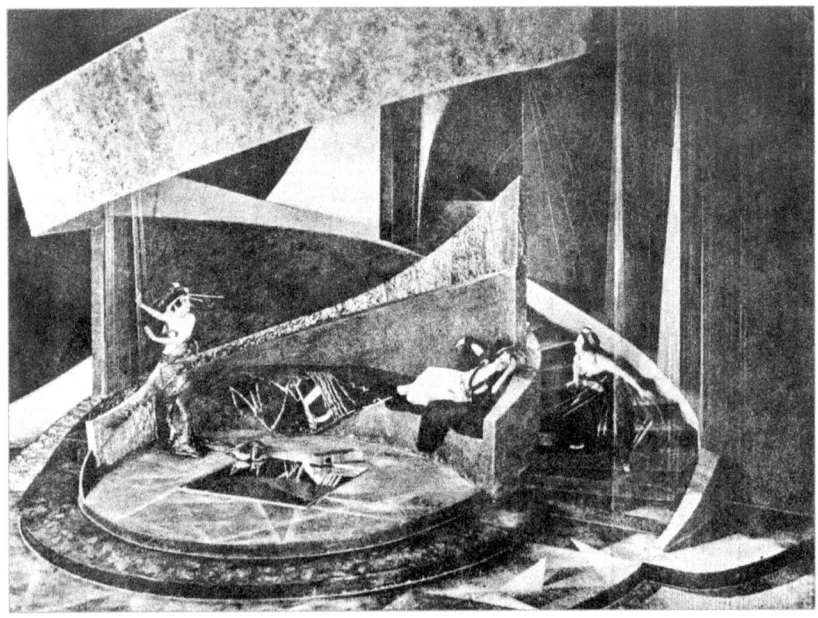

Fig. 8. Aelita, The Queen of Mars

---

message was criticized as superficial; regardless, it was a major hit at the box office and was regularly mentioned as a favorite film in audience surveys for the next several years.[14]

Despite the bias against untested filmmakers, in 1924 Lev Kuleshov directed his début film, *The Extraordinary Adventures of Mr. West in the Land of the Bolsheviks* (*Neobychainye prikliucheniia mistera Vesta v strane bol'shevikov*). It was an entertaining exposition of his theories and one of the most popular films of the decade. This high-energy satire of the problems of the NEP and American misconceptions about the Bolsheviks starred future directors Vsevolod Pudovkin and Boris Barnet as well as Kuleshov's wife, the marvelously eccentric actress Aleksandra Khokhlova.

The conflict between the "old" and the "new" generations of directors sharpened in the mid-1920s. This competition was not necessarily detrimental to the development of Soviet film art. There were two basic issues, the first an ideological debate about the role of cinema in a socialist society. The avant-garde directors, who were drawn from the ranks of the youth, argued that a revolutionary cinema would be revolutionary in form as well as in content. If the mass audience did not understand this type of cinema, they simply needed to be educated. The old guard directors, joined by some young directors who preferred a realistic style, countered by promoting the virtues of entertainment; workers wanted to be entertained and they deserved to get what they wanted.

The second issue that became a generational dispute was closely related to the ideological debate. During the NEP the film industry, although it remained nationalized (except for the Mezhrabpom studio), was expected to pay for itself through ticket sales. Sovkino, the state film trust, encouraged the studios to make entertainment films that would attract audiences, yielding a profit. This profit could then be used to finance the less popular, but more politically correct, films of the revolutionary avant-garde. Another profit-making policy was to import large numbers of foreign films,

---

[14]   Richard Taylor and Ian Christie, eds., *Inside the Film Factory*, chap. 5, in Further Reading.

with the result that for most of the 1920s, the majority of films on Soviet screens were foreign. The foreign films ensured the film industry's financial stability, but backfired politically. Foreign and other "bourgeois" films were clearly more popular than the films of the "revolutionary" artists of the avant-garde. Middlebrow films had their own fan magazine, *Soviet Screen*, replete with full-page photos of foreign and Soviet stars and gushing letters from star-struck moviegoers, mainly young women.[15]

Sovkino's policies put most of the young generation of directors at a clear disadvantage. A comparison of Eisenstein's and Vertov's early work with Protazanov's demonstrates this. Protazanov followed the box office success of *Aelita* with two more popular films. *His Call* (*Ego prizyv*, 1925), a melodrama superficially about the campaign to recruit young communist party members after Lenin's death, focuses on a naïve young girl swept off her feet by a murderous White Guardist who has returned to the USSR to try to retrieve his family fortune. *The Tailor from Torzhok* (*Zakroishchik iz Torzhka*, 1925), starring the popular comic actor Igor Il'inskii, is a rollicking comedy that promoted the state lottery, focusing on a bumbler trying to retrieve his lottery winnings and avoid marrying his landlady. These highly entertaining and well-crafted films did not break new artistic ground, but Protazanov never had any trouble with financing and distribution because he knew how to make films that drew audiences in droves.

In contrast, Eisenstein's work is powerfully original. His first film, *Strike* (*Stachka*, 1925), which dramatized the workers' movement during the revolution of 1905, centering on their betrayal to the police and eventual slaughter, introduced Eisenstein's radical ideas about film editing to amazed critics. This was a brilliant début, but it was his second film, *Battleship Potemkin* (*Bronenosets Potemkin*, 1925), that guaranteed him an enduring place in film history. *Strike* and especially *Potemkin* catapulted the young director to international fame and exacerbated his rivalry with Vertov. However, despite the praise of leftist critics, neither film was a success with working class

---

15   Denise J. Youngblood, *Movies for the Masses,* chap. 3, in Further Reading.

viewers, who were puzzled by the lack of individual heroes and the absence of a classical narrative. Attendance was inflated with mandatory screenings at factories and clubs.[16]

Undaunted, Eisenstein forged ahead with *October* (*Oktiabr'*, Fig. 9), a film loosely based on American journalist John Reed's *Ten Days that Shook the World*. Commissioned to honor the tenth anniversary of the Bolshevik Revolution in November 1927, *October*

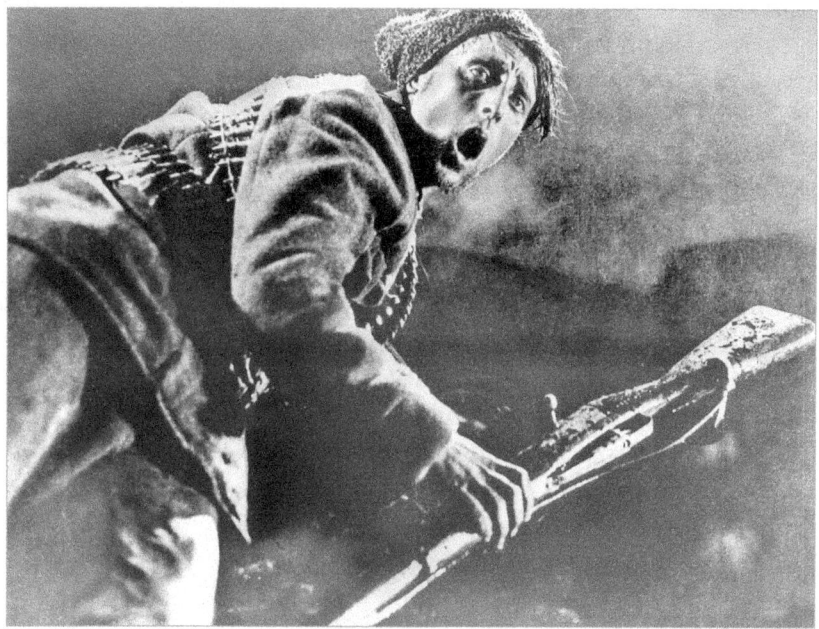

Fig. 9. October

was not released until 1928. Although some of its scenes are among the most famous in Eisenstein's oeuvre, like a girl and a dead horse falling slowly off a bridge, the film lacks the propulsive rhythms and dramatic intensity that make *Battleship Potemkin* so mesmerizing.

There were political problems as well. Eisenstein intended the film to be a celebration of the revolution, but he found himself out

---

[16]   Denise J. Youngblood, *Soviet Cinema in the Silent Era, 1918-1935*, 83-85, in Further Reading.

of step with the Party line. Disgraced Bolshevik leader Leon Trotsky had to be excised from the film, but even then, the final version was problematic. The most developed character is Alexander Kerensky, the dictatorial head of the Provisional Government, a fact that greatly disturbed Lenin's widow, Nadezhda Krupskaia. The portrayal of Kerensky sharply contrasted with that of Lenin, impersonated by a worker who bore a strong resemblance to Lenin, but who completely lacked the leader's energy and personal magnetism. In addition, Krupskaia panned Eisenstein's symbolism, particularly the series of shots of gods and idols.[17]

Dziga Vertov also found it difficult to make movies that attracted a mass audience. His first important body of work was his *Cinema Truth* (*Kino-pravda*) series of documentaries, which began in 1922. His first full-length film was *Cinema Eye* (*Kino-glaz*, 1924), which was criticized as a mere curiosity. It was not until his feature length documentaries *Stride, Soviet!* (*Shagai, Sovet!*) and *One-Sixth of the World* (*Shestaia chast' mira*), both released in 1926, that his style fully matured. These two films exemplify the principles of constructivism in film and are a valuable archive of images of socialist construction. They show the process of building socialism and the positive impact of the revolution on daily life in the USSR. *Stride, Soviet!* looks at the achievements of Soviet power—electrification, education, health, cooperatives—but reveals the problems of NEP society as well: banditry, speculation, poverty and hooliganism. *One-Sixth of the World,* which makes heavy use of the split screen and fast motion photography, is mainly an amalgam of scenes of Soviet industry. Not surprisingly, the proletarians for whom Vertov intended the films did not like them. After laboring all day in a hot and noisy factory, most did not relish the idea of spending their limited leisure time watching workers—working.

Other members of the avant-garde found themselves in a similar position vis-à-vis the mass audience. Kuleshov continued to develop as an artist, but his later, bolder efforts failed to find an appreciative audience of either workers or critics. *By the Law* (*Po zakonu*, 1926),

---

[17]   Youngblood, *Soviet Cinema*, 55, 174-75.

his stunning adaptation of "The Unexpected," Jack London's tale of crime and punishment in the Klondike, met with an even more negative audience and critical response than his failed attempt at science fiction, the wildly disjointed *Death Ray* (*Luch smerti*, 1925). *By the Law's* final scene—a husband and wife (brilliantly portrayed by Aleksandra Khokhlova) struggling up a hill pushing a man they have sentenced to be hanged—is unforgettable.

The directing duo of Grigorii Kozintsev and Leonid Trauberg never penetrated an audience outside the leftist cultural elite. Nevertheless, their films for the adventurous Leningrad studio are artistically important and deserve more careful study than they have found to date. Their experimental narratives such as their 1926 films *The Devil's Wheel* (*Chertovo koleso*) and *The Overcoat* (*Shinel'*, an adaptation of the Gogol' story) perfectly achieved Kozintsev and Trauberg's desire to realize the principles of Expressionism and Eccentrism in film. The plot of *The Devil's Wheel* sounds conventional—an innocent young sailor is sucked into the underworld by his girlfriend—but the execution is not. The film's distortion of reality, which includes shots from odd angles, bizarre cuts, whirling images, figures blurred by the camera lens, was artistically justifiable but wearisome to the eye. *The Overcoat* gave free rein to Kozintsev and Trauberg's love for the grotesque; their style was perfectly suited to the subject, the tale of a poor bureaucrat whose new coat (his only desire in life) is stolen shortly after he obtains it. Nevertheless, like *The Devil's Wheel*, it was a critical failure.[18]

Another avant-garde artist of importance was the Ukrainian Alexander Dovzhenko, the greatest artist to emerge from the non-Russian cinemas. Moviemaking in the multi-ethnic USSR was not an exclusively Russian enterprise, but most leading filmmakers were either Russian or self-identified as Russian. Distribution politics made it difficult for films from Ukraine, Georgia, and Armenia to be considered as more than exotica, at least for the Russian movie-going public. Dovzhenko alone broke this barrier.

---

[18] Youngblood, *Soviet Cinema*, chap. 4.

Dovzhenko first garnered widespread critical attention with his fourth film *Zvenigora* (1928), a romantic and inventive celebration of folklore and folklife in Ukraine. None of Dovzhenko's previous work, which included the short comedy *Love's Little Berry* (*Iagodka liubvi*, 1926), a farce about a woman trying to get the father of her child to marry her and the spy thriller *The Diplomatic Courier's Pouch* (*Sumka dipkur'era*, 1927), about the British waylaying some Soviet diplomatic couriers, prepared viewers for the visual feast that was *Zvenigora*. Subtitled a "cinema poem," *Zvenigora* is lyrical and plotless, in the first part, a fable of wealth hidden beneath Ukrainian earth and an old man's dreams of finding this treasure and meeting legendary heroes. Sergei Eisenstein was thrilled by the kaleidoscope of images; studio and film trust administrators were bemused; ordinary movie-goers were reportedly confused. Nevertheless, a star had been born.[19]

The artistic achievements of Kuleshov, Kozintsev and Trauberg, and Dovzhenko notwithstanding, the most consistently successful of the young avant-garde directors in adapting revolutionary style and content for the tastes of mass audiences was Vsevolod Pudovkin. Because he utilized well-developed plots and characters that had realist overtones, his films were less radical than those of some of his colleagues but still incorporated some avant-garde montage techniques. His directorial debut was *Mother* (*Mat'*, 1926), the story of a worker's rise to revolutionary consciousness that was freely adapted from Maxim Gorky's famous novel. The film was greeted with universal praise.

Pudovkin followed this with other critically acclaimed films on revolutionary themes, *The End of St. Petersburg* (*Konets Sankt-Peterburga*, 1927), which was commissioned for the tenth anniversary of the October revolution, and *The Heir of Genghis Khan* (*Potomok Chingiz-khana*,1928), also known as *Storm over Asia*. With these two films, Pudovkin came into his own as a director. *The End of St. Petersburg* is a particularly brilliant example of Pudovkin as an innovator. This time, a young peasant becomes a revolutionary.

---

[19]   Youngblood, *Soviet Cinema*, 180-81.

But unlike *Mother's* Pavel, this hero is an unnamed "Everyman." The superior camera work of cinematographer Anatolii Golovnia, which reflected the excitement of the revolutionary through the unexpectedness of his technique, is a major factor. As a film actor himself, Pudovkin displayed a remarkable ability to elicit strong performances from his actors. *The Heir of Genghis Khan* was about the British attempt to turn a young Mongol into a puppet ruler, ending in the "puppet" turning against them, leading an armed revolt. It is a powerfully physical film, and Pudovkin's sense of drama and ability to work with actors is obvious. Despite the fact that purges were underway in the film industry, this profoundly formalist movie received only praise from the critics.[20]

Yet even Pudovkin could not compete commercially with the old guard, epitomized by Iakov Protazanov, who continued to evolve as a Soviet realist filmmaker. Known in his pre-revolutionary period as a director of literary adaptations and melodramas, Protazanov continued to make highly polished, well-acted and entertaining movies, albeit with revolutionary themes. One of his best and most popular films was *The Forty-First* (*Sorok pervyi*, 1927), adapted from Boris Lavrenev's novella about a Red Army sharpshooter who eventually kills her lover, a White officer, making him her forty-first victim. With a sizzling romance like this, Protazanov could not fail, and the film is arguably the most entertaining of the decade.

As good as his melodramas were, Protazanov also became known as the premiere director of satirical comedies. Films like *The Case of the Three Million* (*Protsess o trekh millionakh*, 1926), *Don Diego and Pelageia* (*Don Diego i Pelageia*, 1928), and *St. Jorgen's Feast Day* (*Prazdnik sviatogo Iorgena*, 1930) skewered the absurdities of modern life, both Soviet and "bourgeois." *Don Diego and Pelageia* was a particularly pointed exposé of the absurdity of Soviet power, showing a petty and pedantic stationmaster, the quintessential bureaucrat, persecuting an old peasant woman who has crossed the tracks against the warning sign. After a ridiculous trial, she is sentenced to three months in jail before being rescued by two

---

[20]   Youngblood, *Soviet Cinema*, 150-52, 213.

Communist Youth League (Komsomol) members and the local Party secretary. All the lazy officials are fired. Although some critics were suspicious of Protazanov's intentions in this film—was he supporting the Party or not?—*Don Diego and Pelageia* was generally appreciated for what it is, a great comedy.[21]

Several young realist filmmakers also came to the forefront: Boris Barnet, Fridrikh Ermler and Abram Room. Boris Barnet, who had played Cowboy Jeddy in Kuleshov's *The Extraordinary Adventures of Mr. West in the Land of the Bolsheviks*, left the Kuleshov collective to work in films independently. His directorial debut, with Fedor Otsep, was *Miss Mend* (1926), a serialized spy spoof loosely based on Marietta Shaginian's popular novel. This was an auspicious début for Barnet, demonstrating that a western film genre could be adapted to the Soviet worldview. Barnet followed *Miss Mend* with two sparkling comedies on the problems and contradictions of NEP society, *The Girl with a Hatbox* (*Devushka s korobkoi*, 1927), about the shady dealings of NEP-era entrepreneurs, and *The House on Trubnaia Square* (*Dom na Trubnoi*, 1928), on the class struggles of NEP society.

Fridrikh Ermler was a different kind of realist director. Among a minority of leading directors who were members of the Communist Party, Ermler made penetrating social dramas about the problems of life during the NEP. Ermler always foregrounded class consciousness and social criticism, but it is simplistic to dismiss his films as propaganda. In fact, critics sometimes chided him for being insufficiently Party-minded in his work.

He first came to the notice of the movie-going public with his second feature, *Kat'ka the Apple Seller* (*Kat'ka bumazhnyi ranet*, 1926), a touching love story, with a dash of adventure, that explored the Soviet criminal underworld of black marketers and speculators. His next film, *The Parisian Cobbler* (*Parizhskii sapozhnik*, 1927, released 1928) showed a supposedly upstanding member of the Komsomol conspiring to have a gang of ruffians attack and rape his pregnant girlfriend. A hit with moviegoers, this dark melodrama—so different from *Kat'ka the Apple Seller*—caused an unwelcome stir

---

[21]   Youngblood, *Movies for the Masses*, chap. 6.

among film critics for its sensational subject matter and negative portrayal of communist youth. However, the critical reception of *The Parisian Cobbler* was pleasant compared to the chorus of opprobrium following the previews of *House in the Snowdrifts* (*Dom v sugrobakh*, 1927, limited release 1928). This film was based on Evgenii Zamiatin's short story "The Cave," a tale of moral degradation during the terrible winter of 1919. Zamiatin had gotten into trouble with the authorities for his dystopian novel *We*, which was seen to be an allegory of Soviet power. It seemed that even a communist director like Ermler could not be counted on to make politically reliable films.[22]

Abram Room was not in the same league as Barnet or Ermler in terms of mass popularity. He must, however, be included in this brief survey because of the box office success and notoriety both at home and abroad of his 1927 film *Third Meshchanskaia Street* (*Tret'ia Meshchanskaia*), known in the English-speaking world as *Bed and Sofa*. Unlike Protazanov, Barnet and Ermler, Room actively participated in the cultural debates of the NEP, especially as a proponent of the acted film. Yet Room's first two features, *The Bay of Death* (*Bukhta smerti*) and *The Traitor* (*Predatel'*), both 1926, were lively but not particularly distinguished examples of the revolutionary detective genre.

Room found his talents realized in *Third Meshchanskaia Street*. A psychologically complex story of a bored housewife who lives out her movie-fueled fantasies of romance in a one-room basement apartment, the film broke new ground in terms of sexual suggestiveness. The film was the biggest box office hit of 1927. "Right wing" moralizers in the Party were deeply disturbed that a film about a *ménage à trois*, with a *petite-bourgeoise* as a heroine, should be so popular with Soviet audiences. The film's critics were not satisfied with the positive finale and excoriated Room for failing to punish the miscreant males, who surely could not stand as representatives of the working class.

---

[22]   Youngblood, *Movies for the Masses*, chap. 8.

By the late 1920s, as the New Economic Policy era was coming to a close, Soviet cinema was flourishing. Cinema theaters had reopened in all provincial cities and cinematic road shows served rural areas, although there was much work to be done in the "cinefication" of the countryside. A lively film press reflected a variety of political and aesthetic positions. Production had grown to about 150 titles per year, despite the stiff competition from European and especially American films.

Yet clearly there were problems on the horizon. The mass audience did not like the films the critics liked — and vice versa. The young avant-garde directors were encouraged to be more realistic and accessible, while the old guard and the young realists were supposed to be less "bourgeois." From the Communist Party's perspective, the artistic diversity of NEP cinema was unacceptable. There was a strongly politicized drive toward a uniform cinema. More stringent controls — before, during, and after — filming ensued and as a result, film production began to plummet.[23]

1929-1930

Three major factors contributed to the Cultural Revolution in cinema. First, in 1927, sound became more widely used. This had significant artistic impact in all movie-producing countries, but an impoverished, developing state like the USSR could not readily afford to develop the technology and use it widely. Too much had already been invested in silent projectors. Second, "proletarianist" professional organizations like RAPP (the Russian Association of Proletarian Writers) and ARRK (the Association of Workers in Revolutionary Cinematography) were infiltrated by extremist elements that cared more about politics than art or entertainment. These cadres supported the government's aim to turn the Soviet film industry into a vehicle for propagandizing the campaigns to industrialize and to collectivize agriculture. The first All-Union Party Conference on Cinema Affairs laid the groundwork for this; the

---

23   Youngblood, *Soviet Cinema*, chap. 6 and appendix 1.

avant-garde was vigorously denounced at this meeting.[24] Third, in 1929, Anatolii Lunacharskii, the leading proponent of diversity and artistic freedom in cinema (and in all aspects of culture) was ousted from his cabinet-level position as Commissar of Enlightenment. Massive purges of the film industry followed, lasting through the end of 1931.[25]

Nevertheless, these troubled times saw the production of five great films that marked the end of the silent era in the USSR, although silent films continued to be shown (and a few made) throughout the 1930s. Fridrikh Ermler's *The Fragment of the Empire* (*Oblomok imperii*, 1929) tells the story of an amnesiac who suddenly recovers his memory ten years after the revolution to learn that tsarist Russia has been replaced by the communist USSR. After finding work in a factory, he finally remembers that he had a wife and manages to track her down. Her new husband is a well-placed, hypocritical bureaucrat, and she enjoys her life as a member of the Soviet bourgeoisie. In the end, although her new husband beats her, she cannot bear the thought of returning to a working class life. This was Ermler's most experimental film, skillfully employing unusual camera angles and cutting to show the man's overwhelming confusion as he discovers the new world.[26]

Grigorii Kozintsev and Leonid Trauberg cemented their reputation as the most daring experimenters of the Soviet avant-garde with the highly stylized expressionist film *New Babylon* (*Novyi Vavilon*, 1929), set during the Paris Commune of 1870. The plot—a shop girl is executed for her activity on the revolutionary barricades—is merely an excuse for the visual pyrotechnics. The film is a veritable encyclopedia of film technique: flashing titles, out-of-focus photography, fast-motion photography, double exposures and canted shots. The montage is excellent: the frenzy of the music hall is contrasted with preparation for battle; starkly realistic scenes of the common people are juxtaposed with the studied grotesquerie

---

[24] Youngblood, *Soviet Cinema*, chap. 7.

[25] Youngblood, *Soviet Cinema*, chaps. 7-8.

[26] Youngblood, *Movies for the Masses*, 149-52.

of the bourgeoisie. Yet, as critics noted, the film does not affect the viewer emotionally due to its lack of character development.[27]

In *The Man with the Movie Camera* (*Chelovek s kinoapparatom*, 1929), Dziga Vertov strolls around Moscow, brilliantly realizing his "cinema eye" theory. This delightful look at daily life in a big city is seen not only through the camera's eye, but also through the photographer's. At last the cameraman and not the camera is the star of a Vertov movie.[28] The film was accused of "narrow formalism" and "technological fetishism." It had distribution difficulties, and the director was criticized for his usual cost overruns. By this time, poor Vertov had few defenders.[29]

Alexander Dovzhenko made two films during the Cultural Revolution, *Arsenal* (1929) and *Earth* (*Zemlia*, 1930). A sweeping, yet lyrical, epic of war and revolution in Ukraine, *Arsenal* was widely criticized because it seemed to suggest that Dovzhenko's love for his native land was more important than his allegiance to the Soviet state and the Communist Party. Dovzhenko sought to evoke the pathos, not the grandeur, of the revolutionary struggle, making it unique in the annals of Soviet silent films about the revolution. The central character, Timosh, always labeled a "Ukrainian worker," is an enigmatic figure far removed from the positive hero that is at the heart of the developing aesthetic of Socialist Realism. The action is intentionally difficult to follow because Dovzhenko wanted to show the chaos that characterized Ukraine during the Civil War, a time when nationalism and revolutionary ardor were inseparable. Try as Dovzhenko might, the political signals in his films were too mixed to satisfy Soviet cinema's increasingly alert watchdogs.

Dovzhenko's dazzlingly beautiful Earth (1930), ostensibly intended to support Stalin's campaign to collectivize the country-side, was more remarkable in its celebration of the traditional way of life in rural Ukraine. Beginning with the death of an old

---

[27]   Youngblood, *Soviet Cinema*, 204-07.

[28]   Vlada Petrić, *Constructivism in Cinema: The Man with the Movie Camera, a Cinematic Analysis* (Cambridge: Cambridge University Press, 1987).

[29]   Youngblood, *Soviet Cinema*, 207.

grandfather in an apple orchard in the warm summer sun and climaxing with the death of the young hero, shot while he is dancing in the moonlight, Earth is a fable that transcends class warfare in the countryside. The dénouement, which shows the bitter anguish of the dead man's lover and the crazed guilt of the rich peasant who killed him, moves the film well beyond politics and into the realm of pure emotion.

The press denounced all five films as "formalist," a code word meaning that they failed to conform to the state's preference for a simple style accessible to the millions. This was soon to be known as Socialist Realism, a principle enshrined as the foundation of Soviet culture. Filmmakers who did not conform would not find work.

At this time, the sound film was making headway. Some directors and critics opposed the use of sound in cinema, but others, most notably Eisenstein, Pudovkin and Grigorii Aleksandrov, issued a manifesto in 1928 that celebrated the artistic potential of sound, although they firmly rejected the talkies.[30] A few leading artists of the silent era attempted to adapt their experimental talents to the sound film. These efforts met with little success. For example, Vertov's *Enthusiasm* (*Entuziasm*, 1930) and Kuleshov's *The Great Consoler* (*Velikii uteshitel'*, 1933) were lambasted for their "formalism." The embittered Vertov began making documentaries that showed little of his original talent, while Kuleshov spent the rest of his career sidelined into teaching at the State Film Institute. Others, notably Eisenstein, Kozintsev and Trauberg, later adapted to the new aesthetic with varying degrees of artistic success. Some, such as Ermler and Dovzhenko, made films that openly curried Stalin's favor.[31]

Nevertheless, the legacy of Soviet cinema's golden age lived on. In the West, Soviet revolutionary cinema became a staple of film

---

[30]   Richard Taylor and Ian Christie, eds., *The Film Factory*, doc. 92.

[31]   Youngblood, *Soviet Cinema*, chap. 9. Also see Peter Kenez, *Cinema and Soviet Society from the Revolution to the Death of Stalin* (London: I.B. Tauris, 2001), chap. 8.

courses and festivals, with Eisenstein's *Battleship Potemkin* regularly appearing on lists of the greatest films ever made. Today, the editing style of music videos owes a great deal to "Russian montage," particularly to Dziga Vertov, whether or not the directors are aware of it. The style of the radical Soviet filmmakers of the 1920s has become part of the cinematic vernacular. In the Soviet Union, the revival of cinema during Khrushchev's Thaw was made possible in part by the filmmakers who learned the art of the cinema from the masters of the Golden Age.

Further Reading

Cavendish, Philip. *Soviet Mainstream Cinematography: The Silent Era.* London: UCL Arts and Humanities, 2007.

Taylor, Richard. *The Politics of the Soviet Cinema, 1917-1929.* Cambridge: Cambridge University Press, 1979.

------, and Ian Christie, eds. *The Film Factory: Russian and Soviet Cinema in Documents, 1896-1939.* Translated by Richard Taylor. Cambridge, MA: Harvard University Press, 1988.

Youngblood, Denise J. *Soviet Cinema in the Silent Era, 1918-1935.* Austin: University of Texas Press, 1991.

------. *Movies for the Masses: Popular Cinema and Soviet Society in the 1920s.* Cambridge: Cambridge University Press, 1992.

Further Viewing

Arsenal. DVD. Mr. Bongo Films, 2011.

Landmarks of Early Soviet Film (Stride, Soviet!, The Fall of the Romanov Dynasty, The House on Trubnaia Square, By the Law, The Extraordinary Aventures of Mr. West in the Land of the Bolsheviks, The Old and the New, Turksib, Salt for Svanetia). DVD. Flicker Alley, 2011.

October. DVD. Image Entertainment, 1998.

Strike. DVD. Kino International, 2011.

Three Soviet Classics (Earth/The End of St. Petersburg/Chess Fever). DVD. Kino Video, 2003.

Zvenigora. DVD. Mr. Bongo Films, 2011.

THE EXTRAORDINARY ADVENTURES
OF MR. WEST IN THE LAND OF THE BOLSHEVIKS

Neobychainye prikliucheniia
mistera Vesta v strane bol'shevikov

1924

86 minutes

Director: **Lev Kuleshov**

Screenplay: **Nikolai Aseev, Vsevolod Pudovkin, Lev Kuleshov**

Cinematography: **Aleksandr Levitskii**

Art Design: **Vsevolod Pudovkin**

Production Company: **Goskino**

Cast: **Porfirii Podobed (Mr. West), Aleksandra Khokhlova**
("Countess" von Saks), Boris Barnet (Jeddy), Vsevolod
Pudovkin (Zhban), Valia Lopatina (Ellie), Sergei Komarov
(One-eye), Leonid Obolenskii (Dandy)

Lev Vladimirovich Kuleshov (1899-1970) came from an impoverished Tambov gentry family and studied art at the Moscow School of Painting, Architecture and Sculpture during 1915-16, but soon fell in love with cinema and went to work for Khanzhonkov's company, eventually becoming set designer for Bauer's later films and even acting in *Toward Happiness* (*Za schast'em*, 1917). Many film industry workers emigrated after 1917, but as an enthusiastic supporter of the Bolsheviks, Kuleshov stayed, seeing an opportunity to build a new Soviet cinema. His workshop at the State Film School trained actors according to his theories; among the participants were future directors Boris Barnet and Vsevolod Pudovkin, as well as successful actors, such as Kuleshov's wife, Aleksandra Khokhlova, Sergei Komarov, Vladimir Fogel' and Leonid Obolenskii. When film stock was not available during the early twenties, Kuleshov's collective delighted Moscow audiences by performing "films without film," sketches and miniatures in cinematic style. As an American-style comedy with elements of slapstick, the action-adventure film and the western, with heroes modeled on Harold Lloyd (Mr. West) and Douglas Fairbanks (Jeddy), *Mr. West* was a hit with Soviet audiences.

The remainder of Kuleshov's career was difficult. In later years he had only two successful films, *By the Law* (*Po zakonu*, 1926) and *The Great Consoler* (*Velikii uteshitel'*, 1933), and stopped directing after 1943. During the late 1920s-30s he was attacked as a formalist and his *The Merry Canary* (*Veselaia kanareika*) and *Two-Bul'di-Two* (*Dva-Bul'di-Dva*), both 1929, were labeled apolitical and bourgeois. Refused funding for his films, Kuleshov turned to teaching and administrative work at VGIK, the state film school, where he remained for the rest of this life, making only films on juvenile topics during World War II. At VGIK his teaching influenced several generations of filmmakers.

Kuleshov made theoretical contributions in two areas: montage and acting. He studied the creative potential of montage, defining what came to be called the "Kuleshov effect" (the alteration in meaning of an image through juxtaposition with another image) and "creative geography" (the cinematic construction of fictional entities, whether locations or human beings, through editing together different shots). Kuleshov's ideas about the actor derive from contemporary theatre practice, as in Meyerhold's biomechanics. Kuleshov described the actor as a "model" (*naturshchik*), as opposed to the Stanislavskian psychological actor. Rather than emphasizing inner feeling, the model is trained, through metrical-spatial exercises and the cultivation of physical skills, such as acrobatics, to control all parts of the body to be expressive. Facial movements are separated from inner psychological feeling and any part of the body can express any emotion.[1] The actor-model uses little makeup, instead exploiting his or her individuality: "We know that film

---

[1]   See Mikhail Yampolsky, "Kuleshov's Experiments and the New Anthropology of the Actor," in *Inside the Film Factory*, ed. Richard Taylor and Ian Christie (London: Routledge, 1994), 31-50, and Mikhail Yampolsky, "Mask Face and Machine Face," *The Drama Review* 38, no. 3 (Fall 1994): 60-74.

does not need stage actors, we know that an ordinary person with a body mechanism perfect in a humdrum way is unacceptable to the cinema. We need unusual, striking people, we need 'monsters'."[2]

Poet Nikolai Aseev wrote a scenario for *Mr. West* which turned out to be unfilmable and was radically rewritten by Pudovkin and Kuleshov so as not to lose the commission. The Russian film industry had still not returned to normalcy after the Civil War; in the face of shortages of construction materials and technical staff, Kuleshov's actors pitched in on all aspects of the production process.[3] The plot of the film is as follows: The naïve Mr. West, president of the YMCA, must travel to Russia, but has been convinced by the American media that the Bolsheviks are murderous savages. At his wife's insistence, he takes cowboy Jeddy with him as a bodyguard but is kidnapped by a gang of thieves soon after his arrival. Meanwhile, Jeddy gets into various scrapes which land him in prison, but he is soon released by an affable Bolshevik with the help of Jeddy's American friend and love interest, Ellie. The gang plays upon Mr. West's fears, showing him a ruined Moscow and using various stratagems, from a mock troika-style trial to a staged rescue to seduction-blackmail to get Mr. West's dollars. In the end he is rescued by a black leather-clad Bolshevik secret police officer, who shows him the real Moscow and convinces him that the Soviet Union is an enlightened country.

The unusually long title of *Mr. West* references the literary tradition of the foreign adventure tale e.g., *The Legend of the Glorious Adventures of Tyl Ulenspiegel in the Land of Flanders and Elsewhere* or *20,000 Leagues Under the Seas or the Marvelous and Exciting Adventures of Pierre Aronnax, Conseil His Servant, and Ned Land, a Canadian Harpooner*. Mr. West was not alone in his fear of the Bolsheviks. Western countries were horrified by the excesses of the 1917 revolution, the execution of the tsar and his family, and

---

2   "Now If...," in Lev Kuleshov, *Fifty Years in Films*, trans. D. Agrachev and N. Belenkaya (Moscow: Raduga Publishers, 1987), 56. (First published in *Kino-fot*, no. 3 [1922]).

3   The director described the difficult working conditions in Lev Kuleshov, *The Art of the Cinema*, in *Fifty Years in Films*, 161-62.

the brutality of the civil war. The United States officially recognized the Soviet Union only in 1933. The New Economic Policy (NEP), Lenin's return to a limited form of free enterprise in business and agriculture to promote economic recovery after the civil war, was in full swing during the mid-twenties. NEP created a wealthy new business-professional class with a concomitant criminal world of conmen and thieves. The boy who steals Mr. West's briefcase is a *bezprizornik*, a civil war orphan who survives by working for the gang. Zhban ("Jug," a thief's nickname) and his associates are thus a mix of former members of the upper classes who have degenerated into crime and lower class criminal elements.

Mr. West both satirized the American bourgeoisie and adopted American cinematic discoveries. The film contains passing moments of serious social criticism, such as gender inequality in American business, as opposed to early communist initiatives on women's issues: a male office worker at the American company notices the paper in which Mr. West's briefcase had been wrapped lying on the floor and with a glance directs a woman secretary to pick up the offending object. The film pokes fun at American ethnocentrism in the broadest sense: Mr. West's almost unconscious materialism (his Rudy Vallee fur coat and sock garters, his pile of suitcases, his endless supply of dollars); his reflexive and defensive patriotism (flag-waving upon arrival to protect against attackers, Fig. 10) and the famous flag socks that lead Zhban to salute America as the most cultured nation; his attempt to behave "like a real American," i.e., fight hard when attacked by the false Bolsheviks, and his middle-class sexual mores (his prudish reaction to the Countess's advances and the oversized framed picture of his wife he carries next to his heart). In a foreign country Jeddy dresses and behaves like the cowboy he *is*—shooting bottles for target practice, riding atop Mr. West's car, lassoing a coachman, and getting into fist fights. But he is also a working man, having repaired electric lights in the US, and his eccentricities disappear after his release from jail and acquaintance with the understanding Bolshevik. The satire is relatively gentle and good-natured, for Mr. West and Jeddy—the innocents abroad— are naïve and well-intentioned, much more positive types than the villainous Russian conmen.

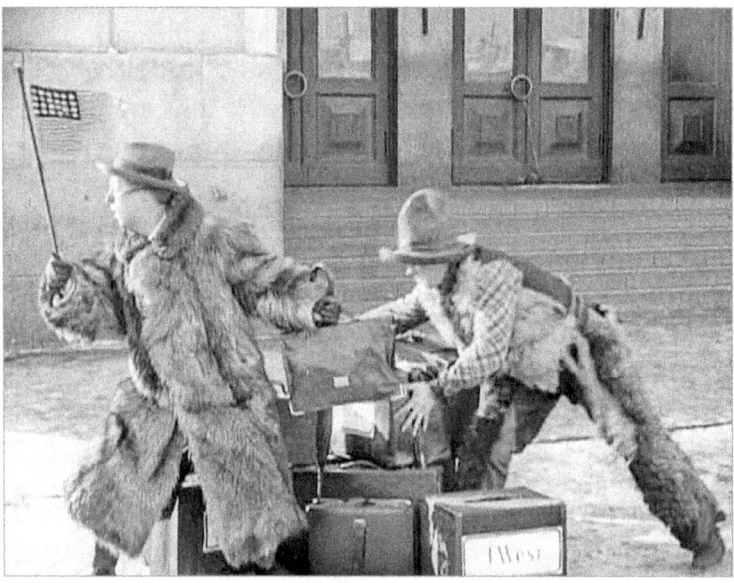

Fig. 10. Mr. West Arrives in Moscow

Mr. West has also been read against the grain (but not always fully convincingly) as inverted commentary on the Soviet system, and it is tempting to see comic scenes such as the imprisonment of Mr. West's briefcase and Jeddy's vision of Soviet cavemen roasting a well-dressed woman over a fire as allusions to Bolshevik methods. (See Petrić article in this section.) A more subtle reading suggests that Kuleshov's choice of American subjects here and in other films, such as *The Death Ray, By the Law* and *The Great Consoler*, allowed him to take up vexed ethical-moral issues which were equally relevant, though unmentionable, in Soviet society. The object of parody in *Mr. West* then becomes the preconceived notion itself, not only in relation to the American bourgeois hero, but as it bears upon Soviet filmmakers. Kuleshov warns against superficial, illusory, propagandistic thinking, utopian simplification of the past and present, and the filming of ideological stereotypes in place of an understanding of reality and human concerns.[4]

---

[4]   I.M. Shilova, "Vremia stat' inostrantsem," *Kinovedcheskie zapiski* 6 (1990): 6.

Mr. West adheres to the machine and efficiency principles of Russian Constructivism (influenced by American efficiency engineering), as applied to acting style, development of the narrative and the production process. In introducing the film to audiences, Kuleshov wrote: "We are presenting this picture not as a demonstration but as a *verification* of our working methods in montage and in the structuring of the frame."[5] In many ways, the film is a compendium of Kuleshov's early ideas on the principles governing cinema. Influenced by American cinema, in *Mr. West* Kuleshov uses continuity editing, close framing, fast cutting, chases, stunts (Jeddy crosses hand over hand on a rope suspended between two buildings),[6] slapstick (Mr. West hooks the Countess's garter on his glasses and loses his pants escaping prison) and chaplinesque tricks (one of the trial "judges" produces a bowl for ink from his sleeve and a quill pen from his collar). In a visual pun, Zhban is accidentally hit by a namesake jug. Peace-loving Mr. West's kissing two doves (possibly a poke at Woodrow Wilson) was filmed in a slow tempo and the fake Bolshevik prison followed *Dr. Caligari* and *Dr. Mabuse*, both parodies of the psychological style. Kuleshov also employs creative geography in the Red Square episode. (See Kepley article in this section.) The director argued that a good intertitle must function exactly like a shot, for it is the same kind of cinematic material as the exposed pieces of film lying on the table before the director.[7] In *Mr. West* intertitles like "Comfort is a relative concept" do not recount action, but instead supply additional meanings.

The acting in the film illustrates Kuleshov's discoveries. Aleksandra Khokhlova uses her distinctive physical traits (large eyes, huge mouth, angular body) to grotesque effect (Fig. 11).

---

[5]   Kuleshov, "Mr. West," in *Fifty Years in Films*, 58. (First published in *Zrelishcha*, no. 79 [1924]: 14).

[6]   According to Kuleshov, Barnet did not train properly for the stunt and had to be rescued by firemen. He was replaced by one of the best actors in the collective, Vladimir Fogel' (Lev Kuleshov, *Praktika kinorezhissury*, in *Sobranie sochinenii v trekh tomakh*, vol. 1 [Moscow: Iskusstvo, 1987], 294).

[7]   Kuleshov, *The Art of Cinema*, 163.

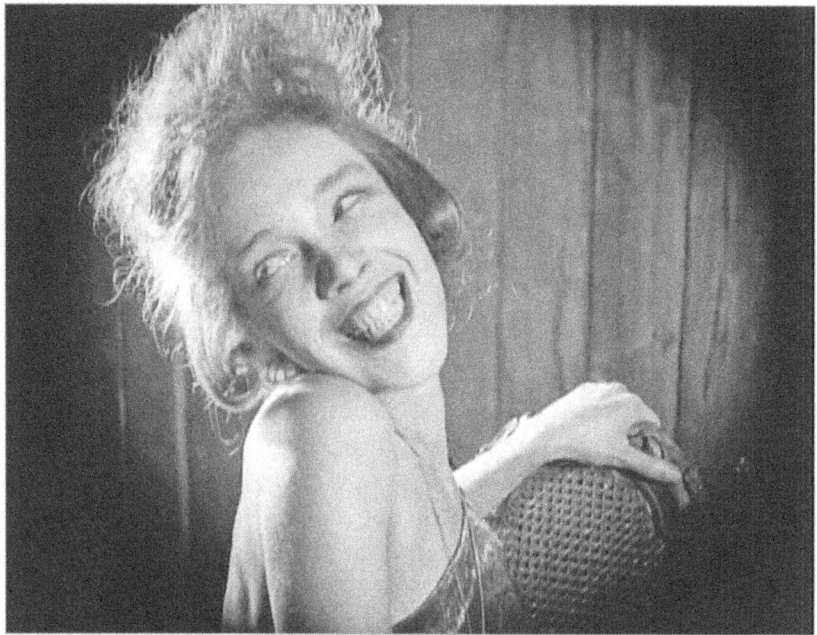

Fig. 11. The Countess

Kuleshov attached importance to developing smooth, horizontal eye movements, which she also uses to advantage. When tied to a stake (a parodic reference to homoerotic images of St. Sebastian), the Countess expresses her glee at the progress of the scam by wiggling sensuously with her entire body. Since any part of the trained body may express any emotion, the executioner at the mock trial repeatedly sucks in and releases his bare stomach, an expression of threat. Following Delsarte, Kuleshov defined opposing facial movements as expressions of extreme emotion; when Zhban is annoyed by noise outside the room, his jaw moves right and eyes left in quick succession. The woman who is frightened by Jeddy's street antics exemplifies action within Kuleshov's metric-spatial grid, an imaginary three-dimensional network of squares along which actors move rhythmically, so as to exist most effectively within the horizontals and verticals of the film frame. The woman leans back from the pole, pauses, leans forward, grasps the pole and pauses, slides down the pole, throwing her legs out in front of her, pauses just above the ground, then falls to the ground and ultimately turns a somersault, ending in a position of prayer.[8]

In the avant-garde's reaction to pre-revolutionary cinema's preoccupation with depth and a surfeit of realistic objects, Kuleshov advocated the emptiness of the film frame (*pustota kadra*) and an emphasis on surface: "The ideal shots are those that look like the flat and primitive paintings on antique vases."[9] The sets of *Mr. West* are geometrically simple, mostly constructed of reversed sheets of plywood. (This was also necessitated by the shortages of the time.) Kuleshov believed that the human face, objects and movements are best filmed against a dark background. "In a number of foreign films, we saw the merest suggestion of décor, just enough for one to imagine the setting in which the action unfolded."[10] Hence the early episode of Mr. West and his wife was filmed against a black background with only a desk and chair on the set.

---

[8]   See Kuleshov, The *Art of the Cinema*, 170-77, and Gerry Large, "Lev Kuleshov and the Metrical-Spatial Web: Postmodern Body Training in Space and Time," *Theatre Topics* 10, no.1 (March 2000): 65-75.

[9]   Lev Kuleshov, "The Art of Creating with Light," in *Fifty Years in Films*, 35-6. (First published in *Kinogazeta* 12 [March 1918]: 12).

[10]   Kuleshov, *The Art of Cinema*, 150-51.

MR. KULESHOV IN THE LAND OF THE MODERNISTS

Vance Kepley, Jr.

The Constructivist ethos, as the phrase might suggest, covered a range of artistic ambitions that cut across several media; but in all its manifestations it was identified with the modern experience. The ethos typically dismissed the received view of the artist as visionary, substituting a notion of the artist as engineer. "Art is finished!" Aleksei Gan hyperbolized in 1922. "It has no place in the human labor apparatus. Labor, technology, organization!"[1] And, as Gan's industrial analogies indicate, Constructivism hailed the process of industrialization.

If the artist was to be an engineer, organizing raw materials into a workable whole, the art work itself was to take on the characteristics of a machine—practical, efficient, utilitarian. The art work's function—and the emphasis was decidedly on the functional—was to alter public consciousness, to help prepare the Soviet population for the machine age.

[...] Most compelling, perhaps, for Kuleshov was the Constructivist argument that a machine aesthetic promoted a modern sensibility, and he set out to explore the presumed affinity between cinema and modernity. He endorsed the Soviet proposition that "a good piece of film educates the viewer." That educational function, however, resided not simply in the film's ideology, but in its form: "If we take a film perfectly well worked out ideologically and produce it poorly from the standpoint of form, despite ideological skill, it will turn out to be a counterrevolutionary film."[2] A film must *manifest* efficiency in order to *advocate* efficiency.

---

[1]   Aleksei Gan, "Constructivism, 1922," in John E. Bowlt (ed.), *The Russian Art of the Avant-Garde* (New York: Viking Press, 1976), 223.

[2]   L. Kuleshov, *Kuleshov on Film*, ed. and trans. Ronald Levaco (Berkeley, CA:

The constructivist ethos could hardly have been more specifically applied, and the process of its application took Kuleshov to the Hollywood cinema. American industry's mass production provided the most convenient model for the Soviet ideal of economic development, and Kuleshov did not hesitate to link the dynamic style of American films to the energy of the American industrial economy. Such films inculcated "boldness and energy" in the population, he asserted, and he envisioned such values transferring to the Soviet Union where they would prove "indispensable to revolutionary struggle, to revolution."[3]

He claimed to base his association of American filmmaking with social dynamism on empirical observation. American and European films dominated the Russian market in the early and middle 1920s while the Soviet film industry struggled to rebuild.[4] The situation familiarized Kuleshov and his students with both state-of-the-art American filmmaking and the Soviet popular response to it. In visits to commercial cinemas, Kuleshov and his protégés watched audiences as carefully as they did films. They noted that American movies generated the most pronounced emotional responses from spectators. Hollywood adventure films and slapstick comedies, characterized by accelerated action and rapid editing, presented an invigorating alternative to the staid literary adaptations and drawing-room dramas of Russian pre-Revolutionary cinema.[5] Kuleshov came to prefer the lean style of the imports to bloated Russian productions which Kuleshov dismissed with the term Khanzhonkovism, a pejorative reference to the pre-Revolutionary Russian studio.[6] To Kuleshov, the very act of generating energy, a characteristic of American film, served the cause of social progress.

University of California Press, 1974), 131.

3   Ibid., 191.

4   Vance and Betty Kepley, "Foreign Films on Soviet Screens, 1922-1931," *Quarterly Review of Film Studies*, vol. 4, no. 4 (1979): 429-42.

5   *Kuleshov on Film*, 44-7.

6   M. Levidov, *Lev Kuleshov* (Moscow: Kinopechat', 1927), 3.

Not only did American films foreground action, but American film style, the classical Hollywood style—to use more recent parlance—also epitomized efficiency, in this case an efficiency of filmic discourse. The canons of classical Hollywood style which would have prompted Kuleshov's enthusiasm are familiar enough today: a clear, economical linear narrative; the careful articulation of time and space through such devices as matches-on-action and eyeline matches; and the organization of the space of a scene around the 180-degree axis.[7] Such devices, as we know, functioned to reduce any threat of spectator disorientation. All this fit Kuleshov's preconception that "the material of the cinema must be extremely simple and organized" in order to assure the spectator's involvement in the film.[8]

[…] Perhaps the ultimate test of the power of *konstruktsiia* resided in the use of newsreel footage for fictional narratives. Newsreel footage should, we might presume, retain a secure, unimpeachable link with its referent, documenting as it does real objects and events. Kuleshov first tested this presumption in his 1920 film *On the Red Front*. He recorded documentary footage of actual battles in the Soviet Civil War and later fashioned a fictional narrative about the conflict. He then used continuity devices to weave his fictional characters into battles that had been fought months earlier.[9]

The usurpation of documentary footage by narrative constructions is also evident at the end of Kuleshov's feature *The Extraordinary Adventures of Mr West in the Land of the Bolsheviks* (1924). […] The case in point comes near the film's end when the title character is taken on a tour of Moscow in order to disabuse him of the mistaken impressions of the Soviet Union he received on his earlier extraordinary adventures. At one point a Soviet guide directs Mr West's attention off-screen. Kuleshov there inserted documentary footage of a Red Army parade in what resembles a borrowing from

---

[7] David Bordwell, Janet Staiger and Kristin Thompson, *Classical Hollywood Cinema* (London: Routledge & Kegan Paul, 1985), 1-84.

[8] *Kuleshov on Film*, 58.

[9] Levidov, *Kuleshov*, 6-7.

a stock shot library. In this case, the documentary footage has been coopted by an eyeline match and thereby incorporated into a fictional world. The real Red Army, in this context, was reduced to the object of a filmic glance by a purely fictional Mr West.

[…] Kuleshov had to confront the status of the photographic image as a perfect intractable analogy to reality if he was to make it serve his Constructivist ambition. His answer was through control of the mise-en-scène of the individual shot. Directors must carefully control what went in front of the camera. The image would then become the analogy, not of unfettered reality, but of a human construct, of an artificially created scene.

In indicating how to effect that control, Kuleshov applied rules of simplicity and legibility, just as he had with editing. The director's task was to strip away excess detail that might detract the spectator's attention from the key narrative function of the shot. Here Kuleshov could look again to the classical Hollywood model with its conventions of centered and/or balanced framing, and the frontal positioning of actors.[10] Indeed, he noted with admiration the simplified, ordered compositions of American films, but he went beyond these practices to advance quite rigid formulas of mise-en-scène. Whereas the Hollywood system "personalized space," making it primarily the venue of character-centered drama, Kuleshov was prepared to go so far as eliminating any spatial context, setting actors off against completely black backgrounds if necessary. This tactic was used periodically in *Mr West* to focus spectator attention exclusively on character behavior: "We wanted the action ... to be most lucid, in relief, and the background to be shaded, to serve only a subsidiary role."[11]

But characters must also interact with a physical environment— a fact that required the creation of surrounding decors. On this issue, Kuleshov developed a purely geometrical formula for the space of a shot, an idea consistent with the Constructivist ethos. Film space, Kuleshov submitted, need not be conceived as a natural continuum,

---

[10]   Bordwell, Staiger and Thompson, *Classical Hollywood Cinema*, 50-5.

[11]   *Kuleshov on Film*, 71.

but as the aggregate of smaller, finite spaces, each of which would be defined and measured geometrically. The director could then position objects and characters in the shot with a precision that only geometry allowed. Kuleshov described the film frame as a grid, consisting of vertical and horizontal axes running at regular intervals parallel to the borders of the frame. He then argued that compositions should obey the design of the grid with a few strong vertical, horizontal or diagonal lines dominating the image. Thus could a director avoid random, imbalanced and, in Kuleshov's view, confusing compositions. Movement within the frame would prove more dramatic if it followed the grid-lines as well.[12]

These restrictive covenants in Kuleshov's theory would clearly threaten to curtail in an artificial manner a director's choices for staging action, and it led to Kuleshov's rather notorious edict that filmmakers should prefer a carpentered world for settings (bridges, buildings, etc.) to natural landscapes where forms would prove less geometrically predictable.[13] In his own filmmaking Kuleshov was often hard pressed to practice this particular preaching. One can, however, find it in evidence in certain scenes of *Mr West*. An example might be Jeddy's daring trip between two tall buildings along a wire stretching between the two structures. The wire defines a horizontal which is framed by the vertical lines of the two buildings. Kuleshov would doubtless make the case that the dramatic effect of the action derived not simply from the actor's acrobatics, but from the geometric design of the shot—a horizontal set off against two graphically powerful verticals. Kuleshov's geometrical conception of space was not limited to the two dimensions of the movie screen. He extended his system to the calculation of compositions into the depth of the camera's view-field. He described that field as a tipped pyramid, the apex of which resided in the center of the camera lens. His grid could then be extended through the length of the pyramid, with the lines converging at the apex. This design allowed directors to place actors and objects "into … basic quadrangles which provide

---

12   Ibid., 62-6, 111.

13   Ibid., 58, 100.

an outline for movement with such precision that they occupy very clear, close, and easily decipherable positions in terms of the rectangular screen."[14] For example, placing an object in the extreme foreground, near the apex of Kuleshov's imaginary pyramid, would exaggerate the object's relative size, and the degree of exaggeration would be subject to perfect reckoning as the product of an exponential. The director could then calculate mathematically the relative consequences of placing objects in the foreground, middle ground or background. Kuleshov tried out the equation in an action scene in *Mr West* wherein he placed a jug precariously on a pedestal in the foreground while a knock-down-drag-out fight ensued in the background. The outsized jug dominates the mise-en-scène, threatening to detract from the fight which takes place behind it— a set-up which might seem to violate Kuleshov's admonition against letting items of the décor compete with character action. In this case, however, it becomes clear that Kuleshov placed the jug in the foreground for a reason; its function is to crash into pieces at the height of the battle, which crash dutifully takes place. Kuleshov's calculation of the effect of the camera's perspective determines the jug's prominence, which, in turn, governs the dramatic effect of the crash.

---

[14]   Ibid., 67.

A SUBTEXTUAL READING OF KULESHOV'S SATIRE
THE EXTRAORDINARY ADVENTURES OF
MR. WEST IN THE LAND OF THE BOLSHEVIKS (1924)

Vlada Petrić

Mr. West demonstrates, in the clearest manner, all the aspects/ characteristics of Kuleshov's directorial style. The collective's first full feature, *The Extraordinary Adventures of Mr. West in the Land of the Bolsheviks*, (working title: *How Will This End?* [*Chem eto konchitsya?*]) was advertised as "the pamphlet on the capitalists' lies about the Soviet Society and an American citizen who believes in such propaganda: conceived and executed in the style of the most popular genre of the bourgeois cinema—the detective film (*kinodetektiv*)."[1]

The reviews testify that the Soviet viewers were entertained by the burlesque "adventures" of the American senator Mr. West,[2] who childishly believes that a group of street hooligans (who kidnapped him upon his arrival to Moscow) are genuine Bolsheviks. But it is also possible that the same audience saw the film as a parody on the Soviet system as well, a system in which such adventures could not take place—even in a fictional world. With little comparative deliberation, one could realize that the underground "network" of the hoodlums is inconceivable in a totalitarian police state like the USSR. As a consequence, the film's plot could be read both as a satire on the American propaganda against the Communist society, and as a humorous—and quiescent—*critique* of the existing autocratic political order in the Soviet Union. It seems plausible, therefore, that the Soviet audience, while laughing at the "absurd" situations of Mr. West (who by his looks and behavior resembles Harold Lloyd), intimately related the kidnappers' "atrocities" to

---

[1] See Nikolai Lebedev, *Ocherk istorii kino SSSR* (Moscow: "Iskusstvo," 1965), 219.

[2] Mr. West is president of the YMCA (RS).

the methods used by the GPU (Stalinist secret police) behind the closed doors of their monstrous enterprise. The Soviet audience probably laughed at Mr. West's crazy exploits, while discreetly chuckling at the presentation of an environment that was a parody of what they knew was the practice common to the Bolshevik establishment.

Mr. West is structured in a way that affects the viewer on both narrative (diegetic) and psychological (subliminal) levels: The naïveté of the plot (dramatic conflicts) and the stylistic exaggeration of the action (mise-en-scène) invest Kuleshov's satire with numerous subtextual implications. No doubt, from today's perspective it is easier—and more appropriate—to recognize the film's subtext as a parody of both capitalist and Bolshevik social orders; however, one should not dismiss the possibility of the film's "subversive" impact on the consciousness of the contemporary Soviet audience. At least the sophisticated viewers were capable of accepting the formal/stylistic execution of the film as a means of associating the parodized world with the conditions that initiated, even requested, such a parody.

Absurdity of dramatic conflicts and oddity of mise-en-scène are carried to the extreme that generates a distrust in the film's primary signification. As a result, the manifest message becomes transparent, henceforth turning against the filmic text, in the process of which the film's form dissociates itself from the plot, fostering its own import that subverts the intentionality of the narrative. For example, the caricature of the countess (Khokhlova), particularly her fancy dresses—in spite of her pompous conduct (intended at mocking the vamp as seen in the American silent movies)—could readily affect the viewer's nostalgia for such clothing (condemned as "alien" to the Socialist society), perhaps even nurture a discontent in those spectators who were dispossessed (by force) of their bourgeois belongings. One should keep in mind that Soviet actresses like Khokhlova were privileged to purchase (abroad, or in the special stores inaccessible to the ordinary people) luxurious outfits and wear them in public, without being denounced as bourgeois. In Protazanov's science fiction parody *Aelita* (1924), for example, the Moscow bourgeoisie attend the clandestine ball:

Dressed in worn-out garments, under which they wear a luxurious wardrobe, they dance and drink champagne while remembering "the old beautiful times," before they wrap themselves again in shoddy rags to return to their Soviet reality!

Another twofold signification of Kuleshov's satire is Mr. West's trial, which, in many respects, reflects the Bolshevik's own legal system: The death penalty (*smertnyi prigovor*), reached without any deliberation by two "cojurors" who constantly nod while looking at the "people's judge," could be seen as a mockery of autocratic justice. The most transparent scene is that in which a "positive" character (the party official and/or representative of the GPU) appears deus-ex-machina at the door of the room in which Mr. West is incarcerated by his kidnappers. Patronizing in attitude, wearing a leather jacket (associated with the Soviet secret police), he points his pistol toward the crooks. To dramatize the situation, Kuleshov first shows a leather-gloved hand slowly appearing through a slightly open door, then the pistol in close up, and finally the "liberator's" head covered with a leather cap, all of which stimulates the viewer's associations outside the narrative context. The very casting of a typage for the part of the Bolshevik (lacking any personal, let alone emotional, expression) also contributes to the audience's "second thoughts" about the character. Near the end of the film, when the same Bolshevik guides Mr. West through the Moscow streets, bringing him to Red Square, the face of the "liberator" remains equally impersonal—a bureaucratic executioner of the Party's order to make sure that the foreigners' impressions of the Soviet Union correspond to Lenin's claim that it is "the most advanced society in the history of mankind." Along the same line of propaganda, an intertitle (after Mr. West had realized that his kidnappers were not true Bolsheviks) irresistibly ridicules common official slogans stating that the Bolshevik society is superior to the capitalist one. Personally, I recall how, immediately after the war in Eastern Europe, people discreetly laughed at a popular song whose "libretto" claimed that "America as well as England/ Soon will be proletarian lands!"

A similar ideological anticipation is contained in the intertitle that announces Mr. West's telegram to his wife in America:

DEAR MADGE, I SEND YOU GREETINGS FROM SOVIET RUSSIA. BURN THOSE NEW YORK MAGAZINES, AND HANG A PORTRAIT OF LENIN IN MY OFFICE. LONG LIVE THE BOLSHEVIKS! YOUR JOHN.

The wording of this radiogram is typical of the Bolshevik dictums launched during the campaign against capitalism, denounced as the greatest evil of humankind. Conceived as a personal message, the intertitle turns into a derision of Party rhetoric, especially its unrealistic attitude toward social values. Even the use of the famous "Kuleshov effect,"[3] which creates the impression that Mr. West himself inspects the military parade in Red Square, sharing company with well-known Party dignitaries (including President Kalinin) has an ironic overtone: Such an extraordinary treatment, especially of an outsider, has been considered inconceivable, if not ludicrous. Again, the audience has been tempted to respond with laughter both to the *coup de cinéma* achieved by the juxtaposition of the authentic archival footage (marching soldiers, Party bosses) and the staged shots involving dramatis personae: This cinematic fantasy, evidently, was possible only in the movies!

Ideologically, the most dubious shot is the final close-up of Mr. West looking directly into the camera with an expression of enormous relaxation. The viewer naturally wants to know the actual source of the protagonist's pleasure. Does it emerge from his realization that the Bolsheviks are not so bad as the Americans think, or from the fact that he has finally been liberated from the type of torture imposed on him in the guise of the Bolshevik common practice? But what actually was Mr. West's experience in the "true" land of the Bolsheviks, on the basis of which he sent a laudatory cable to his wife? On the diegetic level, it was merely a brief stroll through Moscow streets, followed by an unexpected observation of the military parade, supervised by the Party guide! In addition, just before the finale, a short montage sequence of the factory machines

---

[3]   This is "creative geography," which combines documentary and fictional footage (RS).

and workers (edited in the style of Vertov's "film truth" news-reel) has been attached to Mr. West's "adventures," *lacking any image of his own*. Obviously, this was the director's concession to political censorship (apparently, the insert was not anticipated in the original script), which makes Mr. West's conclusive excitement even more ambiguous in regard to his capacity of distinguishing between the reality and the fantasy about the land of the Bolsheviks. In contrast to Mr. West's obliviousness, the "experienced" Soviet viewer couldn't be unaware of this distinction, though unable to express it publicly.

The Communist vision of the future has always been self-serving, totally divorced from natural historical development, albeit based on the Marxist concept of history. With this contradiction in mind, it would be interesting to find out how Mr. West was seen by those Russian intellectuals who were acquainted with the American utopian novel *Looking Backward: (2000-1887)*, written in 1887 by Edward Bellamy and widely popular in Russia both before and after the October Revolution. In 1917, 85,000 copies were reprinted; in 1918, 200,000; and in 1919 and 1922 new reprints were made.[4] The protagonist of Bellamy's novel, the American citizen Mr. West, returns to the year 1887 from the year 2000, when the utopian scheme of industrial organization allows an equal share allotted to all persons in the products of the nation. Kuleshov's protagonist, Mr. West, after visiting the first Socialist country at the outset of the twentieth century, returns to the United States, where the "outdated" social system continues to exist.

---

4   See Sylvia Bowman, *Edward Bellamy Abroad* (New York: Twayne, 1962), 11.

FURTHER READING

Christensen, Peter G. "Contextualizing Kuleshov's *Mr. West*." *Film Criticism* 18, no. 1 (1993): 3-19.

Christie, Ian. *"The Extraordinary Adventures of Mr. West in the Land of the Bolsheviks."* In *The Cinema of Russia and the Former Soviet Union*, edited by Birgit Beumers, 25-34. London: Wallflower Press, 2007.

Tsivian, Yuri. "Cutting and Framing in Bauer's and Kuleshov's Films." *Kintop* (1993): 103-113.

Yanoshak, Nancy. "Mr. West Mimicking 'Mr.West': America in the Mirror of the Other." *Journal of Popular Culture* 41, no. 6 (2008): 1051-1068.

BATTLESHIP POTEMKIN

Bronenosets Potemkin

1925

1820 meters original length, 5 reels; 69 minutes (2007 version)

Director: **Sergei Eisenstein**

Screenplay: **Sergei Eisenstein, Nina Agadzhanova-Shutko**

Art Director: **Vasilii Rakhal's**

Cinematography: **Eduard Tisse**

Intertitles: **Nikolai Aseev, Sergei Tret'iakov**

Producer: **Iakov Bliokh**

Production Company: **First Goskino Factory**

Cast: **Aleksandr Antonov (Vakulinchuk), Vladimir Barskii (Capt. Golikov), Grigorii Aleksandrov (Chief Officer Giliarovskii), Aleksandr Levshin (Petty Officer), Mikhail Gomorov (Matiushenko), Beatrice Vitoldi (Woman with baby on Odessa Steps), N. Poltavtseva (Schoolmisress with pince-nez on Steps)**

Sergei Eisenstein (1898-1948) is one of the great pioneers of cinema, both as filmmaker and film theorist. He had a roller-coaster career in the Soviet Union, alternately benefitting from state commissions and suffering from official rebuke. All of his films use unlikely combinations of formal and narrative elements to challenge viewers into engaging actively in the process of making meaning from visual experience.

Eisenstein was born in Riga, the son of a well-known architect; his parents divorced when he was eleven and he remained with his domineering father, while his mother moved to St. Petersburg. Eisenstein was headed for a career in engineering

when the Revolution intervened. In the Civil War he fought on the Bolshevik side (though he would never join the Communist Party) and afterwards worked for the revolutionary theatre troupe, Proletkult, but soon left the theatre for film. Between 1924 and 1929 he made four feature films, all on themes of revolution and building socialism: *Strike* (1924), *Battleship Potemkin* (1925), *October* (1928) and *The General Line* (renamed *The Old and the New*, 1929). *Potemkin* made Eisenstein famous around the world for its extensive use of radical montage, or juxtaposition of shots for dramatic emotional and political effect.

In 1929 Eisenstein travelled to Europe and the United States, ostensibly to study new sound technology, but also to explore the possibilities of making films in the West and raising money for the strapped Soviet film industry. Eisenstein's stay in Hollywood produced three treatments and zero films. He was about to return home when the socialist writer Upton Sinclair offered to fund a film about Mexico. Eisenstein spent more than a year shooting *Que viva México!*, a film about the endurance of traditional and indigenous cultures in modern, urban Mexico. Eisenstein loved Mexico; he made many friends there, had his first sexual relationship there with a man, and reignited his love of drawing. The film project had to be abandoned, however, when wild cost-overruns and the discovery of a cache of sex drawings led Sinclair to halt the project. At just the same time, when Stalin received word that Eisenstein was to assist on an American anti-Stalinist film, he called Eisenstein back to Russia under threat of being declared a deserter.[1] Sinclair promised to send Eisenstein's footage to Moscow, but he kept it and allowed other filmmakers to edit parts of it, which Eisenstein experienced as a traumatic betrayal.

In his absence, the Soviet Union had gone through a major upheaval with the consolidation of Stalin's power. Exhilarating ideas of the 1920s about art serving society had become rigid

---

[1]   Oksana Bulgakowa, "Kremlevskii kinoteatr, 1929-1953: Dokumenty (review)," *Kritika*, 8.2 (Spring 2007): 459.

guidelines administered by artistic institutions controlled by the Communist Party. Movies were to be made "for the masses" and they had to follow strict conventions in terms of narrative and style. Eisenstein (along with many other artists) struggled to conform to these new requirements, unable to shed his rebellious imagination. Each of his proposals for new projects was denied. In the meantime, he became a popular teacher at the All-Union State Film Institute and he embarked on writing several works of film theory. He was subject to harsh criticism during this period for the "formalism" of his theory and his lack of productivity.

Political attacks culminated in 1937, when Eisenstein was nearing completion of a film based on a story by Ivan Turgenev, *Bezhin Meadow*, but organized around a sensationalized incident in which a young boy, Pavlik Morozov, was murdered after allegedly denouncing his father as a counter-revolutionary. Eisenstein turned the film into an Abraham and Isaac parable. The head of the film industry, Boris Shumiatskii, stopped production and denounced Eisenstein to the Central Committee, which, however, decided to allow Eisenstein to continue working as a director. Then, in a horrifying turn of events, Shumiatskii was arrested and subsequently shot.

In 1938 Eisenstein produced his most conventional film, a hagiographical depiction of a medieval ruler Alexander Nevsky. It became his most popular film, though he considered it something of an embarrassment. If *Bezhin Meadow* threatened his life, *Alexander Nevsky* saved it and then brought him to the heights of fame and success: in 1939 he won the Order of Lenin; in 1941 *Nevsky* won the Stalin Prize. He was given cash, a new apartment and a car. He was made Artistic Director of Mosfilm.

In January 1941, Eisenstein was commissioned to make a film about Ivan the Terrible as part of a campaign to recruit tsarist rulers as historical precedents for Russian state nationalism and authoritarian rule. Eisenstein wrote a screenplay that emphasized two achievements: the establishment of a centralized state against the will of the aristocratic élite, the boyars; and the successful defeat of non-Russian neighbors in the east and in the west. A draft of the screenplay was finished in spring 1941, but shortly after that Germany invaded the Soviet Union. In October, the film studios were evacuated to Alma-Ata, where Eisenstein would develop ideas for a complex psychological treatment of Ivan's evolution from visionary revolutionary to murderous tyrant. Filming took place between 1943-45. Part I was approved in late 1944, released in early 1945, and received the Stalin Prize in late 1945. Part II was finished in early 1946, but was banned by the Central Committee in March. Eisenstein was in the hospital when the film was screened for Stalin, having suffered a heart attack the night he finished Part II. Part II would not be released until 1958 and Part III was never finished. A life of intense work in difficult circumstances took its toll on Eisenstein. He died of a second heart attack in 1948, at age fifty, hard at work at his desk.

From the very beginning of his career, Eisenstein was as interested in thinking about the way we perceive films as in making them: theory and practice were always intertwined. Eisenstein believed that cinema was the highest of the arts, because it was capable of incorporating the history of all the arts into a new form that utilized movement, making its images correspond more closely to the cognitive and emotional responses of our brains. His work in the 1920s was focused on the cognitive and emotional effects of images following one another in cinematic time. "Montage," or editing, compelled the viewer to supply significance to streams of incongruous images. His work in Mexico brought him into contact with ethnography and cultural evolution, expanding ideas about montage. He came to believe that an art work could achieve greatness when it was constructed in ways that corresponded to universal structures of human cognitive perception. Unlike earlier montage, which focused more narrowly on visual constructions, his concept in the 1930s and 1940s incorporated sound, color, movement, and complex dialectical structures to reproduce something like synaesthesia. The viewer was still to be provoked but now the challenges were organized around multiple layers of dialectical visual cues, including everything from set details, to patterns of actors' movements, to synchronization of musical score with visual images, to rhythms of continuity and disruption, to narrative flow and misdirection. He left numerous unfinished manuscripts when he died, as well as thousands of drawings.

Joan Neuberger

* * *

Battleship Potemkin was commissioned for the twentieth anniversary of the 1905 revolution. It was first conceived as a vast panorama of the events of that year, including the Russo-Japanese war, the Bloody Sunday massacre and anti-semitic pogroms, but after the film crew moved from Leningrad to Odessa to take advantage of better weather, Eisenstein decided to focus on a relatively minor incident, the June 1905 mutiny on the *Prince Potemkin*, the fastest and most powerful battleship in the Russian fleet. In the film a rebellion is sparked by maggot-infested meat offered as rations to the crew. When the sailors refuse to eat, the captain threatens to execute some of the rebels, causing a melee in which several officers are thrown overboard and the crew takes control of the ship. Vakulinchuk, the leader of the rebellion, is shot by the officer Giliarovskii. His body is brought to Odessa harbor where it attracts the sympathy of townspeople, whose numbers grow until they line the Richelieu steps connecting the harbor to the city. Fearing an uprising, the authorities dispatch cossacks to massacre innocent citizens. In response, the *Potemkin* fires a salvo, destroying military headquarters. The *Potemkin* now faces the Black Sea fleet, which they invite to join them in rebellion. After a few tense moments, the Russian navy allows the *Potemkin* to pass.The mutineers have triumphed.

In 1926 the negative of the film was sold to Germany because the USSR did not have the facilities to duplicate it for international distribution. The German censor cut up the negative and then sold this version back to the Soviets in 1940 in the wake of the Molotov-Ribbentrop pact. The most complete restoration of *Potemkin* is the 2007 Kino version, which claims to include all the material cut by the German censors in 1926 and 1928, as well as a complete rendering of the original intertitles, and is accompanied by Edmund Meisel's score, which was created for the film's Berlin premiere.

Because of its incendiary message, *Potemkin* was banned or censored in Europe and the US. For us, more than 85 years later, its revolutionary content is overshadowed by Eisenstein's revolutionary discoveries in filmmaking. Eisenstein's Constructivist heritage is evident in the geometric organization within the frame: the intersecting, almost abstract lines of the sailor's hammocks, the triangle of the ship's deck and Vakulinchuk's tent within the rectangular film frame, the triangular pattern of a flag, the strong geometries of the Potemkin's leather-cased, phallic guns, the rigid lines of sailors on deck under the officers' command that dissolve into randomness during the mutiny.[1] *Potemkin* illustrates Eisenstein's ideas on typage, attractions and several categories of montage. Eisenstein was interested in portraying realistic human types—a typical student, school teacher, bourgeois lady, beggar, revolutionary orator, a drunkard—and used many amateurs in the film. Nevertheless the main roles were played by trained actors and, interestingly, most of the participants in the Odessa Steps sequence were also professionals.[2] Even Vakulinchuk, the rebel hero who dies early on in the film, is a generic type— a strong, healthy physical specimen (one of the male bodies Eisenstein admires in the hammocks episode), who nevertheless can be replaced in the revolutionary struggle by Matiushenko, another sailor who takes charge of the Potemkin.

Eisenstein's idea of "attraction" was borrowed from reflexology and materialist psychology (Pavlov, Bekhterev) and defining it, he also explained his cinematic strategy: an attraction is "any demonstrable fact (an action, an object, a phenomenon , a conscious combination, and so on) that is known and proven to exercise

---

[1]   The hammocks are also part of the pervasive "canvas" motif of the film and initially enclose the men in a symbolic cocoon from which Vakulinchuk arouses them by his speech.

[2]   Naum Kleiman, "Arguments and Ancestors," in *Eisenstein Rediscovered*, ed. Ian Christie and Richard Taylor (London: Routledge, 1993), 35.

a definite effect on the attention and emotions of the audience and that, combined with others, possesses the characteristic of concentrating the audience's emotions in any direction dictated by the production's purpose. From this point of view a film cannot be a simple presentation or demonstration of events: rather it must be a tendentious selection of, and comparison between, events, free from narrowly plot-related plans and moulding the audience in accordance with its purpose."[3] In his polemics with Dziga Vertov and the Cine-Eye group, Eisenstein argues: "It is not a 'Cine-Eye' that we need but a 'Cine-Fist'."[4] The montage of attractions, a succession of filmic blows or shocks meant to act on the audience's emotions, is illustrated in the super-sized maggots on the rotten meat, the smashing of the plate at the end of part one, the woman's suddenly jerking head at the beginning of the Odessa steps sequence, and culminating in the schoolteacher's shattered pince-nez, her bloodied eye and silent scream.

In *Potemkin* Eisenstein uses associational montage, in which contiguous diegetic shots create linkages: the priest slaps a cross in the palm of his hand, followed by an officer stroking the cross-hilt of his sword (religion associated with the threat of military violence). In another scene the priest again slaps the cross in his hand; a shot of a life preserver emblazoned with the name of the ship, "Prince Potemkin," follows, which in turn is followed by the imperial double-headed eagle on the ship's prow (religion and violence linked to state power). Rhythmic montage, as used in the Odessa Steps sequence, determines shot length by content, along with a change in the speed of the metric cuts, to produce complex meanings. Eisenstein's less clear-cut category of tonal montage, which is concerned with expressive visual qualities, such as light values, degree of focus and graphic shapes, is illustrated in the

---

[3]   Sergei Eisenstein, "The Montage of Film Attractions," in *Sergei Eisenstein, Selected Works: Writings, 1922-1934,*vol. 1 (1924 typescript, Eisenstein archive, RGALI), 40-41.

[4]   Sergei Eisenstein, "The Problem of the Materialist Approach to Form," in *Sergei Eisenstein, Selected Works*, vol. 1, 58. [First published in Russian, in *Kinozhurnal ARK*, 1925, no. 4/5: 5-8].

fog sequence of the film, which has "gloom" as its dominant tonal quality.[5]

Ultimately, *Potemkin* turns on the imbrication of political and aesthetic concerns. Attractions, typage and montage all serve to manipulate audience reaction. Eisenstein's emphasis on typage and the masses as hero corresponds to the Bolshevik commitment to collectivity, and the relationship between shots is presented in Marxist terms: "We must look for the essence of cinema not in the shots but in the relationships between the shots just as in history we look not at individuals but at the relationships between individuals, classes, etc."[6]

For the production history of *Potemkin* and a close analysis, see Taylor in Further Reading.

---

[5]   See David Bordwell, 132, in Further Reading. For other categories of montage, such as metric, overtonal, intellectual and vertical montage, defined (often vaguely) by Eisenstein over the years, see 131-33.

[6]   Sergei Eisenstein, "Béla Forgets the Scissors," in *Sergei Eisenstein, Selected Works: Writings*, 1922-1934, vol. 1, 79. [First published in *Kino*, 10 August 1926.]

MONUMENTAL HEROICS: THE SILENT FILMS

David Bordwell

Eisenstein's silent films were, like those of his Left contemporaries, didactic works. Yet he saw no contradiction between creating propaganda and achieving powerful aesthetic effects. Indeed, central to his thinking was the belief that only if propaganda was artistically effective—structurally unified, perceptually arousing, emotionally vivid—would it be politically efficacious. This urge to plumb the artistic capacities of film made Eisenstein the most ambitious and innovative director of Soviet cinema.

His experiments drew on diverse sources. Certainly Constructivism, particularly its theatrical manifestations, strongly influenced his films. Yet Constructivism's moment had passed when Eisenstein began filmmaking. Moreover, the movement's reliance upon abstract design was not suited for a medium that would, in the Soviet state, have to utilize representational imagery. Kasimir Malevich quickly recognized this, criticizing film directors for plagiarizing academic realist art and refusing to use pictorial abstraction to expose the materials of "cinema as such" (Malevich 1925, 228-229).

Eisenstein's films can usefully be understood as part of a broad tendency toward "heroic realism" in 1920s Soviet art. This trend had its immediate sources in the Civil War period, which generated lyrical, episodic portrayals of collective action. In agit-dramas and novels the hero became the mass, and appeal to the spectator was posterlike in its directness. By the mid-1920s, when the avant-garde had declined, most painters, writers, and theatre workers accepted the obligation of celebrating the Revolution or portraying Soviet society through some version of "realism" (although the exact meaning of this concept was hotly debated). […]

In constructing a cinematic mythology of the new regime, Eisenstein drew upon cultural formulas and iconography from

his youth. For example, propaganda and popular legend already defined the key events of the *Potemkin* mutiny—the spoiled meat, the death of Vakulinchuk, the display of the body. (See Gerould, 1989.) Public celebrations also furnished filmmakers a wealth of tales and storytelling strategies. From soon after the October revolution through the 1920s, the government sponsored mass spectacles to celebrate public holidays and commemorate historical turning points. On May Day in 1920, for instance, 4,000 participants performed in the "Mystery of Liberated Labor" for an audience of 35,000. Such spectacles, and the festivals and processions associated with them, were echoed in Eisenstein's films. The ritual of parading zoo animals dressed as class enemies finds its equivalent in *Strike*, while the mass spectacle "Storming of the Winter Palace" in October 1920 forms a plot outline for *October.*

Eisenstein was prepared to romanticize revolutionary action. In his films, men (and occasionally women) fight, women and children endure, and all may die at the hands of the oppressor. The enemy slaughters innocents: the Odessa Steps are populated by mothers, infants, old men and women, a male student, and amputees. Yet these films never show a slain enemy. *October*'s Bolsheviks are murdered, but the government's side appears to suffer no casualties. In *Potemkin*, Vakulinchuk is shot, but the officers are merely tossed overboard. Sometimes the film flatly ignores the question of revolutionary justice; *Potemkin*'s priest, feigning death in the hold, is never seen again; in *Old and New*, the kulaks who poison the bull go unpunished. Eisenstein concentrates on the spectacular moments of upheaval, suffering, and victory and avoids confronting the ethical problems of insurrectionary violence. [...]

Toward Plotless Cinema

Indeed, one could argue that Soviet heroic realism was most richly realized in the new medium. Pudovkin, Dovzhenko, Ermler, and others were working in this tradition, with occasional contributions from the FEX collaborators Kozintsev and Leonid Trauberg. Whereas mainstream entertainment film was derived largely from tsarist cinema, as well as from doses of German, French, and American

influence, these directors offered a distinctly "Soviet" alternative. Eisenstein helped shape this alternative, and he often took it further than his contemporaries.

In his time, Eisenstein's innovations were taken as exemplary of the trend of "plotless" cinema. This was not filmmaking that avoided narrative altogether; it was, rather, a new sort of narrative cinema. Plotless films, Adrian Piotrovsky pointed out, did not present the action as "a consequentially motivated development of individual fate." Moreover, plotless cinema relied on "exclusively cinematic means of expression," which included unrealistic manipulations of time and the use of "non-diegetic" and "associative" montage (1927, 105). From these aspects of the "plotless" film Eisenstein created what Piotrovsky called his "monumental heroics" (106).

The prototypical Soviet film sought to show that history was made by collective action, and most directors provided narratives that treated characters as typical of larger political forces. Still, the characters are usually individualized, with distinctive traits and psychological motives. Often a figure is derived from an instantly recognizable type—the bureaucrat, the worker, the middle-class woman, the Red Army soldier. Although Eisenstein is associated with the practice of "typage," he did not take credit for originating it, and it is common throughout Soviet film of the period.

In Eisenstein, however, typage follows from his idiosyncratic tendency to build his plots around the "mass protagonist." A scene will employ a crowd to manifest the central role that Marxist doctrine ascribes to class action as the motor of history. Most members of the crowd who get picked out lack psychological qualities. Their actions are more often determined by their historical or organizational roles. It is as if Eisenstein took literally M. N. Pokrovsky's dictum: "We Marxists do not see personality as the maker of history, for to us personality is only the instrument with which history works" (quoted in Willett 1978, 106). In Eisenstein's films, history is a process—of defeat in *Strike*, of gain in *Potemkin*, of victory in *October*, of building socialism in *Old and New*—and the plot is built around stages in the unfolding of a large-scale dynamic. [...]

The Battleship Potemkin (1925)

The Battleship Potemkin was long considered the masterwork of the silent cinema. In 1958 an international critics' poll voted it the greatest film of all time. In later years, however, the film slipped into the shadows, an object of casual acceptance or debunking dismissal. Even for Eisensteinians the rediscovery of *Strike* and the reevaluation of *October* made *Potemkin* seem a tame official classic.

For our purposes, *Potemkin*'s importance is manifold. Within Eisenstein's career, its stringent unity represents an attempt to turn the experimentation of *Strike* to fresh purposes. With respect to film form, Eisenstein's subtleties run deeper than is generally supposed. The careful organization of the film's chapters and episodes is matched by rich development of visual motifs. Eisenstein also explores certain staging and editing options with an unprecedented rigor, a tendency that reaches its culmination in the Odessa Steps sequence. More generally, *Potemkin* can be seen as a synthesis and transcendence of contemporary tendencies in literature and theatre. Owing less to Constructivism than to NEP "heroic realism," *Potemkin* lays down one path for a distinctively Soviet cinema.

At the time, Eisenstein insisted that *Potemkin* was not simply the successor to *Strike* but a contemporary answer to it. As the NEP assimilated market economics, he claimed, so *Potemkin* deliberately adopts the "pathos" of "right art": sentiment, lyricism, psychological portrayal, and passionate fervor. And as NEP policy aimed to achieve socialism through a deliberate swerve in the *opposite* direction—that is, through capitalism—so *Potemkin* seeks to arouse emotion and partisanship by more traditional cinematic means. Putting aside the possibly disingenuous comparison with the NEP, we can see that Eisenstein considers *all* stimuli potentially of equal value in creating the desired effect on the spectator. The mists of Odessa Harbor become no less powerful than a slaughtered bull (1926b, 68).

Another source of emotional engagement in the film is Eisenstein's decision to restrict our knowledge. *Strike*, *October*, and *Old and New* utilize omniscient narration that shuttles freely between protagonist and antagonist, always supplying the spectator with the maximum amount of information. In *Potemkin*, with the exception of a few moments showing the plotting of the ship's officers, Eisenstein confines us wholly to what the affirmative characters know and feel. The attack on the Odessa Steps startles the viewer because there has been no indication of what the cossacks have been planning. Similarly, suspense is aroused at the climax by Eisenstein's refusal to take us aboard the tsarist fleet and divulge the officers' reaction to the *Potemkin*'s passage. In general, by restricting our range of knowledge to the progressive forces in the struggle, the narration solicits a stronger emotional tie with them.

Potemkin, then, aims at revolutionary pathos. "*Strike* is a treatise; *Potemkin* is a hymn" (1926b, 69). It is no less an attack on the audience, but by more unified and "motivated" means: not an agit-guignol but a Communist epic. Eccentrism survives only in subdued form, as the somersaults of officers hurled overboard or the mild caricature of the priest. Whereas *Strike* uses the Civil War aesthetic of agitation to pay homage to aborted insurrections, *Potemkin* is Eisenstein's first saga of revolutionary triumph. The Lenin epigraph in *Strike* serves as a warning, but the epigraph for *Potemkin* launches a national *epos*:

> Revolution is the only lawful, equal, effectual war. It was in Russia that this war was declared and begun.
>
> —Lenin

The generalized composite of events offered by *Strike* is replaced by a precise delineation of three days in 1905 when mutinous sailors were caught up in the spirit of revolution. In *Potemkin*, the Bolshevik appropriation of revolutionary impulses finds concrete and heroic manifestation.

That manifestation, as we might expect, owes more to mythmaking than to historical fidelity. Although Eisenstein was proud of his research into records and the mutineers' memoirs, and although he used the student agitator Konstantin Feldman as a performer and a historical consultant, the film takes great liberties. (See Amengual 1980, 155-159; and Wenden 1981.) Eisenstein synthesizes 1905 events: the mourning over Vakulinchuk in Odessa refers to an interlude during the Moscow uprisings, and the Steps sequence fuses the Odessa massacre with one in Baku. Through the use of typage, the sneering anti-Semite at Vakulinchuk's tent becomes a premonition of the reactionary Black Hundreds society that emerged as a response to the 1905 uprising. Most notably, the triumphant ending cuts the historical episode short, omitting reference to the eventual exile and imprisonment of the mutineers. "We stop the event at this point where it had become an 'asset' to the revolution," Eisenstein admitted (1926b, 67). Twenty years later he explained that the ending shows 1905 to be "an objectively victorious episode, the harbinger of the triumph of the October Revolution" (1945b, 29).

As in *Strike*, history is made collectively: the sailors are driven to rebellion, the Odessa citizens are stirred by Vakulinchuk's sacrifice, the fleet refuses to fire on the *Potemkin*.[1] But *Potemkin*'s referential dimension, as well as its urge to arouse emotion, allows for a new relation between the individual and the mass. In *Strike* the bourgeois forces, though typed, are far more individuated than the Bolsheviks. By contrast, accounts of the *Potemkin* mutiny had already created a gallery of heroes: the agitator Matyushenko, the martyr Vakulinchuk, the student Feldman, and others. Though broadly portrayed in Eisenstein's film, these individuals have more distinctive identities than do the agitators and workers of *Strike*. Even the anonymous townspeople slaughtered on the Steps are more vividly characterized than the massacre victims in the previous film. Tretyakov commented that playwrights had trouble "in shifting from the depiction of human *types* to the construction of the *standards* (exemplary models)" (Stephan 1981, 184). *Strike* failed to make this shift; *Potemkin* succeeds. Its creation of "exemplary models" marks a new phase in heroic realism in Soviet cinema.

The film breaks into five distinct parts, each corresponding to a reel and bearing a "chapter title." Most reels contain two or more segments, yielding a total of ten distinct sequences. This

---

[1]   According to Hill 1978, the film's original epigraph was from Trotsky: "The spirit of insurrection hovered over the Russian land . . . The individual was dissolving in the mass, and the mass was dissolving in the outburst" (74-86).

"plot-carcass," as Eisenstein called it (1926c, 75), presents an ever-expanding revolutionary impulse. Like the waves that crash on shore in the opening shots, rebellion steadily gathers force, spreading from agitators to a faction of the crew, to the entire crew, to all sectors of the populace of Odessa, and finally to the tsarist navy.

Structure of *The Battleship Potemkin*

I. Men and Worms
    1.Vakulinchuk and Matyushenko meet on the bridge.
    2. Crew's quarters: The first mate whips a sleeping sailor; Vakulinchuk agitates.
    3. Morning: The crew objects to the rotten meat.
    4. Lunch: The crew refuses the soup.
II. Drama in Tendre Harbor
    5. The captain prepares to execute the dissenters; the crew mutinies. Vakulinchuk is killed.
    6. A launch takes Vakulinchuk's body to shore in Odessa.
III. An Appeal from the Dead
    7. Morning: Odessa's citizens discover Vakulinchuk's body lying in state. Agitators arouse the populace.
IV. The Odessa Steps
    8. Citizens bring supplies to the Potemkin. Onlookers on the Steps are massacred.
V. Meeting the Squadron
    9. The sailors meet and resolve to confront the navy.
    10. After a night of tense waiting, the Potemkin meets the squadron and is allowed to pass through.

Within each part the curve of dramatic intensity rises. In "Men and Worms,"[2] for instance, the discontent of the crew grows:

---

[2] Throughout this chapter I provide a literal translation of the Russian titles rather than standard translations. As we shall see, "Men and Worms" has a significance not captured by the "Men and Maggots" of the standard English-language version.

a sleeping sailor takes a casual whipping; the men object to the worm-ridden meat; they refuse to eat the soup; at the end of the reel, the abused sailor disgustedly smashes a plate. Similarly, reel two's insurrection builds up gradually, from the men's calm breaking of ranks, through the intensification of suspense during the execution, to the long-suppressed outburst ("Brothers!") and Vakulinchuk's rallying cry: "Kill the dragons!" *Strike* takes it for granted that the workers have long suffered exploitation, but *Potemkin's* mutiny is the culmination of a series of vividly particular indignities.

After Eisenstein left Proletkult, a colleague recalled, he transformed his initial experiments "into an orderly aesthetic system" (Levshin 1966, 64). The rigorous architecture of *Potemkin* shows just how highly organized this new approach was. Each reel, for instance, concludes on a dramatic note: the sailor smashing the plate, Vakulinchuk's body lying on the jetty, the red flag (hand-colored) snapping atop the mast, the *Potemkin's* bombardment of the generals' headquarters, and the low-angle shot of the battleship's prow slashing upward across the screen.

Similar parallels inform the sequences as units. In a 1939 essay Eisenstein points out that most of the reels split into contrasting parts. Thus the tension on the quarterdeck erupts into the mutiny; the calm mourning for Vakulinchuk leads to the angry meeting. In each reel, a pause marks the transition from one phase to another. Eisenstein also suggests that the same structure is found in the film as a whole, with the misty opening of "An Appeal from the Dead" serving as a large-scale caesura (1939f, 14-15).

One could also see the five parts as forming a headpiece and two pairs of structurally comparable segments. Part I is expository and relatively elliptical in its presentation of several episodes spread out over a night and a morning. But then we have symmetry. Part II (Drama in Tendre Harbor) and Part IV (The Odessa Steps) both concentrate on a single day's events, and both explode into violence. Parts III (An Appeal from the Dead) and V (Meeting the Squadron) have a somewhat different structure: each part moves from night to dawn, then traces a rising tension that culminates in the assertion of group unity.

In another sense, of course, Part V neatly answers Part I in that the rebellion that began on the ship reaches its culmination in the unity of all sailors. In addition, Part II, with its foiled execution and the cry of "Brothers!" is echoed by Part IV, with its aborted battle and the same cry to alliance. Eisenstein argued for a rhythmic affinity between the Steps sequence in Part IV (based on the mechanized "drumroll" of marching feet) and the confrontation in Part V (which picks up the same mechanized pulsation; 1945b, 220). One could also see the plot as presenting phases of oppression (Part I) and uprising (Part II), which are then reversed when the Odessa uprising (Part III) is put down (Part IV).

Such large-scale symmetries are made possible by Eisenstein's decision to build his plot out of elaborately worked-out scenes, a strategy not prominent in the more fragmentary and episodic *Strike*. In *Potemkin* he organizes a swmall body of material to a very high degree. Consider, for example, sequence 5, the first scene in "Drama in Tendre Harbor." This initially demarcates an open, unified space for the action, the deck

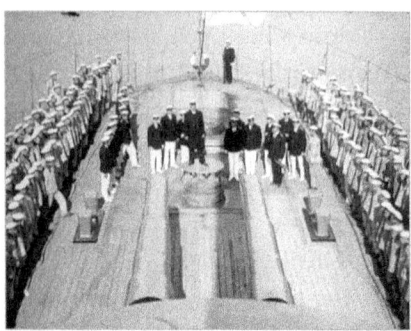

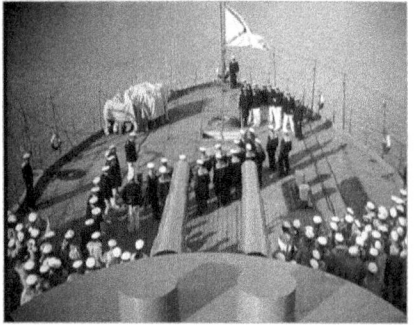

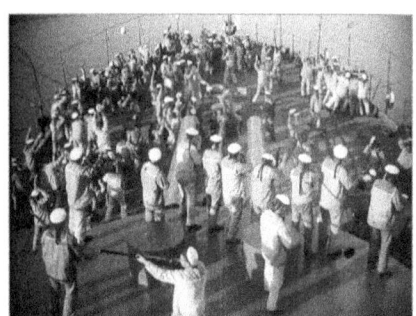

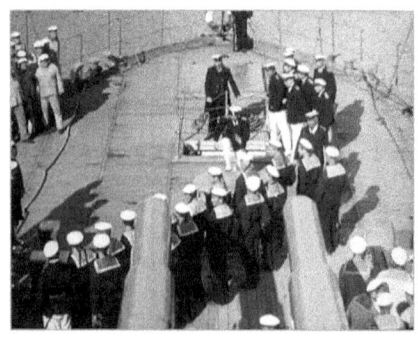

Fig. 12-15

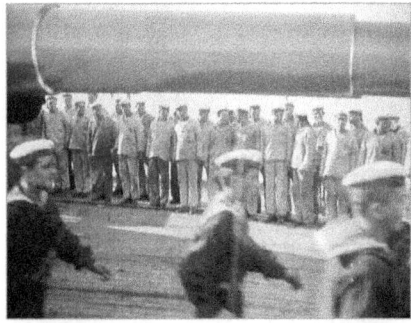
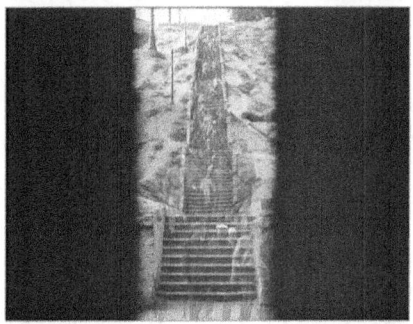
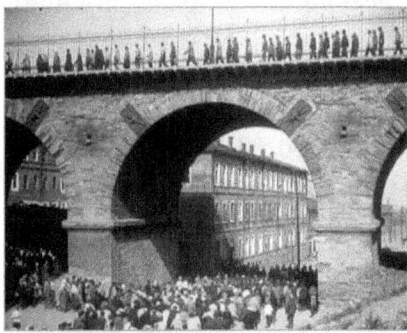
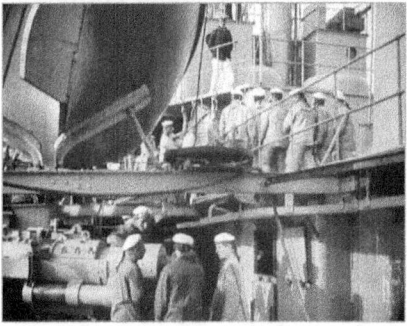

Fig. 16-19

viewed from above the turret (Fig. 12). This camera position, which will reorient us at crucial moments, also serves as a constant against which to measure the progress of the action (Fig. 13, 14).

In the segment's first half, this unified space is analyzed into discrete chunks, often filmed from the same camera angle as the establishing shot (Fig. 15). Gradually the cutting departs from the quarterdeck, presenting shots of other parts of the ship. Despite such expansions of the dramatic field, though, most of this portion of the sequence is static, portraying a tense confrontation between officers and crew, then one between the firing squad and the dissenters. But once Vakulinchuk seizes the top of the turret, defining himself as "above" the action and occupying a vacant white space in the closer views, the mutiny erupts.

The scene splinters into several lines of action. One involves the sailors seizing weapons and battling the officers. A parallel line of action centers on Gilyarovsky's murderous pursuit of Vakulinchuk. Other episodes are briefly highlighted: the captain is dragged away, an officer climbs onto a piano and is seized, crewmen toss officers into the sea. At the climax, Dr. Smirnov is hurled overboard. As the crew takes over the ship, Gilyarovsky manages to shoot Vakulinchuk, and the sequence ends with his body carried up the gangway. Thus images of Vakulinchuk—his seizing of the turret and his death—frame the mutiny. In such ways, a vast number of details of the locale are assimilated into the unfolding drama. Shklovsky praised Eisenstein for "exhausting" the dramatic potential of the Odessa Steps as a locale in the same way (Amengual 1980, 620).

Such stringent organization affects the presentation of motifs. *Potemkin* justifies its recurrent elements in terms of plausibility. In *Strike*, for the sake of maintaining the circle motif, the agitators met amidst discarded wheels or drainage pipes. In the later film, graphic motifs spring more naturally from the locales. The ship establishes the drama as one of both horizontals and verticals (Fig. 16). The same graphic motifs are stressed in the city of Odessa, which is depicted as strongly vertical (as in the masking that introduces a flight of steps, Fig. 17) and horizontal (the quays). Eisenstein often films the city so that it has the split-level structure of the ship (Fig. 18, 19).

The motif of the cross undergoes a similar development. Thematically it points to an alliance between religion and military oppression. The cross first appears during the scene on the quarterdeck, carried by the priest arising from below deck. As the firing squad aims at the tarpaulin, Eisenstein turns the cross into a weapon by cutting to the priest, who slaps the cross into his hand like a blackjack (Fig. 20, 21). Two shots later Eisenstein compares

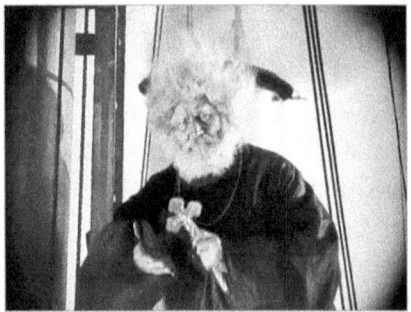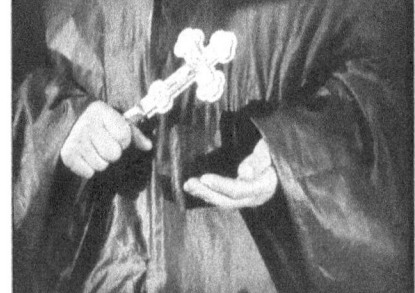

Fig. 20   Fig. 21

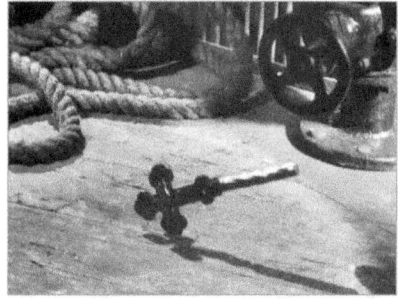

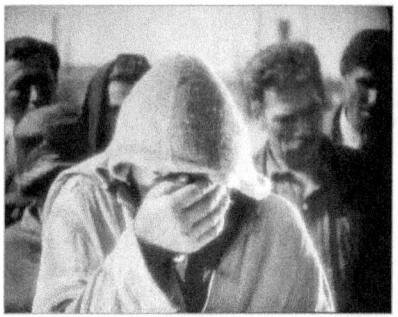

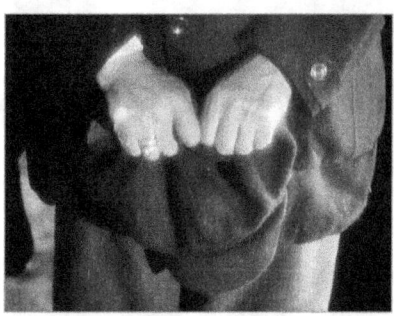

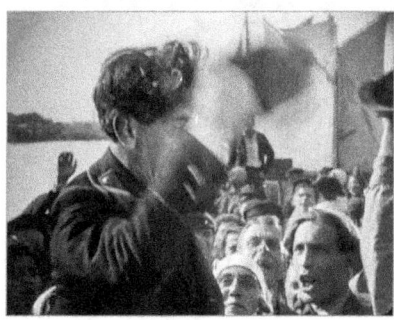

Fig. 22-25

this gesture to an officer's hand stroking his dagger. During the combat on deck, the priest wields the cross as a club. And when the priest is hurled backward, the cross thuds into the deck like a knife (Fig. 22).

By now, Eisenstein's "orderly aesthetic system" requires a moment-by-moment control over the metaphorical or emotional implications of each motif. Consider, for instance, a passage during the mourning for Vakulinchuk. It is, as Eisenstein pointed out in a 1928 note, an instance of "harmonic montage," in which "sadness" arises out of the interaction of several cinematic parameters: the bent posture of an old man, a lowered sail, an out-of-focus tent, fingers kneading a cap, tearful eyes, and so on (Aumont 1987, 166). But the passage also displays a dynamic emotional development by means of repeated gestures. As the townspeople weep, Eisenstein emphasizes their grief through close-ups of hands wiping away tears or covering eyes (Fig. 23). A pair of hands twisting a cap (Fig. 24) introduces a new prop, which becomes dynamized when the student agitator shakes his cap at the crowd and others thrust their caps up (Fig. 25). The sorrowful hands knot into fists (Fig. 26). Another agitator, this time a woman, raises her fist (Fig. 27). Now the weeping woman of an earlier shot recapitulates the movement from sorrow to rage: clutching her handkerchief, she makes a sweeping fist (Fig. 28, 29). As if

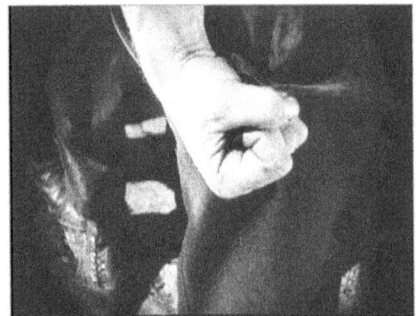
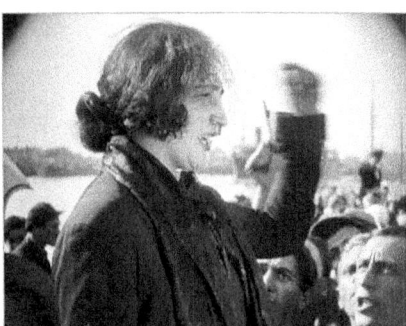
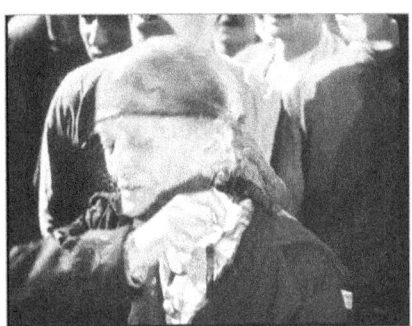
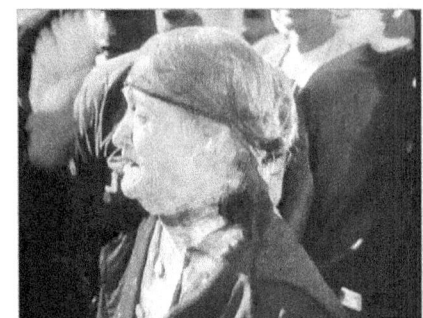

launched by her gesture, other arms burst into the air, and soon the entire crowd is shaking its fists in anger (Fig. 30). *Strike* has nothing like these minute modulations from one expressive gesture to another.

The same fine-grained process governs the use of intertitles. "All for one" cuts to a group of four workers; "And one—" is followed by a shot of the dead Vakulinchuk; "—for all" cuts to an extreme long-shot of the people gathered by the pier. This intertitle becomes a motif in itself.

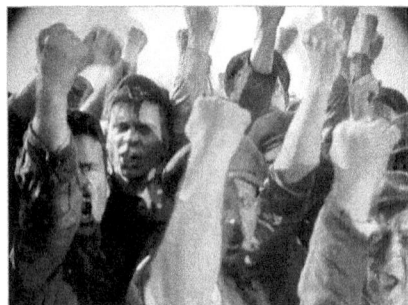

Fig. 26-30

In Part V the *Potemkin* confronts the squadron, and the title "One against all" precedes a shot of the cannon swiveling to the camera; "All against one" follows soon after—the titles emphasizing the separation that is soon to dissolve into the joyous cry of "Brothers!"

Eisenstein often coordinates intertitles with images to create metaphorical motifs. A shot of boiling soup is followed by shots of sailors angry about the rotten meat, and a title tells us that the men's rage "overflowed" all bounds. A similar tactic gives a poetic cast to titles in the opening of segment 6. "With the night, a mist spread . . . ," and shots of mist lead to "From the pier a rumor spread . . ." Then come shots of the city awakening, accompanied by the title, "Along with the sun, the news made its way into the city . . ." The news of the rebellion is compared to the natural processes of mist and daylight seeping from the sea into the port. Such verbal-visual associations form part of Eisenstein's conception of "film language" at the time and anticipate notions of "intellectual" montage. In his theoretical writings, as we will see, Eisenstein considers both verbal and visual metaphors to be extensions of basic kinesthetic ones.

Across the entire film we find the same detailed reworking of motifs. Meat hangs, mess tables hang, and eventually men and eyeglasses hang. The hammocks of sequence 1 anticipate the tarpaulin tossed over the condemned seamen in sequence 5, which is soon used to wrap officers before they are chucked over the side. Similar stretches of canvas become Vakulinchuk's tent (Part III) and the sails of the boats that bring supplies to the ship (Part IV). In the final reel, the tarpaulin finds its authentic function when men use it to cradle shells lugged to the cannons.

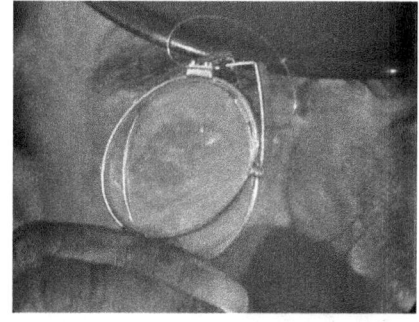

Fig. 31

A more central motif is that of the single eye. It is introduced in sequence 3 when Dr. Smirnov examines the meat (Fig. 31) and declares that the worms are only maggots. The single eye is initially linked to a power that simply denies visible truth. During the mutiny (sequence 5)

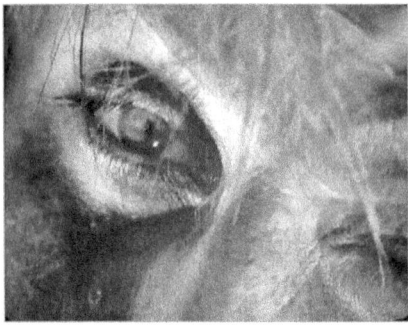

Fig. 32

the motif becomes a sign of duplicity when the priest feigns unconsciousness but checks his surroundings by opening one eye. Soon after this, as Gilyarovsky fires at Vakulinchuk, Eisenstein gives us an extreme close-up of his eye widening (Fig. 32). But in segment 8, a title tells us that "Alert and sharp-sighted, the shore watched over the battleship," transferring the power of vision to the townspeople. At the end of the scene, however, the old schoolmistress on the Odessa Steps suffers a hide

ous wound to the eye (Fig. 33). Like the animal motif in *Strike*, the single-eye motif now evokes not the strength or cunning of the oppressors but the suffering of their victims.

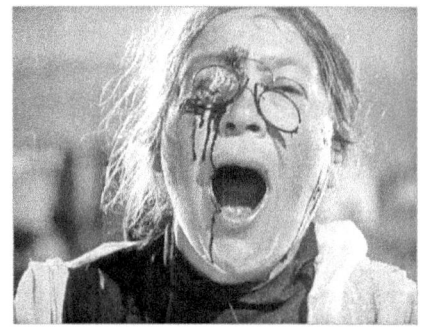

Fig. 33

So tightly intertwined are *Potemkin's* motivic "lines," though, that the eye motif cannot be fully understood apart from a larger imagistic cluster. Another way into the network is provided by the motif of eyeglasses. Smirnov is characterized by his pince-nez, which he uses to scrutinize the rotten meat (Fig. 34). This prop carries stereotyped associations with the petty bourgeoisie and the bourgeoisie.[3] But since Eisenstein's aim

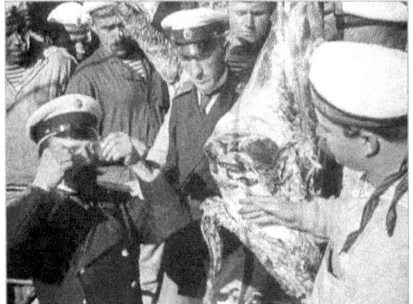

Fig. 34

---

[3] The association would not be unique to Eisenstein's film. In Bely's novel *Petersburg*, for example, spectacles, pince-nez, and lorgnettes are associated with upper-class life.

is to show Russia uniting against tsarist rule, he presents many of Odessa's middle-class citizens as aligned with the rebellion. Well-

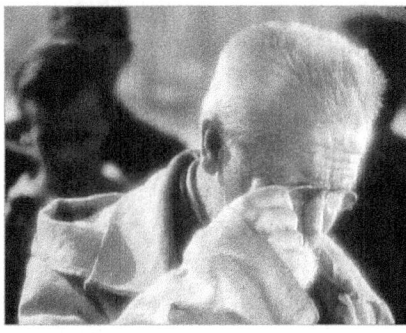

Fig. 35

dressed women with parasols join workers at the tent sheltering Vakulinchuk's body. An old man, typed as a pensioner or a shopkeeper, takes off his pince-nez to weep (Fig. 35). A student with spectacles, a rich woman with a lorgnette, and a schoolmistress with a pince-nez cheer the *Potemkin* at anchor. On the Odessa Steps, how-

ever, the troops indiscriminately open fire. Thus the image of the schoolmistress' wounded eye and smashed pince-nez (Fig. 33) bears witness to a brutal widening of the struggle. All classes fall victim to tsarist oppression.

The motivic linkage of the eye and the pince-nez nicely exemplifies the principle of the "double blow" that Eisenstein would articu-

late in his pedagogy of the 1930s. The wounding of the woman's eye is repeated and intensified in the cracking of the lens of her pince-nez, just as the effect of the worms wriggling on the meat is amplified by Smirnov's folded-over pince-nez, which he uses as a magnifying glass (Fig. 36).

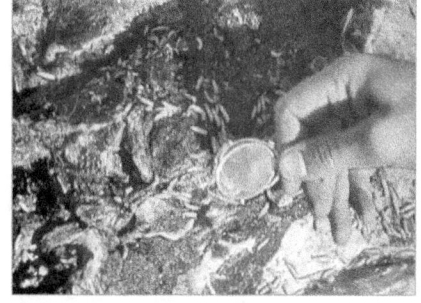

Fig. 36

These elements are suspended within a still broader web of metaphorical motifs. One nodal point involves the rotten meat. The first reel's "chapter title," "Men and Worms," initiates a complicated series of analogies. When the crew complains of the rotten meat, Smirnov's point-of-view shot shows wriggling worms. "These are not worms," he announces, "only dead maggots." Apart from portraying his denial of the truth, the episode clinches the metaphor: the navy's oppression reduces the men to parasites, with rotten meat their natural food. But when Smirnov is thrown overboard, an intertitle compares him with the meat ("He has gone to the bottom to feed the worms") and a brief image shows the infested meat. In this new parallel, the old order is rotten. By contrast, the opening of sequence 8, in which Odessa's boats bring fresh bread and meat to the battleship, shows the Russian people nourishing the uprising.

Smirnov is another motivic knot. After he confronts Vakulinchuk over the meat, the two are made parallel. Smirnov is thrown overboard; Vakulinchuk tumbles over. Smirnov clutches at ropes in resist-

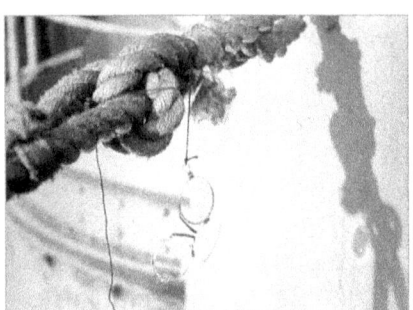

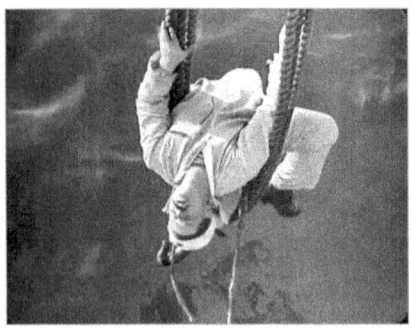

Fig. 37, 38

ing the mutineers; Vakulinchuk's body is snagged by ropes from the winch. And when Smirnov is flung overboard, his pince-nez is shown dangling from the rigging (Fig. 37). Apart from strengthening the eyeglass motif, the shot is quickly paralleled with the image of the slain Vakulinchuk, hanging above the sea (Fig. 38). Interestingly, it is not the elimination of Captain Golikov that marks the crew's victory but rather the dunking of Smirnov, the real embodiment of tsarist oppression; at almost the same moment the leader of the rebellion becomes its first martyr.

Integral to *Potemkin*'s conception of "heroic realism," then, is a core of realistically motivated elements—eyes, eyeglasses, meat, worms, dangling objects, and so on—that can radiate into a network of emotional and thematic implications. Instead of creating isolated, posterlike "attractions," Eisenstein assumes that ever-expanding metaphorical fields will stimulate complex emotional associations in the spectator. Writing in 1929 about shot-to-shot organization, he notes that in cinema, an action is effective only when presented "in montage pieces, each of which provokes a certain association, the sum of which amounts to a composite complex of emotional feeling" (1929c, 178). Although he does not make the point, longer-range motif-based associations also govern his filmmaking.

A comparable rigor and concentration inform *Potemkin*'s staging and editing. Certain cutaways, especially during the mutiny, comment on adjacent action in straightforward ways. For example, after an officer is flung overboard, Eisenstein cuts to the still-mounted life preserver that will not help him. Eisenstein's new emphasis on extensively developed scenes also allows him to push his rapid cutting further. Alexander Levshin recalls that he usually filmed retakes from different angles so that during cutting he "could literally swim in editing pieces" (Levshin 1966, 67). Many passages have a jittery quality, rendering a single actor or action in a flurry of shots that jump to and fro between two angles. Sometimes an action notably overlaps from shot to shot, as when the mess attendants

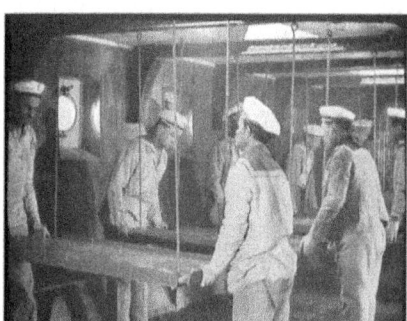 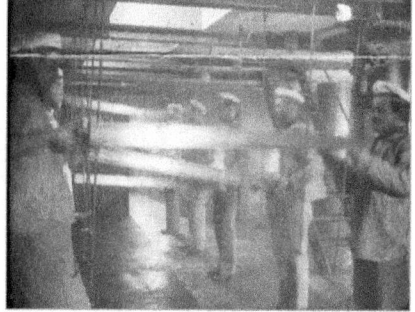

Fig. 39   Fig. 40

lower the hanging tables (Fig. 39, 40). Eisenstein also relies on a device explored occasionally in *Strike*: accentuating an action by repeating it almost *in toto* in succeeding shots (Fig. 41, 42, 43). But such overlapping cuts typically alternate with smoother or more elliptical ones, so Eisenstein gains many possibilities for rhythmic emphasis.

Above all, Eisenstein's cutting on movement generates oscillating conflicts. In a hail of overlapping shots, a sailor knocks an officer off a cannon; at each moment his swing slices in opposite directions. When the tarpaulin is tossed, a cut to the opposite side

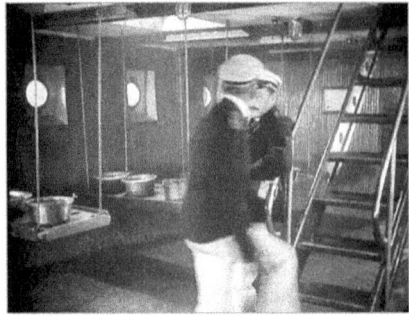

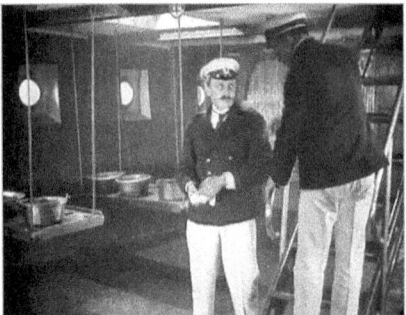

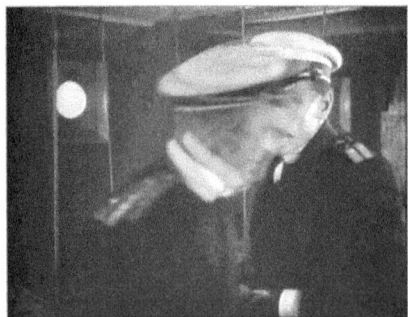

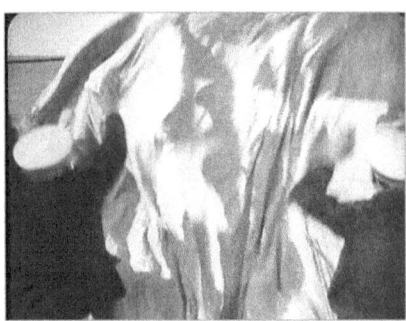

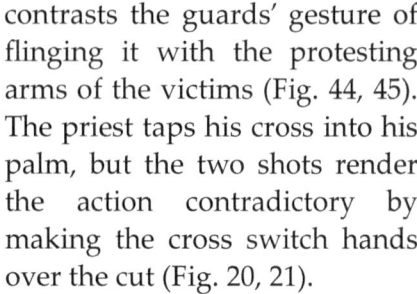

contrasts the guards' gesture of flinging it with the protesting arms of the victims (Fig. 44, 45). The priest taps his cross into his palm, but the two shots render the action contradictory by making the cross switch hands over the cut (Fig. 20, 21).

The film's dramaturgical and stylistic concentration reaches its apogee in the sequence on the Odessa Steps (Part IV). As already suggested, its didactic function is to show the punishment exacted on all classes for the spread of the revolutionary impulse. Narratively, the episode develops out of sequence 7, which shows Vakulinchuk's body lying in the tent. This presents the people uniting with the sailors' cause while introducing some of the "cast" of the Steps scene. In addition, the earlier part of 7 iden-tifies Odessa with several flights of steps. People pour

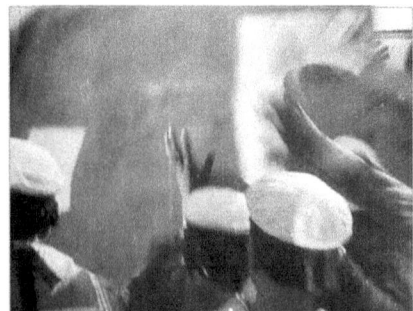

Fig. 41-44   Fig. 45

down them to the pier, which serves as a middle ground joining sea and city, sailors and citizens. At the end of the sequence, Odessa is bound more tightly to the ship when Eisenstein shows various classes of people on flights of steps waving to the sailors.

In the first half of the Steps scene, citizens bring supplies to the ship while the people on shore watch over them. Again, braided motifs bind the shots together. Eisenstein discusses some graphic elements in one passage, as we shall see in Chapter 5; for now we can notice a particularly careful knitting of elements during the crowd's waving to the ship. The modulating motifs are italicized:

1. (ms): Old *woman* with *pince-nez* and younger girl, the latter *waving* with her *left* hand (Fig. 46). This shot introduces the schoolmistress, who will furnish one of the "counter-movements" of the sequence; the shot also picks up the pince-nez motif.

2. (mcu): *Well-to-do woman* with *lorgnette* (Fig. 47); she starts to *twirl* it in her *right* hand. Her gesture is continued by:

3. (ms): *Well-to-do woman* with *parasol*; she *twirls* it in her *right* hand as she *waves* her *left* hand (Fig. 48).

4. (mis): Another *parasol* is opened (Fig. 49); a legless *man* comes into the shot and waves his *right* hand (Fig. 50).

5. (mcu) as 2: *Well-to-do woman* with *lorgnette twirls* it with her *right* hand (Fig. 51). Her gesture matches that of the man in 4.

6. (mis) as 4: The legless *man* grabs his *cap* and *waves* it in his *right* hand (Fig. 52).

By intertwining various items in the image—woman/man, rich/poor, right/left, waving/twirling, pince-nez/lorgnette/cap—

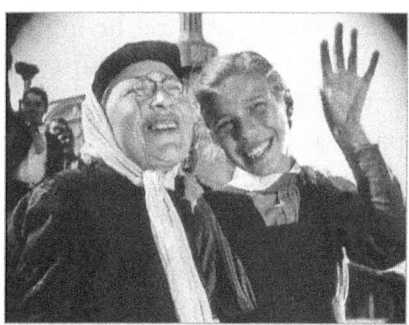

Fig. 46

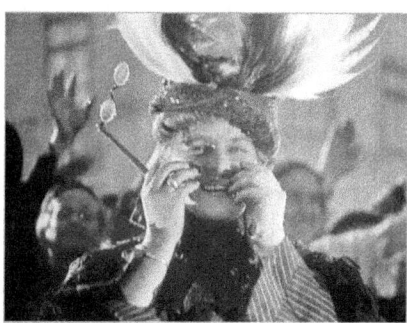

Fig. 47

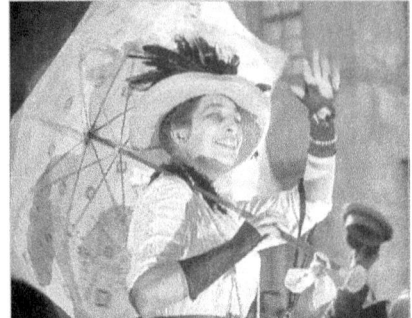

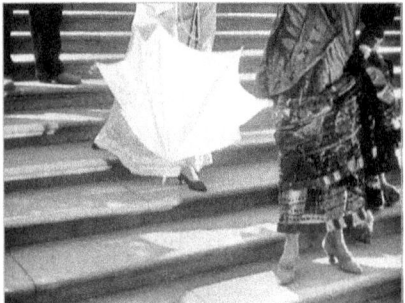

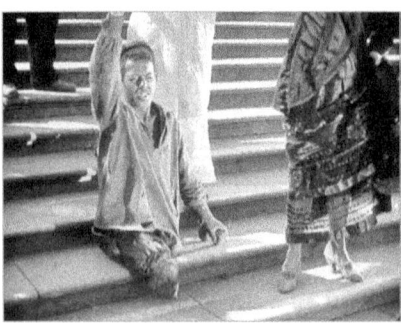

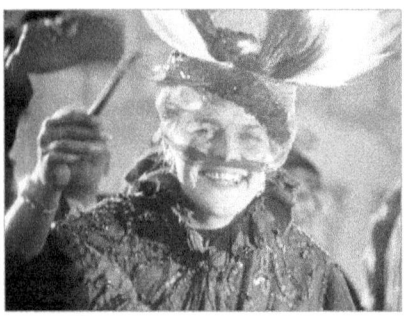

Fig. 48-51

Eisenstein presents the cross-class solidarity aroused by the *Potemkin*'s rebellion. The caps and fists shaken in anger in Part III have become caps, hands, and eyeglasses waved in fraternal greeting.

"Suddenly": one of the most famous titles in world cinema introduces four percussive shots of a woman's body jerking spasmodically (Fig. 53). Barely comprehensible in projection, the jump-cut series of shots functions, Eisenstein remarks, as the detonator in an explosion (1964, 85-86). But it also breaks apart the unified diegetic space of the scene. Where is this woman located? (The blank white background gives no information.) What exactly has happened to her? Are we seeing her staggered again and again by a fusillade, or is this a single convulsion presented repeatedly (as scenes aboard the *Potemkin* repeat events like the laying of the mess tables)? This four-shot series begins to loosen up the space of the Steps, presenting "quasi-diegetic" images: never completely outside the story world (as are the butcher and bull in *Strike*), yet not firmly located in it, they function as immediate perceptual and emotional stimuli.

As soldiers stalk down the staircase and begin firing, the action breaks into several lines. The overall momentum is provided by the crowd, which descends en masse. (As Shklovsky notes, the use of two amputees emphasizes the steps as such [1926a, 7].) Within the crowd's flight two parallel lines of action are crosscut. One centers on the schoolmistress with the pince-nez, who huddles with a group. The other line of action involves a mother whose little boy is shot. The two lines of action create an upward thrust that opposes the descending troops. But the expressive qualities of the two lines differ sharply. The schoolmistress leads her group upward in an imploring attitude, trying to appeal to the soldiers. The mother, half-demented, carries her son up the steps to confront the riflemen and demand help. Cutting between the shots contrasts expressive gestures of beseeching and defiance (Fig. 54, 55).

The mother is shot down mercilessly, and the old woman's companions fall to another volley. There emerges a third line of action, one involving another mother and her baby. She is shot,

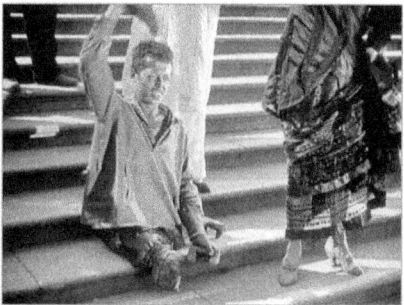
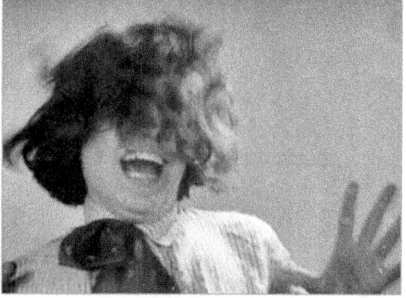
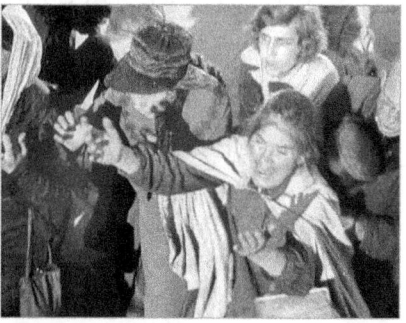
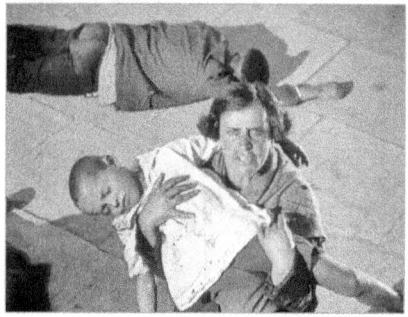

Fig. 52-55

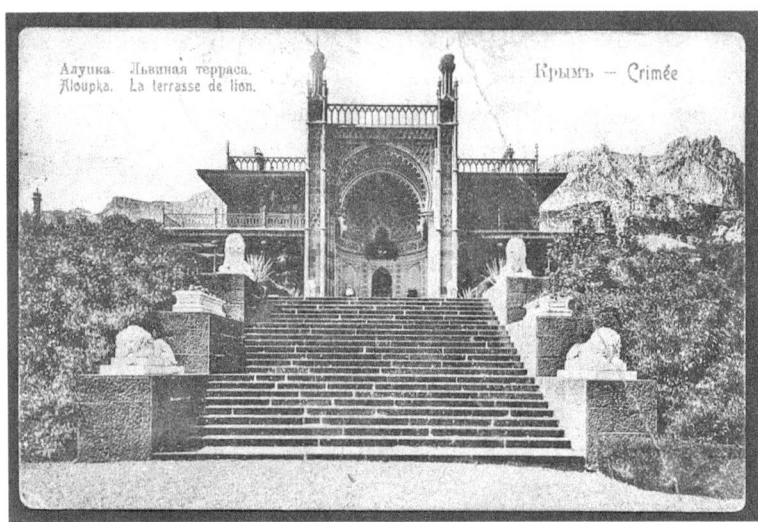

Fig. 56. The Lions' Terrace, Vorontsov Palace, Alupka

and her crumpling fall sends her baby carriage jouncing down the steps. As the cossacks cut off the crowd at the foot of the stairs, the carriage intensifies the descending movement of the crowd. And now another series of close-ups frees the imagery from the dramatic space. The schoolmistress' face is intercut with the baby carriage, but we cannot be sure that she is watching it. The carriage upends, its destiny suspended. A cossack fiercely slashes with his saber, but nothing firmly establishes him as attacking the infant. After four shots of him slashing (twice) we are shown the old woman's smashed eye (Fig. 33); is this a saber gouge or a bullet wound? The scene thus climaxes in a string of galvanizing attractions. Their force comes partly from their sharing a concrete diegetic realm, and partly from their being pushed toward a purer, more direct arousal.

The move into a realm that is only loosely diegetic is repeated and intensified when the *Potemkin*'s guns target the military headquarters. The attack reiterates, at a higher level, the unity between sea and city forged by the citizens' trips out to the ship. As the cannons swivel, three shots of bronze Cupids adorning the theatre are edited to suggest their panicky flight from the onslaught. After the bombardment, three shots of sculpted lions combine to

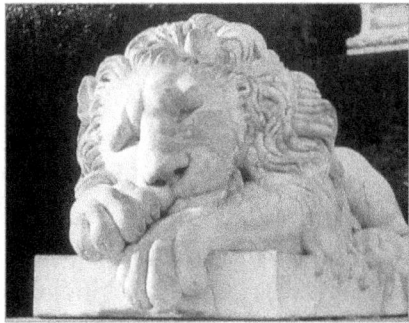
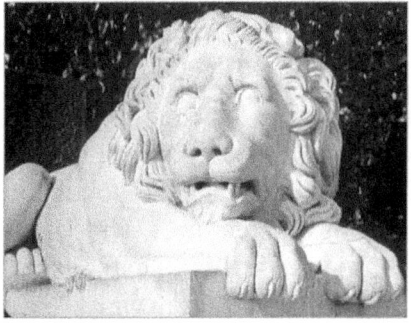
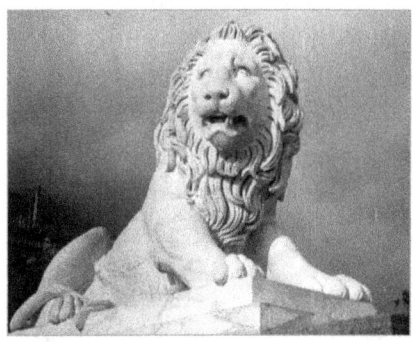

Fig. 57-59

create the image of a single lion leaping to his feet (Fig. 57, 58, 59). Since the lions were prominent Crimean landmarks (Fig. 56)[4], Eisenstein probably assumed that they would not be taken as existing in the abstract realm of *Strike*'s slaughtered bull. Like the jerking woman at the beginning of the sequence, they are quasi-diegetic. But what is their function in the climax of the sequence?

In general, the shots imply an upheaval that shakes even statues to life. Like many of Eisenstein's cinematic tropes, however, the passage is polysemous. Perhaps the leaping lions represent the generals stirred to rage by the bombardment. But the lion is usually associated with courage, a quality unlikely to be ascribed to the forces that ordered the Steps massacre. The lions may also be taken to symbolize the Russian people, aroused by the massacre and reasserting themselves in the ship's counterattack. This reading would be consistent with Eisenstein's somewhat oblique formulation: "The marble lion leaps up, surrounded by the thunder of *Potemkin*'s guns firing in protest against the bloodbath on the Odessa Steps" (1929c, 174).

---

[4] The image used in the original publication was not available (RS).

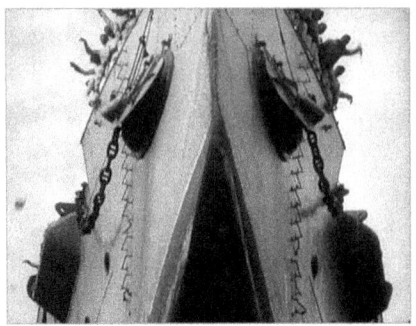

Fig. 60

But "symbolic pictorial expression" (1929c, 172) is only part of Eisenstein's purpose. His writing gives far more attention to the emotional and perceptual side of the passage. The rampant lion, he says, exemplifies the "artificially produced representation of movement" that yields a "primitive-psychological" effect (1929c, 172, 174). As literal filmic "animation," it snaps the spectator to attention.

More specifically, the shots have an auditory effect. In whipping a snoozing lion into a roar, the editing synesthetically evokes the tumult of the barrage. "The jumping lions entered one's perception as a turn of speech—'The stones roared'" (Eisenstein 1945a, 314). Thanks to the lion shots, Pudovkin noted admiringly, "The explosion on the screen was literally deafening" (Pudovkin 1928, 199). In Eisenstein's later theory, this passage would epitomize what he saw as an ecstatic "leap" into a new quality. The rampant lion, concluding the reel as the colored flag had ended the previous one, constitutes what he would in 1939 call the "point of highest ascent": when black-and-white becomes color, or when visuals burst into sound, the film's form is "suddenly hurled to another dimension" (1939f, 26).

Its blend of broad action, sharply developed detail, and metaphorical richness makes the Odessa Steps sequence profoundly typical of *Potemkin* as a whole. In these respects it also instantiates a trend in Left art of the mid-1920s away from modernist fragmentation and toward socialist "epics." [...]

Like the agitational *poema*, *Potemkin* subordinates experimentation to the interests of emotional exhortation. Still, Eisenstein remains the *montageur* of attractions. Cossacks slash at the viewer, the mother carrying her child shouts in anger at the camera, a woman with an exploded eye howls in close-up, and cannons lift to aim directly at the audience. In the last shot, the *Potemkin*'s keel splits the frame, overcoming the audience (Fig. 60). Heroic realism, on Eisenstein's understanding, drives its kinesthetic and emotional energy into the very fibers of the spectator.

In 1989 Leonid Trauberg was asked to name the best film ever made. Gazing out a window, he answered softly: "*Potemkin*. We jumped up from our chairs" (Van Houton 1989, 146).

Bibliography

Amengual, Barthélémy. 1980. *Que viva Eisenstein!* Lausanne: L'Age d'Homme.

Aumont, Jacques. 1987. *Montage Eisenstein*. Trans. Lee Hildreth, Constance Penley, and Andrew Ross. Bloomington: Indiana University Press.

Eisenstein, Sergei. 1926a. "Béla Forgets the Scissors." In Sergei Eisenstein. *Writings, 1922-34.* Ed. and trans. Richard Taylor. Bloomington: Indiana University Press, 1988, 77-81.

Eisenstein, Sergei. 1926b. "Constanta (Whither *The Battleship Potemkin*)." In Eisenstein. *Writings*, 67-70.

------. 1926c. "Eisenstein on Eisenstein, the Director of *Potemkin*." In Eisenstein. *Writings*, 74-76.

------. 1929c. "The Dramaturgy of Film Form." In Eisenstein. *Writings*, 161-80.

------. 1939f. "On the Structure of Things." In Eisenstein. *Nonindifferent Nature: Film and the Structure of Things*. Trans. Herbert Marshall. Cambridge: Cambridge University Press, 1987, 3-37.

------. 1945a. "Nonindifferent Nature." In Eisenstein. *Nonindifferent Nature*, 216-396.

------. 1945b. "The Twelve Apostles." In *Notes of a Film Director*. Ed. R. Yurenev, trans. X. Danko. Moscow: Foreign Languages Publishing House, 1958, 9-31.

------. 1964. *Immoral Memories: An Autobiography*. Trans. Herbert Marshall. Boston: Houghton Mifflin, 1983.

Gerould, Daniel. 1989. "Historical Simulation and Popular Entertainment: The *Potemkin* Mutiny from Reconstructed Newsreel to Black Sea Stunt Men." *Drama Review* 33, no. 2 (Summer): 161-184.

Hill, Steven P. 1978. "The Strange Case of the Vanishing Epigraphs." In *The Battleship Potemkin*. New York: Avon, 1978, 74-86.

Levshin, A. 1966. "Eisenstein and the 'Iron Five'." In *The Battleship Potemkin*. Ed. Herbert Marshall. New York: Avon, 1978, 63-67.

Malevich, Kasimir. 1925. "And Images Triumph on the Screens." In *Essays on Art*. Vol. 1. Trans. Xenia Glowacki-Prus and Arnold McMillan. Copenhagen: Borgen, 1971, 226-232.

Piotrovsky, Adrian. 1927. "Towards a Theory of Film Genres." In *The Poetics of Cinema*. Ed. Boris Eikhenbaum. Trans. Richard Taylor. Special issue, *Russian Poetics in Translation* 9 (1981): 90-106.

Pudovkin, V.I. 1928. "S.M. Eisenstein (From *Potemkin* to *October*)." In *The Film Factory: Russian and Soviet Cinema in Documents, 1896-1939*. Eds. Richard Taylor and Ian Christie. London and New York: Routledge, 1988, 198-200.

Stephan, Halina. 1981. *"Lef" and the Left Front of the Arts*. Munich: Sagner.

Van Houton, Theodore. 1989. *Leonid Trauberg and His Films: Always the Unexpected*. 's Hertogenbosch: Art and Research.

Wenden, D.J. 1981. *"Battleship Potemkin*: Film and Reality." In *Feature Films as History*. Ed. K.R.M. Short. London: Croom Helm, 37-61.

Willett, John. 1978. *The New Sobriety: Art and Politics in the Weimar Period, 1917-1933*. London: Thames and Hudson.

FURTHER READING

Aumont, Jacques. See above.

Bordwell, David. *The Cinema of Eisenstein*. New York and London: Routledge, 2005.

Doise, Eric. "Unorthodox Iconography: Russian Orthodox Icons in *Battleship Potemkin*." *Film Criticism* 33, no.3 (Spring 2009): 50-66.

Eisenstein, Sergei. *Selected Works: Writings, 1922-34*. Vol.1. Edited and translated by Richard Taylor. London: I.B. Tauris, 2010.

Gerould, D. See above.

Goodwin, J. *Eisenstein, Cinema, and History*. Urbana, IL: University of Illinois Press, 1993.

Håkan, Lövgren. *Eisenstein's Labyrinth: Aspects of a Cinematic Synthesis of the Arts*. Stockholm: Almqvist & Wiksell, 1996.

Mayer, David. *Eisenstein's Potemkin: A Shot-by-Shot Presentation*. NY: DaCapo Press, 1972.

Nesbet, Anne. *Savage Junctures: Sergei Eisenstein and the Shape of Thinking*. London and NY: I.B. Tauris, 2007.

O'Mahony, Mike. *Sergei Eisenstein*. London: Reaktion Books, 2008.

Taylor, Richard. *The Battleship Potemkin: The Film Companion*. London: I.B. Tauris, 2000.

Thompson, Kristin. "Eisenstein's Early Film Abroad." In *Eisenstein Rediscovered*. Edited by Ian Christie and Richard Taylor, 53-63. London: Routledge, 1993.

Wenden, D.J. See above.

BED AND SOFA

Tret'ia Meshchanskaia

1927
2025 meters, 68 minutes
Director: **Abram Room**
Screenplay: **Viktor Shklovskii, Abram Room**
Cinematography: **Grigorii Giber**
Art Design: **Vasilii Rakhal's, Sergei Iutkevich**
Production Company: **Sovkino**
Cast: **Nikolai Batalov (Kolia), Liudmila Semenova (Liuda),
    Vladimir Fogel' (Volodia), Leonid Iurenev (Building
    Supervisor), Maria Iarotskaia (Nurse)**

Abram Matveevich Room (1894-1976) attended the Petrograd
Psycho-Neurological Institute from 1914-17, and then studied
medicine at Saratov University until 1922, also serving as a Red
Army doctor during the Civil War. In Saratov he taught and directed
in the local theatre school and in 1923 joined the Theatre of the
Revolution in Moscow, where he worked with Meyerhold. In 1924
he began directing films, working for Goskino-Sovkino-Soiuzkino,
Ukrainfilm and, beginning in 1940, at Mosfilm. He also taught at
VGIK, the State Film School, from 1925-34. Unlike Eisenstein and
the other montage filmmakers of the twenties, Room was interested
in psychological drama, the individual hero and narratives of
everyday life. Shot in 1926, amidst the debate over the new Family
Code, *Bed and Sofa* generated much controversy because of its frank
portrayal of sex with multiple partners and the director's refusal
to provide a correct socialist solution to the situation. The film ran
successfully on the continent, but was not released in the US because
of its scandalous content and was distributed in England only in the

early thirties. By 1934 Room was under attack for financial problems with *One Summer (Odnazhdy letom)*. He was accused of being a careerist, and the film was taken away from him. In 1936 *Bed and Sofa* was removed from the list of films approved for distribution in the USSR, and in the same year Room's new film, the imaginative *A Strict Youth (Strogii iunosha)* was banned for Formalism and a lack of realism. Room managed to revive his career in 1945 with *The Invasion (Nashestvie)* and made safe films for the rest of his working life, concluding with a trilogy of literary adaptations, of which the most famous is *The Garnet Bracelet (Granatovyi braslet, 1964)*.

The plot of *Bed and Sofa* remains interesting and relevant even today. Kolia, a construction foreman, and his wife Liuda live in a small, crowded apartment on Third Meshchanskaia Street in Moscow. Volodia, a young print worker, comes to the city looking for work and happens to run into his old army buddy Kolia, who invites the homeless Volodia to stay on the couple's sofa. Volodia is helpful and kind to Liuda, unlike the insensitive Kolia, and, when the husband goes on a business trip, Liuda and Volodia begin an affair. Kolia moves out of the apartment but, after realizing that Volodia is hardly an ideal partner, Liuda invites him back to live on the sofa. Liuda soon realizes she is pregnant, but does not know which of the men is the father, and both men send her off to a private clinic to have an abortion. At the last minute Liuda decides against the operation and leaves Moscow to live and work on her own. Kolia and Volodia are briefly ashamed of their caddish behavior, but soon return to their accustomed, comfortable way of life.

Bed and Sofa has not lost its appeal over the years. In 1997 *Bed and Sofa: A Silent Movie Opera* (music by Polly Pen, lyrics by Laurence Klavan) was staged in New York and in 1998 Petr Todorovskii directed *Retro vtroem (Retro of Three)*, a remake-tribute to Room's film, set in contemporary Russia. In 2004 Blackhawk films released a digitally mastered version of *Bed and Sofa* with full Russian and English intertitles, made from an original print.

BED AND SOFA

Julian Graffy

The Film's Titles

The film's original title was *Liubov' vtroem* (literally, "The Love of Three"), the Russian term for a love triangle or *ménage à trois*. Considered too bold and scandalous, it was replaced by *Tret'ia Meshchanskaia* [Third Meshchanskaia Street], by which the film is now known in Russia, but in fact *Liubov' vtroem* was restored for the advertising posters,[1] and used in distribution. Contemporary reviews of the film use the two titles interchangeably (a practice not unusual at the time).

For most of the century before the making of *Bed and Sofa*, Russian culture had been preoccupied with the elaboration of new social models. One of the most persistently alluring of these was the idealised *ménage à trois*, which found its most notorious expression in Nikolai Chernyshevsky's 1863 novel *What is to be Done? (Chto delat'?)*, subtitled "From Tales About New People" ("Iz rasskazov o novykh liudiakh"). It was drawn in part from literary models, including the writings of George Sand and Rousseau, and in part from the living arrangements of two famous contemporaries, Alexander Herzen and Nikolai Shelgunov. Herzen, who had himself addressed the question of the love triangle in his 1847 novel *Who is to Blame? (Kto vinovat?)*, participated in two such triangles, first with his wife Natalie and the German Romantic poet Georg Herwegh, and then with his closest friend Nikolai Ogarev and Ogarev's second wife, Natalia Tuchkova-Ogareva. Despite the elevated belief of the

---

1   Both the poster designed by Vladimir and Georgii Stenberg and the one designed by Iakov Ruklevskii, each from 1927, style the film "Liubov' vtroem (Tret'ia Meshchanskaia)."

participants that a continuing harmonious union was possible, both of these triangles ended in bitterness and recrimination. A more rational approach was taken by the radical critic Nikolai Shelgunov, his wife and cousin Liudmila Michaelis and the poet and political activist Mikhail Mikhailov, and this triple union for a time successfully combined political activity and personal tranquillity. After the arrest and death of Mikhailov, Michaelis spent a period in European exile, but she eventually returned to her husband.[2]

In *What is to be Done?*, Dmitri Lopukhov and Alexander Kirsanov are fellow medical students and already the greatest of friends before they meet the heroine, Vera Pavlovna Rozal'skaia, and Vera Pavlovna is initially jealous of their friendship. Lopukhov and Vera Pavlovna marry, but theirs is a relationship based upon Lopukhov's rational idealism and the marriage remains celibate. Kirsanov, realising the nature of his own feelings for Vera Pavlovna, withdraws from their lives. Eventually, though, it becomes impossible to ignore the intensity of the love between Vera Pavlovna and Kirsanov, and *What is to be Done?* becomes the story of Lopukhov's selfless accommodation to this love. While he does, at one stage, propose that all three of them live together, for "economic" reasons, a point that is taken up later by the novel's exemplary radical hero Rakhmetov, who is against the idea of jealousy in a "developed" person and insists to Vera Pavlovna that the trio could have lived calmly and moved into one apartment, the offer is stoutly rejected by Vera Pavlovna. Lopukhov sacrifices himself in the name of her greater love for Kirsanov, even faking his own suicide so that they can be married.[3] At the end of the novel Lopukhov, now resurrected

---

[2] Details of these relationships are taken from Irina Paperno's absorbing *Chernyshevsky and the Age of Realism: A Study in the Semiotics of Behavior* (Stanford, CA, 1988). Herzen is discussed on 141-7, Shelgunov on 147-50.

[3] Lopukhov's proposal is in chapter 3, section 25 of the novel, and Rakhmetov's assessment in chapter 3, section 30. Because of the number of existing editions of Chernyshevsky's novel I have considered it more useful to refer to chapters and sections, rather than to a specific edition. Where, however, I quote directly from the novel, I have used the exemplary translation by Michael R. Katz in N. Chernyshevsky, *What is to be Done?* (Ithaca, NY, and London, 1989).

as the "Canadian" Charles Beaumont, himself marries again and the two couples take up residence in a kind of commune, with adjoining apartments and flexible arrangements for achieving privacy. The behaviour of the characters in *What is to be Done?* is motivated throughout by utopian ideals, virtuous delicacy and a concern for the feelings of others, and it is crucial to note that, despite its reputation, there is no period of *ménage à trois* in the novel. It is also important that the relations of the characters are not affected by pregnancy or the birth of offspring, since the Russian utopian tradition was hostile to children.[4] In the delicacy of its characters' behaviour, the absence of an actual *ménage à trois*, the general erasure of the physical and the specific elision of the complications of pregnancy, the novel's abstraction contrasts markedly with the sardonic realism of *Bed and Sofa*. [...]

Thus the radical thinkers of the mid-nineteenth century, to whom both the politicians and the artists of the post-revolutionary period would naturally turn, had raised questions of sexual morality and specifically had theorised about the *ménage à trois*. But Shklovsky and Room could also draw upon more recent models. During the first decade of the twentieth century the Symbolist poets Dmitri Merezhkovsky and Zinaida Gippius combined a celibate marriage very similar to that of Lopukhov and Vera Pavlovna with a *ménage à trois* with Dmitri Filosofov.[5] During the same decade the younger Symbolist poets Alexander Blok and Andrei Bely, themselves linked over many years by an intense "love-hatred," were both in love with Blok's wife Liubov' Mendeleeva, and events reached a dramatic

---

4   Each of the couples does in fact have a child at the end of the novel, but this information is vouchsafed by Chernyshevsky in passing and the children play no role in the plot. On the "hostility to progeny" of the religious-utopian tradition in Russia, see Eric Naiman, *Sex in Public: The Incarnation of Early Soviet Ideology* (Princeton, NJ: Princeton University Press, 1997), 27-45. For his reading of *What is to be Done?*, see 36-7.

5   For an account of this and other theorised relationships in Symbolist circles see O. Matich, "The Symbolist Meaning of Love: Theory and Practice," in I. Paperno and J. Delaney Grossman, eds., *Creating Life: The Aesthetic Utopia of Russian Modernism* (Stanford, CA, 1994), 24-50.

climax in March 1906 when Mendeleeva almost left her husband for Bely.[6]

After the Revolution, the politician and sexual theorist Alexandra Kollontai addressed the idea of the "love of three" in a famous 1923 article "Make Way for the Winged Eros" ("Dorogu krylatomu erosu"). Stressing that love is not just biologically motivated but also socially articulated, she invokes the treatment of the love triangle by Herzen and Chernyshevsky as attempts to solve an emotional drama created by bourgeois capitalism. She insists that "the key" to the problem of the duality of love is now "in the hands of the proletariat," and suggests that the dilemma of one woman loving two men or one man loving two women can be resolved through the proletarian ideal of "love-comradeship," which will destroy the exclusivity of the bourgeois marriage and place all the participants within the collective. In the "accomplished Communist society, love, 'winged Eros,' will be transformed into something completely unfamiliar to us [...] People's feelings will become collective ones, and inequality between the sexes, as well as the dependence of woman on man, will disappear without a trace, lost in the memory of past centuries."[7] The article has an obviously utopian tone, but "Three Generations," a story Kollontai wrote at the same time, which traces the evolving sexual mores of a mother, a daughter and a granddaughter in the same family, is more circumspect. Olga Sergeevna Veselovskaia, who represents the middle generation, for a while maintains a simultaneous relationship with two men, but ends up estranged from both of them.[8]

---

[6]   On this relationship see A. Pyman, *The Life of Aleksandr Blok. Vol. 1: The Distant Thunder 1880-1908* (Oxford, 1979), especially 236-40.

[7]   A. Kollontai, "Dorogu krylatomu erosu," first in *Molodaia gvardiia*, 3 (1923): 111-24; translated as "Make Way for the Winged Eros," in W.G. Rosenberg, ed., *Bolshevik Visions: First Phase of the Cultural Revolution in Soviet Russia*, 2nd ed. (Ann Arbor, MI, 1990), Part 1, 84-94; quotation on 92.

[8]   "Three Generations" was first published in Kollontai's collection *Liubov' pchel trudovykh* (Moscow-Petrograd, 1923). It is translated by Cathy Porter in Alexandra Kollontai, *Love of Worker Bees* (London, 1977), 182-211.

The most famous real-life triangle of the period was that of the poet Vladimir Mayakovsky, Lili Brik and her husband, the Formalist critic Osip Brik, with whom he also had a close friendship based on their discussion of his poetry. This relationship was very much in the public domain, since his passionate love for Lili had been the main subject of Mayakovsky's lyric poetry for a decade.[9] [...]

All the texts and relationships articulated here had entered the cultural consciousness and worked as subtexts for *Bed and Sofa*, none more so than the life of Mayakovsky and the Briks. Shklovsky was a colleague of Brik through the school of Russian Formalism, and the Formalist critics and the Futurist poets were connected through the Left Front of the Arts (LEF). Room, too, was a close acquaintance, and indeed, as recounted above, the script of *Bed and Sofa* was written while its authors were collaborating with Lili Brik and Mayakovsky on *Jews on the Land*. But, in addition to this, Mayakovsky was such a dominant figure in Soviet culture in the 1920s that his imagery served as a kind of cultural barometer of the period, and many of the images used in *Bed and Sofa* have their source in his poetry.

The title chosen to replace the "scandalous" *Liubov' vtroem* is the name of an actual Moscow street, one of four (First, Second, Third and Fourth Meshchanskaia Streets) which run north from the Inner Ring Road [Sadovoe koltso, Garden Ring], to the east of Tverskaia Street. The streets date from the late seventeenth century when, in 1671, Tsar Aleksei Mikhailovich resettled there the traders and craftsman (*meshchane*, from the Belorussian *mesta*, Polish *miasto*, meaning town) from the Belorussian towns he had won back from Poland. [...]

Initially the word *meshchanstvo* was merely descriptive. It was first introduced into the Russian legal code in a manifesto of 17 March 1775, in which it indicated urban dwellers who were not

---

9   The evolution of the relationship can be closely traced in their correspondence. See Vladimir Mayakovsky, *Love is the Heart of Everything: Correspondence between Vladimir Mayakovsky and Lili Brik 1915-1930*, ed. Bengt Jangfeldt, trans. Julian Graffy (Edinburgh, 1986).

registered in the merchant class (*kupechestvo*). The term was made more inclusive by Catherine the Great, and gradually, during the nineteenth century, it lost its close connection with a specific social stratum and took on ever more pejorative associations in intellectual discourse. It began to imply vulgarity, philistinism and narrowness of vision, very similar to the use of the term *petit-bourgeois* in western European languages.[10] [...]

After the Revolution, of course, both the class and the vices ascribed to it should have disappeared and, when it became clear that they had not, the term was ritually invoked, by both writers and social commentators, to indicate the perverse survival of a force which encouraged the continuation of the old ways, and thus to explain the gap between the ideal and reality. It is precisely in this sense that the term is used by Mayakovsky, who asserts in the poem "About Rubbish" ("O driani"), written in 1920-21, that "From behind the back of the Russian Soviet Federative Socialist Republic the muzzle of the *meshchanin* has emerged," only to go on to insist that he is referring not to a class but to "*meshchane* of all classes and estates indiscriminately."[11] [...]

The Flat: NEP and Byt

Most of *Bed and Sofa* takes place in the one-room flat on Third Meshchanskaia Street and the film's plot revolves around the changing functions of this domestic space. From the opening scenes it is apparent that the flat is cluttered: objects fill every available space and make it difficult for the characters to move around. As well as the bed and the sofa, the room will gradually be revealed to contain a rocking chair, a chest of drawers full of crockery, a mirror, a handsome wall clock, curtains cutting off the kitchen and the entrance hall, a dividing screen, a rug, a wicker case stowed under

---

[10] For a definition of the term "*meshchane*" roughly contemporaneous with *Bed and Sofa*, see the entry in *Bol'shaia Sovetskaia Entsiklopediia*, Vol. 39 (1938), col. 308.

[11] V. Maiakovskii, "O driani," in his *Polnoe sobranie sochinenii v trinadtsati tomakh* (henceforth Maiakovskii, *PSS*), Vol. 2, 73-5.

the bed, potted plants, a samovar, a teapot, a soup tureen, articles Kolia uses in his work and a number of little plaster ornaments. Clothes are strewn over the floor. A calendar and several pictures cover the walls, including a photograph of Liuda herself, portraits of Tolstoy, Stalin and Marshal Budenny, a picture of swans and a cover illustration from the film magazine *Sovetskii ekran* (*Soviet Screen*).[12] [...]

After the Revolution, and especially with the introduction of NEP, a concern that conditions had not changed led to a battle to overcome the old *byt*. The word *byt*, which means "way of life," had come, like *meshchanstvo*, to signify a philistine domination by possessions. The avant-garde were particularly vociferous in their attacks. [...]

The Party, too, engaged in battles over the new Soviet interior. Above all it was to be light and airy, leaving no room for what Lenin called the "dirt of the old world," and people were encouraged to whitewash walls and paint their furniture white.[13] The 1924 volume *Advice for the Proletarian Housewife* urged her: "not to stuff the apartment with unnecessary extra furniture, not to hang useless rags for decoration. These things not only significantly reduce the amount of light, but also harbour dust containing all manner of parasites, and poison the home with throngs of tiny bacteria which are extremely harmful to one's health."[14]

According to the painter El' Lissitzky, the room of the future would be like "the best kind of travelling suitcase," stripped of

[12] We are never given a close-up of this picture. While most critics refer to it as coming from *Sovetskii ekran*, which first appeared on 24 March 1925, some call it *Ekran*, another film magazine which started to appear before the Revolution. While only the word *Ekran* is clearly visible, *Sovetskii ekran* used various formats for its logo, one of which, used for example in issue 7 for 1926, looks very similar to the one in the picture.

[13] On this, and its link to the electrification campaign, see V. Buchli, "Soviet Hygiene and the Battle Against Dirt and Petit-bourgeois Consciousness," chapter 3, 41-62 of his *An Archeology of Socialism* (Oxford and New York, 1999).

[14] *Sovety proletarskoi khoziaike* (Ekaterinburg, 1924), 90-1, quoted in Buchli, *An Archeology of Socialism*, 44.

everything except a mattress, a folding chair, a table and a gramophone.[15] At the end of 1928 *Komsomol'skaia Pravda* would launch a "Down with domestic trash" campaign, challenging its readers to throw out their trinkets, take down their pictures and postcards, and report to the paper on their successes.[16]

Thus, the very darkness of the semi-basement flat on Third Meshchanskaia Street is an affront to the new order, and none of the objects with which it is cluttered is ideologically neutral. Worker viewers of the film would complain that the soup tureen and the metal glass holders (*podstakanniki*) were unproletarian, and the artist Vladimir Tatlin was about to declare war on the chest of drawers.[17] Rugs were considered unhygienic and took too much labour to keep clean.[18]

But the main ideological battle grounds were the bed and the sofa themselves. Rakhmetov, the ascetic hero of *What is to be Done?*, had slept on a strip of felt lined with nails. Eisenstein boasted of having slept on the mirrored door of a wardrobe after the Revolution,[19] and in the "The Tsaritsa's bedroom" sequence at the end of his *October* (*Oktiabr'*, 1927), the ripping of the royal mattress by a sailor from the Amur Fleet is shown as a synecdoche of the revolutionary explosion as a whole. The new "revolutionary" bed was to be multi-functional, easily folded away and invisible.[20] The

15 El' Lisitskii, "Kul'tura zhil'ia" [1926], quoted in Svetlana Boym, *Common Places* (Cambridge, MA: Harvard University Press, 1994), 38. Lopukhov in *What is to be Done?* had also stripped his room of anything that was not absolutely necessary (see chapter 3, section 20 of the novel).

16 Boym, *Common Places*, 35-8.

17 V. Tatlin, "Problemy sootnosheniia cheloveka i veshchi: ob"iavim voinu komodam i bufetam," *Rabis* (14 April 1930): 9, quoted in O. Matich, "Remaking the Bed: Utopia in Daily Life," in J. Bowlt and O. Matich (eds), *Laboratory of Dreams: The Russian Avant-garde and Cultural Experiment* (Stanford, CA, 1996), 59-78 (60).

18 Buchli, *An Archaeology of Socialism*, 44-5.

19 "Dvinsk," in R. Taylor (ed.), *Beyond the Stars. The Memoirs of Sergei Eisenstein,* Vol. 4 of S.M. Eisenstein, *Selected Works* (London and Calcutta, 1995), 138-9.

20 See the illustrations from *LEF*, 3, 1923, reproduced in Matich, "Remaking the

gorka, the pile of well-stuffed pillows that before the Revolution had signified prosperity, was specifically rejected.[21] These pillows had played a memorable role in Nikolai Larin's 1913 film melodrama *Merchant Bashkirov's Daughter* (*Doch' kuptsa Bashkirova*), where they suffocated the "unsuitable" suitor, but Liuda in *Bed and Sofa* ritually plumps them up each morning.

The sofa, too, is usually represented as an article of luxury. The protagonists of *What is to be Done?* only occasionally allow themselves to relax on one. Walter Benjamin describes a well-cushioned sofa as an essential feature of the *petit-bourgeois* NEP interior, and Svetlana Boym stresses that in post-revolutionary households they were both rare and ideologically suspect.[22] Thus the very presence of the sofa in Room's film is yet another indicator of the slide back into *byt*, though it has to be said that the sofa here is not only the sleeping place of the sexual loser, but also both small and uncomfortable, only marginally more acceptable than the office desk.

Bed," 71 and the design by Rodchenko, in ibid., 74.

21   Buchli, *An Archaeology of Socialism*, 44.

22   W. Benjamin, "Moscow" [1927], in his *One-Way Street and Other Writings* (London, 1979), 177-208 (188). Boym, *Common Places*, 130-4.

LIFE INTO ART: LAYING BARE THE THEME IN *BED AND SOFA*

Rimgaila Salys

In an early version of the script for Abram Room's 1927 film *Bed and Sofa* (*Tret'ia Meshchanskaia*) the chairman of the house committee gives a speech exposing the shameful and immoral situation in the apartment. In another variant the film concludes with an abortion, a more focussed farewell note ("Knigi vziala—khochu zanimat'sia. Sama rabotat' masterom," "I've taken the books—I want to study, to be a skilled worker myself") and Kolia's cathartic tears.[1] Yet in the end Room chose to reject these tendentious, didactic and ultimately easy solutions. He insisted that *Bed and Sofa* was concerned with the personal lives of his heroes and that the basic task of the film "was not to solve, but only to sharpen, not to instruct, but only to lay bare and pose this theme for the audience to discuss."[2] This is perhaps still the most complete and useful definition of the film and its aims. Room's discussion of *Bed and Sofa* borrows from the Formalist concept of "obnazhenie priema" ("laying bare the device"), introduced by Jakobson and used by Shklovskii in such works as

---

[1]   Irina Grashchenkova, *Abram Room* (Moscow: Iskusstvo, 1977), 107. *Bed and Sofa* was released by Sovkino March 15, 1927. The screenplay was authored by Viktor Shklovskii and Abram Room. On the significance of the street name in the title, see Steven P. Hill, "*Bed and Sofa*" ("*Tretia Meshchanskaia.*" *Film Heritage* 7, no. 1 [Fall 1971], 19) and Paul E. Burns, "An NEP Moscow Address: Abram Room's *Third Meshchanskaia* (*Bed and Sofa*) in Historical Context," *Film and History* 12, no. 4 (Dec. 1982): 73-4. For information on the genesis of *Bed and Sofa* see Grashchenkova, 85-6, and V. Shklovskii, "Tret'ia Meshchanskaia," in *Za sorok let. Stat'i o kino* (Moscow: Iskusstvo, 1965), 104-07.

[2]   "...osnovnaia zadacha byla ne razreshat', a lish' zaostrit', ne instruktirovat', a lish' obnazhit' i postavit' etu temu na obsuzhdenie zritelia." (Abram Room, interview in *Sovetskoe kino* 2 (1927): 9, quoted in *Istoriia sovetskogo kino*, ed. Kh. Abul-Kasymova et al., vol. 1 [Moscow: Izdatel'stvo "Iskusstvo," 1969], 386).

his 1921 essay on *Tristram Shandy*. The Russian Formalists were interested in writers who "laid bare" the conventions of literary art, destroying its illusory reality through awareness of and toying with form. Through the graphic—and not conventionally covert—love triangle of *Bed and Sofa*, Room "lays bare" the question of sexual morality in the new society.

The thematic focus of *Bed and Sofa* emerged directly from an item that appeared in *Komsomol'skaia Pravda*: two young factory workers and Komsomol members showed up at a maternity home to visit a young mother (also a worker and Komsomol member) and her baby because she did not know which one of them was the father. The trio made no attempt to hide the situation and even tried to give it a theoretical foundation, arguing that love among Komsomol members was not subject to jealousy and could be collective, because it was not based on private ownership.[3] Shklovskii and Room put the viability of collective Communist love to the test by transposing the situation to the much more ordinary reality of two mature working men and a Moscow housewife. Three years after *Bed and Sofa* was made, Shklovskii commented on the film from a perspective that complemented Room's stated purpose in undertaking the project: "There is no villain in the film. These are three good people who have gotten all tangled up in the fact that urban life has changed, while the life of the apartment has not, and that people must now learn by experience what is moral and what is immoral."[4]

Both Kolia and Volodia are ultimately flawed figurations of the Soviet New Man. Hail-fellow-well-met Kolia is a successful worker, a construction foreman, the physiological New Man who loves his body narcissistically, enjoying his morning exercises and hygienic samovar shower. Less physically imposing, but endowed with emotional intelligence, Volodia is the technological New Man, who works only with machines. In the spirit of the time, the camera lingers on the newspaper printing press and his hair standing

---

3   Grashchenkova, 86.

4   Viktor Shklovskii, *Room. Zhizn' i rabota* (n.p.:Tea-kino-pechat', 1929), 10.

upright, charged with static electricity. Nevertheless, by the end of the film both men are revealed as selfish and self-absorbed, mired in bourgeois morality, and ultimately addicted to bourgeois domestic comforts.

Yet while "there is no villain" in *Bed and Sofa* and Room claims not to instruct, the theme it sharpens, lays bare and poses is pervasively feminist: bourgeois patriarchal interests are consistently portrayed as primary and dominant in this corner of Soviet society and Liuda, the female heroine, is commodified and marginalized. The film also raises significant questions regarding the usefulness to women of the 1926 draft Family Code, as it was being discussed in the 1925-26 public debate and treats the abortion issue from a perspective which appears both to support the conservative government position and (perhaps conveniently) allows Liuda to control her own body and future as she opts for motherhood.

I

In *Bed and Sofa* male domination and female subservience are conveyed directly through characterization. Liuda's husband, Kolia, "the husband!," as she calls him scornfully, is master of the house as he reminds her to scrub the hall, demands a glass-holder for his hot milk, and humiliates her by a paperwad to the chest. The more sensitive Volodia's gift of a radio with earphones turns out to be selfishly motivated, as he himself spends evenings listening on the sofa. Both men display *Domostroi*-like behavior: before going on his business trip—and in the context of possible gossip about Liuda and Volodia—Kolia issues a veiled warning: "No one will take her from me." Later, when Liuda refuses to make tea for Volodia, he physically prevents her from leaving the apartment and then locks her inside.[5] Finally, the pregnant Liuda performs heavy physical

---

5   In another version of the intertitles Kolia asserts that Liuda "knows I am very fond of her. But whom one loves, one also chastises, if necessary. She understands that, too." Volodia prevents Liuda from leaving the apartment: "I am your husband and master in the house." *Domostroi* advocates secluded lives for women and instructive corporal punishment: "But if your wife does

labor (scrubbing clothes clean in a trough), separated by a curtain from the central domestic space of the apartment where Volodia doubles for her by serenely frying up some eggs while Kolia does drafting work at a table.[6]

Judith Mayne has pointed out that Kolia and Volodia are the real couple in *Bed and Sofa*, and that male homosocial desire is the moving force of the film.[7] Before his trip to Rostov, Kolia laughingly asserts that Volodia's fears of gossip are rubbish because Liuda is absolutely crazy about him and at the same time feels the muscles on Volodia's bare arms (Volodia has been asleep on the sofa), before flexing his own. Returning from the trip, he jokingly covers Volodia's eyes and tricks him into a kiss meant for Liuda. When Kolia first brings Volodia to the apartment and introduces him, he explains their shared past, how they "fought and froze together in the Red Army" (there is a photo of Budennyi on the wall), and reinforces his point by firmly kissing Volodia on the mouth. This is normal Russian etiquette for men, and not homosexual behavior, yet it nonetheless underscores the primacy of the male bond, as opposed to the mens' relationship with Liuda, who only merits a random peck on the cheek from Kolia as he leaves for work in the morning or goes off to Rostov.

Similarly, the male body is generally more prominent in the film: Liuda simply washes up in the morning under a faucet while Kolia revels in—and the camera lingers on—his samovar shower. Volodia is shown stripped to the waist as he talks to Kolia before the Rostov trip. The female body is effaced, denied erotic or other display: after

---

not...do all that is recommended here, ...then the husband should punish his wife. Beat her when you are alone together; then forgive her and remonstrate with her. But when you beat her, do not do it in hatred, do not lose control. A husband must never get angry with his wife; a wife must live with her husband in love and purity of heart." *The Domostroy*, ed. and trans. Carolyn Johnston Pouncy (Ithaca: Cornell University Press, 1955), 143.

6   Judith Mayne notes the linking net pattern on both Liuda and Volodia's faces. (Judith Mayne, *"Bed and Sofa* and the Edge of Domesticity," in *Kino and the Woman Question* [Columbus: Ohio State University Press, 1989], 115-119).

7   Mayne, 120. See also Eve Kosovsky Sedgwick, *Between Men: English Literature and Male Homosocial Desire* (New York: Columbia University Press, 1985).

her night with Volodia, Liuda's blouse is in slight disarray and she is only permitted to bite the bedframe in remembrance of passion. The bond of male friendship is re-established — and even strengthens — after the affair is revealed, since the men prefer their tea, talk and games of checkers to walks with Liuda. In the aftermath of Liuda's departure, Kolia and Volodia briefly acknowledge their caddish behavior, but soon fall back into the same pattern of domestic togetherness as they make tea and search for the jam.

The dynamic of male domination-female subservience is also conveyed more subtly in *Bed and Sofa* through the symbolic use of space, architecture and artifacts. Room begins the film by establishing a semantics of gendered space. From a long shot of the environs of Moscow we move in toward the city, to the towering Cathedral of Christ the Savior[8] and a building under construction, to the deserted Tret'ia Meshchanskaia Street, Kolia and Liuda asleep on their bed, their sleeping cat and several views of the one-room apartment. After an intercut shot of the railroad tracks and Volodia looking out the train window, the camera reverses direction, moving from the secluded street to a large building, a view of the city, the Cathedral of Christ the Savior, and the Moscow River with its environs.[9] The world is thus presented as a series of gradations forming an organic whole in which the outside — NEP Moscow, the

---

[8] Until it was blown up on Stalin's orders in 1931 to make way for the planned Palace of Soviets, the Cathedral was a prominent Moscow landmark because of its height. When Yurii Zhivago returns from military service in WWI, the cathedral is the first sign of the city he is able to see from a distance: "...the Church of Christ the Savior showed over the rim of the hill, and a minute later the domes, chimneys, roofs, and houses of the city." Boris Pasternak, *Doctor Zhivago* (New York: Ballantine Books, 1983), 165.

[9] Room uses the traditional symbolism here: the railroad upon which Volodia travels in to the city obviously represents the road of life. The crisscrossing tracks are intercut in two separate scenes — once between Kolia and Liuda in bed and Volodia looking out the train window, and a second time between the couple's washing and Volodia's wandering around Moscow — as their life tracks are about to intersect in a fateful manner. In another early scene Volodia stops to look at the Moscow River and kicks a stone into the water, causing ever-widening ripples; his arrival will have the same effect on the couple's lives.

world of modernity with its male-dominated construction projects, trolleys, airplanes and printing presses—is seamlessly connected to the private world of the Meshchanskaia apartment. Room reinforces this unity on a microlevel by connecting space through metonymical contiguity: outdoors, early in the morning, streetcleaners sweep rhythmically with their brooms; the brooms (of other sweepers) then become visible through the half-basement apartment window. A cat sits by the window, jumps down and leads us to the couple's bed. A similar effect is achieved by the shots of Liuda, Kolia and the cat performing their morning ablutions as a car is being hosed down on the street outside.

The male heroes of the film easily negotiate the boundary between social and personal space as they go back and forth to their jobs and travel to and from different cities.[10] Liuda is unemployed (a NEP phenomenon) and confined to the apartment, spends hours by the basement window, becoming progressively more marginalized as the bond between Kolia and Volodia strengthens.[11] She becomes first an eavesdropper from behind a curtain as Volodia explains the new relationship to Kolia and her marginality is underlined by two enlarged shots of her head superimposed on the curtain as she listens.[12] The film thus highlights her marginality: she is prominent in her lack of prominence. Later she is an onlooker from the peripheral window area, as the men occupy themselves with checkers night after night. Liuda leaves the apartment only four times and two of the trips are controlled by the men in her life. Volodia takes her on a plane ride over Moscow and to the cinema, thereby literally and figuratively broadening her horizons,[13] but also seduces her in the process. Both men selfishly compel her to go to the hospital for an abortion. When Liuda goes outdoors on her own

[10]   Mayne, 112.

[11]   Female unemployment in 1921 was 60,975 and in 1927, 369,800. Wendy Z. Goldman, *Women, the State and Revolution, Soviet Family Policy and Social Life, 1917-1936* (New York: Cambridge University Press, 1993), 111.

[12]   Mayne, 119.

[13]   Burns, 77.

Fig. 61.
Kolia Relaxing Atop
the Bol'shoi Theatre

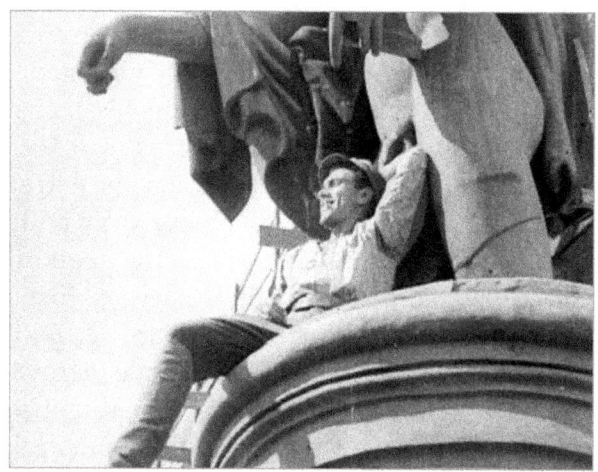

initiative, the motives are entirely different. She instinctively pities the homeless Kolia and runs outside in the rain to bring him back to sleep on the Meshchanskaia sofa. In her final departure she breaks out of spatial and psychic boundaries, reclaiming her identity as she removes her photograph from the picture frame which had hung on the wall, putting herself, so to speak, into her travel bag and leaving the apartment for good.

But prior to Liuda's climactic escape from the constraints of domestic space, freedom and public display are shown to be the prerogative of men. While Liuda typically watches the feet of passersby from the window of her half-basement apartment, Kolia works high up on the roof of the Bol'shoi Theatre.[14] He is clearly very big on himself as well, and the architecture of this scene, as it relates to both Kolia and Volodia, is overcharged with testosterone.

---

[14]   Burns points out that Kolia is refurbishing a pre-revolutionary structure, "just as in his private life he represents the carry-over of pre-revolutionary social attitudes" (77). Upkeep, staff expenses and renovation of this symbol of pre-revolutionary elite culture had been a sore point since 1919. In 1927 Osip Brik complained, "We have been saying for ten years that the Bolshoi Theatre must be closed, and yet this year it is being renovated." For the same reason, Vertov stages the Bolshoi's filmic implosion in *Man with a Movie Camera* (Yuri Tsivian, "Dziga Vertov and His Time," in *Lines of Resistance: Dziga Vertov and the Twenties,* ed. and with an introduction by Yuri Tsivian [Gemona: Le Giornate del Cinema Muto, 2004], 20-22).

Kolia seats himself by P. K. Klodt's sculptures of Phoebus-Apollo with his sun-chariot and horses, mounted on the pediment of the Bol'shoi Theater.[15] Hitching up his pants demonstratively, he settles down to lunch by the horses (brother studs), and then has a smoke leaning comfortably against the god's monumental genitals (Fig. 61). He smiles, stretches luxuriantly and dangles his legs over the edge of the roof—Phoebus' maleness always visible beside him—lord and master of all he surveys. Exhausted, unable to find a place to live, and almost in despair, i.e., occupying a subordinate role in the mythic imaging of the male hierarchy, Volodia sits down in a half-circle of benches in the square opposite the Moscow City Soviet and stares dejectedly at the phallic column of the Freedom Obelisk before him.

Another Moscow monument functions in a similar way as part of the sex plot between Volodia and Liuda. The occasion is the Aviakhim holiday. Stunt planes (more male display) are performing over Moscow and the couple go up in an *agitsamolet*, a Red Army propaganda plane.[16] While the plane trip over Moscow is liberating for Liuda, it also serves Volodia's intentions. He is able to win her over during the flight as he shows her the sights, and she clings to him apprehensively as he puts his hand on her back protectively. After the flight she feels giddy, leans against the plane and throws Volodia a sexy look. The episode culminates in their return to the city via a famous monument, the Triumphal Arch, erected in 1834 at the Tver' Gates.[17] The arch dominates the entire screen as we approach it head on with Volodia and Liuda, and pass through the central aperture. The monument was built to commemorate Kutuzov's

---

[15]   The sculpture was added to the roof of the Bol'shoi Theater when it was rebuilt in 1824. *Bol'shaia sovetskaia entsiklopediia*, ed. A.M. Prokhorov et al., vol. 3 (Moscow: Izd-vo "Sovetskaia entsiklopediia," 1970), 545.

[16]   Aviakhim was a voluntary society for assistance to the aviation and chemical industries.

[17]   The Triumphal Arch was dismantled in 1936 as a hindrance to traffic, and later reassembled in simplified form on Kutuzovskii Prospekt. For a photograph of the original arch, see *Moskva-XX vek*, comp. and ed. Lev Konstantinovich Korniushin (Moscow: "Planeta" and TOO "Kuznetskii most," 1993), 134.

1812 victory over Napoleon, and Volodia has been victorious in his strategy to overcome Liuda's defenses.

Unlike Eisenstein, whose hero was the masses, Room emphasized human psychology and the individual actor in his films.[18] In an essay that is contemporaneous with *Bed and Sofa* he also stresses the superiority of artifacts to actors' facial mimicry in film: "I maintain that sensations come across much sooner when they are expressed with the aid of a thing, an object…. In ordinary life things are mute and insignificant….In film, on the screen a thing grows to gigantic dimensions and functions with the same force (if not greater) as does man himself."[19] Although the apartment filled with objects serves as an example of the petit bourgeois *byt* decried by the Party and the avant-garde, at the same time "things" are central to Room's cinematic method as correlates to people and relationships in the film.

After their day's outing, Volodia makes his move, telling Liuda how attractive she is and taking her by the arm. As he speaks, a *Sovetskii ekran* movie magazine cover hanging on the wall behind them is visible next to him, pointing up the elements of fantasy and unreality in the relationship.[20] A portrait of Tolstoy (the author of *Anna Karenina* and *The Kreutzer Sonata*) hangs on one of the other walls, underscoring the film's preoccupation with sex and morality. When Volodia tells Liuda's fortune that evening, he hints at the sexual relationship by placing the jack of diamonds, the traditional scoundrel, face down, covering the queen of hearts in a lengthy close-up shot. The next morning Liuda rises groggily and places Kolia, the king of hearts, next to the other cards. After Liuda and Volodia's first night together, he is shown sprawling comfortably on the bed (in his shoes) as its new owner. The rug on the wall behind

---

[18]   Hill notes that in later years Room also kept a multi-volume translation of Freud's writings in his home. (Hill, 18).

[19]   A. Room, "Moi kinoubezhdeniia," *Sovetskii ekran* 8 (1926): 5.

[20]   The same point is made just before via montage: Volodia and Liuda are in a movie theatre, the lights are dimmed. Next we see the wall switch in the Meshchanskaia apartment and the hanging lampshade, so that the seduction scene that follows is directly connected to the fantasy world of the movies.

him frames Volodia as predator on the married couple—seduced wife and clueless husband: a wolf growls at one bear cub, while the other cub faces away, looking into the forest and ignorant of events. Just as Volodia's stumbling in on Liuda changing her dress at the beginning of the film prefigures their affair, Kolia's seemingly irate return from Rostov with a noticeable bulge under his coat (a gift basket of berries) points to his anger and her subsequent pregnancy. Fittingly, the aftermath of the discovery of the affair is played out via the symbolism of domestic utensils. Kolia's growing anger at the betrayal is conveyed by his metaphorical manipulation of fork-as-knife. Liuda defuses the situation—literally shutting Kolia up—by offering him a spoonful of stew, really the bribe of domestic comfort which will ultimately reconcile both men to the unconventional living arrangement. In the evening Kolia and Volodia do not simply play checkers; they play for the right to take their turn with Liuda. When Kolia, outwitted by Volodia, returns with rolls for a late tea, a shot of the boiling kettle defines the steamy scene behind the screen.[21] When Volodia prevents Liuda from leaving the apartment, the camera focuses on the heart-shaped lock.

Perhaps the most visible symbol-artifact in the film is the couple's tabby cat. As a part of the menage, the cat denotes domesticity, comfort and affection, but also the indiscriminate sexuality of an animal in heat—in a word, Liuda. At the beginning of the film, the cat parallels the couple's actions: they are shown sleeping in the early hours of the morning, the tabby lies nearby on its side; they are shown washing and the cat too washes itself. An inveterate prankster, Kolia plops the clawy cat on the sleeping Liuda, thereby placing the two in initial proximity. At breakfast Kolia becomes annoyed by the skin on his boiled milk. Disgusted, he first attempts to feed it to Liuda, holding the dripping skin up to her mouth. She refuses, and then gives it to the cat. Later, when the house supervisor comes to ask Liuda about the anomaly of Volodia's presence on their sofa, he sees the tabby perched comfortably on the sofa, a projection

---

21   For a discussion of the uproar over the symbolism of the carafe with boiling water and the "glass of water" theory of sex, see Grashchenkova, 104.

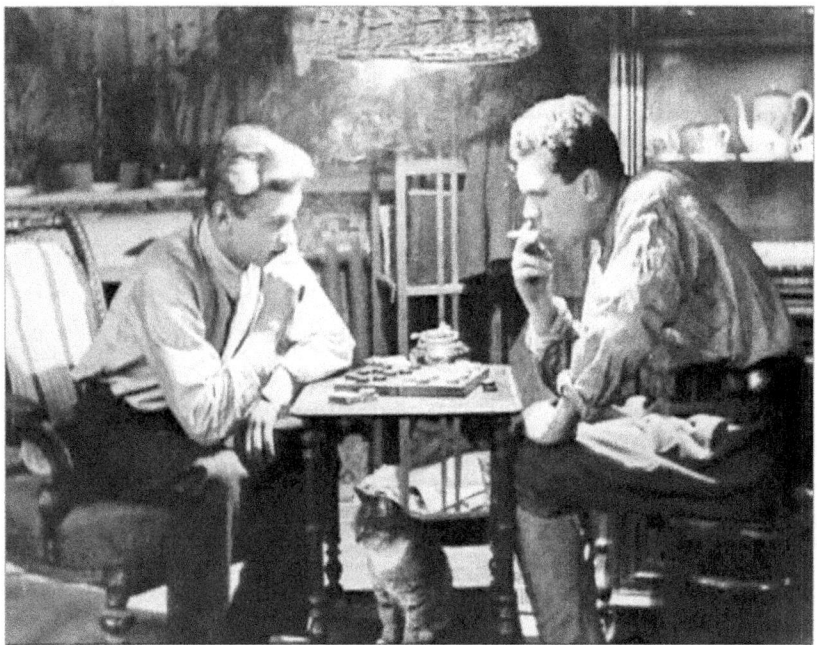

Fig. 62. Volodia, Kolia and Cat

of Liuda's wishful thinking. When Liuda first fails to respond to Volodia's advances, he throws himself on the sofa and, in frustration, pets the tabby (instead of Liuda) as it lies with exposed belly and spread-eagled hinders. After discovering the Liuda-Volodia liaison, Kolia tries sleeping in his office and lies on his desk, dreaming of happier times. In a series of shots superimposed on the interior of the apartment, we first see him at center screen, relaxing in a rocking chair at home. In the next superimposed shot, he appears to the left of his own rocking self, holding and stroking the kitty. As that image dissolves, he materializes on the right, embracing and stroking Liuda. Later, when the two men begin their evening games of checkers, the cat sits under their table, lowly and excluded (Fig. 62), like the marginalized Liuda who broods by the window. And at the end of *Bed and Sofa* the living tabby is transformed into a kitsch cat, a clay figurine (a gift from Kolia), representing Liuda's actuality as pet/bourgeois domestic object. The clay cat weeps a tear that has fallen on it as Liuda holds the figurine, and her own tear-filled eyes appear in a close-up shortly thereafter. She sadly places the figurine in her travelling bag; it is both an act of remembrance and the removal of a now conscious self from an untenable situation. At the end of the film, as the men relax in domestic conviviality, both Liuda and the flesh and blood tabby are absent from the scene.

II

The scenario for *Bed and Sofa* was written during the summer of 1926, at the height of the public debate over the draft of a new Family Code, which was ratified on November 19th and went into effect January 1, 1927.[22] Paul Burns has pointed out the importance of this topic, noting that "Ludmilla's plight would have qualified her for the protection of the new Family Code:" a postcard divorce, half of the property accumulated during the marriage, alimony for six months to a year, and a determination of legal paternity.[23] Given the timing of the scenario for *Bed and Sofa*, I would argue for a closer correspondence between the film and its socio-historical context. The fourth and last draft of the 1926 Family Code was the subject of intense public debate in the press, in urban areas and in the provinces, in schools, factories and at village meetings from October 1925 through November 1926.[24] *Bed and Sofa*, the scenario of which was written before the actual ratification of the Code, thus brings to the fore different points of view which were part of the debate around the new Family Code, and raises questions about the benefits of these various proposals for women. The film does

---

[22] The scenario was written in the Crimea near Mt. Kastello, where Shklovskii and Room were also writing the script for *Evrei na zemle (Jews on the Land)*. See Shklovskii, *Za sorok let,* 104, and Lili Brik's July 2, 1926 letter to Maiakovskii: "The most important news is that I'm working on 'Ozet' (The Society of Jewish Worker Farmers). If you can, go and see the colonies in the Crimea. In a few days Vitya Shklovsky is going there to make a film with Room and Yushkevich (from Goskino). So far I have very little to do and they don't pay me" (Letter no. 239 in *Love is the Heart of Everything: Correspondence Between Vladimir Mayakovsky and Lili Brik, 1915-1930*. Ed. Bengt Jangfeldt, trans. Julian Graffy [New York: Grove Press, 1986], 173).

[23] Burns, 77.

[24] Goldman, 216.

not simply reference the Code, which went into effect in 1927, but is concerned rather with a variety of proposals which were being argued before the new Code was approved.

Two aspects of the debate are most relevant to *Bed and Sofa*: *de facto* marriage and collective vs. single paternity. The 1918 Family Code stressed the need for civil marriage, completely ignoring *de facto* relations. Only married partners were entitled to the rights proceeding from a registered civil marriage. Each successive draft of the 1926 Code further undermined the significance of registered marriage, culminating in the final draft of 1925, which extended alimony and every significant right of marriage to partners in *de facto* relationships. The purpose was both to promote the option of free union and to protect women in *de facto* relationships, giving them a right to property acquired during the period of cohabitation and alimony if unemployed.[25]

After their first night together, and after they wonder "What about Kolia?," Volodia moves his pillow and blankets from the sofa to Liuda's bed and they shake hands, thereby ratifying a *de facto* union. When Kolia learns of the new situation, he is of course angry, but restrains himself. After Volodia states his intention to remain in the apartment, Kolia abandons the field of battle ("Then I'm going. You two live together") and bows to the *de facto* marriage. In the record of the October 19, 1925 debate on the draft Family Code, speakers had pointed out that "the towns have almost completely given up registered marriages" and that "it is impossible to deny that *de facto* marriages preponderate in our life."[26] Kolia seems to recognize that he is no longer in a position to exact the traditional husband's revenge.

Nevertheless, the phenomenon of *de facto* marriage, which was being institutionalized by the draft Family Code, did not simplify matters during a housing shortage. The effortlessness and informality of the *de facto* relationship ultimately make it easier for Liuda to

---

25   Goldman, 203, 204, 212.

26   *Changing Attitudes in Soviet Russia: The Family in the U.S.S.R*, ed. and intro. by Rudolf Schlesinger (London: Routledge and Kegan Paul Limited, 1949), 104.

sleep with both men, but the result is a paternity problem. The 1918 Family Code and the first three drafts of the 1926 Code recognized collective paternity in cases where a woman was unable to identify the father of the child because of multiple partners around the time of conception.[27] The last draft recognized only single paternity, but the collective vs. single paternity debate continued for some time.[28] *Bed and Sofa* points up the complications of collective paternity, when the parties involved have not yet attained a "high level of socialist consciousness": Kolia immediately says he doesn't want someone else's child (even his best friend's) and Volodia doubtless feels the same. Nor does it seem possible to determine which of the men is the father, even in court with a judge making the decision, as was specified by the last draft of the 1926 Code. The film thus raises doubts about the usefulness and viability for women of both collective and single, court-established paternity.

III

Judith Mayne has written about the ways in which the issues of motherhood and abortion were problematic during the early Soviet period, even to those committed to sexual equality, in the face of the need to build socialism, to increase the population after years of social upheaval.[29] Abortion was legalized in Russia in 1920, but the very language of the decree makes it clear that the practice was considered undesirable: "The Workers' and Peasants' Government

---

27   Goldman, 207.

28   Goldman, 246. See for ex., the Kartyshev statement in the record of the October 1925 VTsIK meeting: "As for the point that the court must recognize one father when there are several, and while scoundrels may be cited as witnesses—I feel that this is not just. Each one should be made to pay— this would be fair and in the child's interest. Otherwise it looks as though the court, under pressure from the Women's Department or for some other reason, might recognize as father not our drainage man who earns 40 rubles but the most well-to-do person, even though the latter may be innocent. For this reason we must make each one pay the full sum" (*Changing Attitudes in Soviet Russia: The Family in the U.S.S.R.*, 97).

29   Mayne, 122-29.

is conscious of this serious evil to the community. It combats this evil by propaganda against abortions among working women. By working for socialism, and by introducing the protection of maternity and infancy on an extensive scale, it feels assured of achieving the gradual disappearance of this evil."[30] However, once legalized, the number of abortions in Moscow had been rising steadily: 19 per 100 births in 1921, 31 in 1925, 55 in 1926; and the authorities grew more concerned.[31] In its anti-abortion stance, *Bed and Sofa* thus partially responds to a governmental agenda.[32]

The private hospital to which Liuda goes for the abortion is portrayed negatively as an assembly line operation in which each woman takes (and becomes) a number. The female clientele of the clinic comprise a gallery of NEP types: a nervous young girl with

---

[30] Schlesinger, 44.

[31] Goldman, 289. See Burns, 78 and Denise J. Youngblood, "The Fiction Film as a source for Soviet Social History: The Third Meshchanskaia Affair," *Film and History* 19.3 (Sept. 1989), 54, on *Bed and Sofa* as an anti-abortion film.

[32] The 1925-26 debate over the new Family Code was not orchestrated by the government, nor was it particularly affected by the struggle for power at the top among Stalin, Zinov'ev and Kamenev. Neither the majority wing of the Party nor the left opposition took a position on the new Code (Goldman, 218), and yet a wall calendar of an uncharacteristically relaxed Stalin, legs crossed and smoking a cigarette, figures twice in the film. Kolia tears a page from the calendar for the new day at the beginning of the film; upon returning from Rostov, he tears off nine sheets to bring the calendar up to date without realizing why time has stopped for Liuda and Volodia. Stalin was becoming increasingly prominent by late 1925: his November 7, 1925 article on the anniversary of the Revolution took precedence over Zinov'ev's in *Pravda*; at the Fourteenth Party Congress on December 18-31, he presented the Central Committee's report for the first time; he was elected a full member of the Politburo Jan. 1, 1926, and Stalin's theses condemning the opposition (Trotskii, Zinov'ev, Kamenev) were adopted in a resolution by the Fifteenth Party Conference, Oct. 26-Nov. 3, 1926. Although Stalin had not yet emerged as the decisive victor in the power struggle at the top, he was nevertheless clearly in ascendence during 1926 and qualified for wall-calendar status. At the same time, it is equally possible that the Stalin calendar may be a later addition to the film. (See Youngblood, 56, 59, n.9; and Hill, 17). In any case, Stalin was known to be conservative in his views on family life, so his earlier or later presence in the film is fully consonant with its official anti-abortion message.

her mother, two middle-aged and well-off Georgian or Armenian ladies, a worn-down looking woman of the merchant class, and a high-class Moscow prostitute arrayed like a flamenco dancer who coolly puts out a cigarette, adjusts her stockings and decolleté before going in for the operation. Liuda is the only working-class customer in a hospital that clearly caters to the former privileged classes. The quality of medical care in the establishment is also suspect: at one point there is a sudden commotion in the operating room, the nurse runs in to help, and the young girl faints in her mother's arms. To escape this stifling atmosphere, Liuda throws open a window, looks down and sees a little boy cradling a doll. As she looks again, she sees (or imagines she sees) a baby lying among fancy cutwork sheets. Later the nurse looks down before closing the window and, because Liuda has decided not to have the abortion, sees *two* babies, two more mouths to feed.

When Kolia and Volodia learn of Liuda's pregnancy and begin to insist on an abortion, she bursts out from behind the curtain separating her from the men's space and conversation (the film is full of such instances of ingenious manipulation of space which show Liuda's marginalization in the trio's social dynamic) shouting "Going halves on an abortion! What were you both thinking about?"[33] Unlike the debate on marriage and divorce, the Soviet discussion on abortion, beginning in the early 1920's, was never framed in terms of individual rights and needs because society's reproductive imperatives were always given unquestioning precedence.[34] In *Bed and Sofa* the issue of social obligation vs. reproductive rights is not faced squarely, but is resolved rather conveniently through Liuda's voluntary decision to have the baby. In conformity with government policy, abortion is painted negatively in the film, but *Bed and Sofa* nonetheless advocates the woman's right to make the decision either way. Ultimately, this issue is folded into the larger question of female self-sufficiency and self-determination in all life decisions, as Liuda

---

[33]   Another version of the intertitles: "So you've arranged everything! Who is making this decision?"

[34]   Goldman, 257.

leaves her two husbands and heads for the provinces to start a new life. In accord with Room's stated purpose—neither to instruct nor to solve, but rather to lay bare, pose and sharpen the theme—*Bed and Sofa* dramatizes and represents the full cultural complexity of these difficult questions without providing pat answers or simple solutions.

Further Reading

Graffy, Julian. *Bed and Sofa: The Film Companion*. London & New York: I.B. Tauris Publishers, 2001. [This is the most comprehensive work on the film.]

------. "Commentary." *Bed and Sofa,* Disc 1. DVD. Directed by Abram Room. Chatsworth, CA: Image Entertainment, 2004.

MAN WITH A MOVIE CAMERA

Chelovek s kinoapparatom

1929

66 minutes

Director (Author-supervisor of the experiment): **Dziga Vertov**

Assistant Director: **Elizaveta Svilova**

Chief Cameraman: **Mikhail Kaufman**

Production Company: **VUFKU (Kiev)**

Dziga Vertov was born David Abelevich (later changed to Denis Arkad'evich) Kaufman on 2 January 1896 in Białystok, Poland, then part of the Russian Empire. The pseudonym Dziga Vertov has dynamic, Futurist associations: Vertov comes from the Russian verb to spin, "vertet,'" and Dziga is usually said to resemble the Russian word for gypsy, "tsygan," but also may refer to the Ukrainian word for a spinning top, the whirring of film on an editing table or the click of a camera shutter. Dziga Vertov, the "spinning gypsy," joined the Moscow Cinema Committee in Spring 1918 and made his reputation with the *Kino-Pravda* Soviet newsreel series, so-called by analogy with the Bolshevik newspaper *Pravda*. This series revolutionized the power of the newsreel form to persuade and analyze, rather than simply inform or describe. While these are all short films, his *History of the Civil War* (*Istoriia grazhdanskoi voiny*, 1921) and *Kino-Eye* (*Kinoglaz*, 1924) are among the first attempts at a feature-length documentary and mark him as a pioneer of the form which was taking shape internationally in this decade. Crucially, this period saw Vertov team up with his brother, Mikhail Kaufman, who was the cameraman for all of his silent films, and his wife, Elizaveta Svilova, who edited all the films and played an increasingly important role as assistant and co-director after the split with Kaufman in 1929.

Jeremy Hicks

In the years 1921-1926 Vertov was the major figure in Soviet newsreel and documentary and a seminal influence on the montage film style made famous by Sergei Eisenstein, despite the fierce polemics between the two. His theoretical writings in this period range from the early poetic manifesto "We" to increasingly pragmatic attempts to define documentary according to a minimally staged "Kino-Eye" method of filming, intended to serve as a template for emulation. In 1926 Vertov was able to make two further technically groundbreaking films in Moscow: *Forward Soviet!* (*Shagai sovet!*), a celebration of Moscow's progress since the end of the Russian Civil War in 1921, and *One Sixth of the Earth* (*Shestaia chast´mira*), an apology for the emergent "Socialism in One Country" policy commissioned to promote Soviet exports. However, Vertov's radical conception of documentary, his ambitions for a grassroots movement of film journalists and aspiration that documentary dominate repertoires combined to marginalize him, and he was forced to leave Moscow and to join the semi-autonomous Ukrainian film organization VUFKU in 1926. Here he made three of his most enduring works: *Eleventh Year* (*Odinnatsatyi*, 1928), *Man with a Movie Camera* (1929) and one of the first Soviet sound films, *Enthusiasm: Symphony of the Donbas* (*Entuziazm. Simfoniia Donbasa*, 1931). While *Man with a Movie Camera* is rightly considered his masterpiece, each of these films was formally innovative, although they did not enjoy critical or commercial success.

After *Enthusiasm's* hostile domestic reception, especially because of its innovative approach to sound, Vertov left Ukraine and, overcoming numerous administrative and technical obstacles, made his next film, *Three Songs of Lenin* (*Tri pesni o Lenine*, 1934), on location in the Far East for Moscow's Mezhrabpomfilm. This marked a new stage in his evolution, as he adapted to the more rigid political climate and narrower limitations on the use of sound. Central to this new approach was the emphasis upon the recording of folk music performances as a way of retaining sound with an aura of authenticity and avoiding the stultifying effects of the voice-over. *Three Songs of Lenin* was officially praised, but with noticeable reluctance, due to the marginal role Stalin and Russia (rather than the Far East) occupy in it, and so as not to encourage Vertov unduly. Similarly, when Vertov completed *Lullaby* (*Kolybel'naia*) in 1938, which resembles *Three Songs of Lenin,* but emphasizes Stalin more, it was barely mentioned, in part because Vertov's potential influence on documentary filmmakers was still feared, and he had to be tightly controlled. In the last pre-war years, most of Vertov's projects were rejected, and those that were accepted and completed were undistinguished.

During the war (1941), Vertov was evacuated to Kazakhstan, where he was able to make several more films, the most significant of which by far was *For You at the Front* (*Tebe, front,* 1942). This continued the folkloric approach of *Three Songs of Lenin* and *Lullaby* and is effectively the last work in which one can discern Vertov's distinct artistic sensibility. Once again the film was effectively suppressed and in the anti-Semitic climate that began to intensify in the USSR from 1943 until Stalin's death in 1953, Vertov, ethnically Jewish, was further marginalized, denounced and relegated to editing standardized newsreels. In his last years he rarely worked as his health declined, and he was nursed by his wife, Svilova.

Since his death, in 1958, Vertov's influence has grown steadily after republication of his writings in the 1960s enabled first the Soviet and then international public to acquaint themselves with his rich theoretical legacy, and subsequently with his films. The last decade has seen more works published about Vertov than any other period, as his appeal and influence continue to grow in the twenty-first century.

Synopsis

Man with a Movie Camera begins with a sequence of a tiny cameraman setting up his tripod on a camera twice his size, pointing it at a cityscape before getting off and, in the next shot, going behind the curtains masking the screen in an empty cinema. The auditorium fills up and the projection, accompanied by an orchestra, begins. After a number 1 in an intertitle, we see a woman and the wider urban world asleep, before a cameraman leaves for work in a car and films an onrushing train, appearing to be nearly hit by it, and the woman awakes. Lenses are changed on the camera and it begins to film "the city" waking up, opening up, being cleaned and starting work in numerous ways, all this being filmed by a cameraman we see taking up various poses. We see a camera filming people in a horse-drawn taxi but the frame freezes, and we see more still images, ending with a movie frame with sprocket holes down the side, and follow the work of the film editor making still images come to life. The film then returns to the women in the horse-drawn carriage, who arrive at their destination, and the cameraman walks off.

Man with a Movie Camera then explores various kinds of intersections and changes of direction: stages in human life (birth/death, divorce/marriage), a traffic accident, then cleaning, washing, hairdressing, beauty treatments and sewing, which are likened to editing. The pace of work now becomes frenetic and we see speeded up sequences of factory assembly lines and telephone exchanges, followed by the coalmines and hydroelectric power plants that drive this activity. The factories and machines then grind to a halt, and the workers wash and brush before undertaking a myriad of leisure activities: a liner is launched, people bathe on a beach, play or watch sports, dance, and enjoy fairground rides, and children are entertained by a magician. Other people unwind by drinking beer in a popular bar, which is contrasted with more educational "Leninist" workers' clubs and a shooting range. This sequence ends with a musical performance mostly using everyday objects, rendered through superimpositions, before switching back to the cinema where the film began. The audience watches the camera dance, before seeing various images including more musical performances. We see them being shown fragments summarizing the themes from the film, but with more double-exposures intensifying the earlier motifs of traffic, urban crowds, and the camera filming the well-off people in a horse-drawn taxi, intercut with a clock pendulum ticking ever more furiously and the Bolshoi Theatre collapsing upon itself. The finale merges workers with their work and ends with an eye superimposed on the camera lens.

Structure

Watching *Man with a Movie Camera* for the first time can be a bewildering experience, so a helpful way of beginning to understand it is to think about how it is structured. The initial intertitles give us some pointers here, such as: "excerpt from a camera operator's diary." After the prologue in which we see the start of the film's projection in a cinema, *Man with a Movie Camera* does indeed follow the course of a day, beginning in the early morning, following the awakening and morning routine of a woman and other people, as well as the start of the working day in various shops, factories, transport depots and so forth. The day progresses through the intensification of work, followed by a winding down and various leisure activities in clubs, bars, sports games, and finally in the cinema.

Yet this diary is at the same time not conceivably that of a single day, because, if we watch carefully, we notice the scenes are from places that lie so far apart geographically that they cannot have been photographed by a single person in a single day: iconic images of Moscow, such as the Bolshoi Theatre or the façade of the National Hotel coexist with images of the Volkhov hydroelectric power station near Leningrad and street scenes in Ukraine, along with the beach at Odessa. While the film has been mistakenly described as a "city symphony," analogous to Walter Ruttman's *Berlin: Symphony of a Great City* (1927), in fact the cityscape we see is a composite, and likewise the day is many days rolled into one.[1] Indeed, not only does the film end in a cinema, its first sequence is also a film screening. The effect is to celebrate the power of the camera and of cinema, not so much to record as to analyze, make sense of and construct something new. This is a film about filmmaking and about film, an experiment in film language which springs from the context of the Russian avant-garde.

---

[1]   Jeremy Hicks, *Dziga Vertov: Defining Documentary Film*,124, in Further Reading.

The Avant-Garde

Although he has been described as a Productivist,[2] Cubo-Futurist[3] and Formalist,[4] Vlada Petrić has argued in his book-length study that Dziga Vertov is most helpfully considered part of the Russian Constructivist movement with which he was loosely associated, and which encompassed all of the above named strands of the Soviet avant-garde.[5] Vertov's Constructivist affiliation is evident in his collaboration with the painter, photographer and designer Aleksandr Rodchenko on some of his films and in the publication of some of Vertov's writings in the key Constructivist journal, *Lef*.[6] Certainly both Vertov's theories and practice are very close to that of Constructivism, formulated by Aleksei Gan in 1922 as a commitment to "propaganda by means of facts," in opposition to art as a mystification masking harmful, individualistic, passive and contemplative tendencies.[7] Vertov's development of propagandist newsreel and documentary cinema, in opposition to fictional forms, can be seen as realizing this commitment to factual or documentary forms, and *Man with a Movie Camera* embodies this program through its parody of fictional techniques in the sequence in which the cameraman seems almost to fall beneath a train as a woman dreams. The film then shows how this effect was achieved as the woman awakes, and the camera switches lenses and swings

---

[2]   Graham Roberts, *The Man with the Movie Camera*, 93, in Further Reading.

[3]   Kazimir Malevich, "Painterly Laws in the Problems of Cinema," trans. Cathy Young, in Margarita Tupitsyn, *Malevich and Film* (London and New Haven, 2002),155-56.

[4]   Seth Feldman, "'Peace Between Man and Machine': Dziga Vertov's *The Man with a Movie Camera*," in Barry Keith Grant and Jeanette Sloniowski, eds., *Documenting the Documentary: Close Readings of Documentary Film and Video* (Detroit, MI: Wayne State University Press, 1998), 49.

[5]   Vlada Petrić, *Constructivism in Film—A Cinematic Analysis*, 1-69, in Further Reading.

[6]   E.g., *Lef* 4 (1924).

[7]   Aleksei Gan, *Constructivism* (Tver': Tverskoe izdatel'stvo, 1922 [repr.: Milan: Edizione dello scorpione, 1977]), 25, 53.

to film the outside world. The suggestion is of an analogy between the woman's awakening and the freeing of the cinematic medium from its stultifying slumbers under the spell of fiction and art. This link between the woman waking and film is elaborated through the intercutting of her washing, then opening her eyes, and the washing of windows and opening of shutters, which visually match the camera's lens and her eyes. We also see a shot of a camera lens focusing and flowers coming into focus, stressing the theme of vision, and the woman's awakening as a metaphor for it.[8]

The analogy between the woman and film is further reinforced by the use of a film poster from a saucy 1927 German melodrama entitled *The Awakening of a Woman* (*Das Erwachen des Weibes*), translated as "probuzhdenie," which has a suggestion of "arousal" in Russian, serving as an image of the kind of cinema Vertov is opposing. In fact, the scenes with a woman waking up are the only ones in a domestic setting, the sphere from which Vertov intended to liberate film, and society.[9] In place of these images, which seem to invite the spectator to ogle the woman, Vertov challenges us to look out upon the world and to see from a kaleidoscopic variety of perspectives, especially very low or very high angles and diagonal compositions, which insist upon the mobility of points of view available specifically to the camera: the movie camera is a prosthesis enhancing human sight, analogous to the telescope or microscope, enabling an insight beyond the surface immediately visible to the unenhanced eye and revealing the world in all its dynamism and transformative energy, a perspective unavailable to previous visual arts, such as painting.

Such a view of cinema informs much of the film's thematic sweep, such as the repeated images of machines in motion, dynamically framed, the shots of city street traffic, the Russian words for which, "dvizhenie goroda," also mean "town movement," and appear as a category in the editing sequence (Fig. 63, uppermost label).

---

8   This has been analyzed in detail by Yuri Tsivian, *"Man with a Movie Camera*: Reel One," 51-76, in Further Reading.

9   Vertov, RGALI 2091/2/155. Quoted in Hicks, 35.

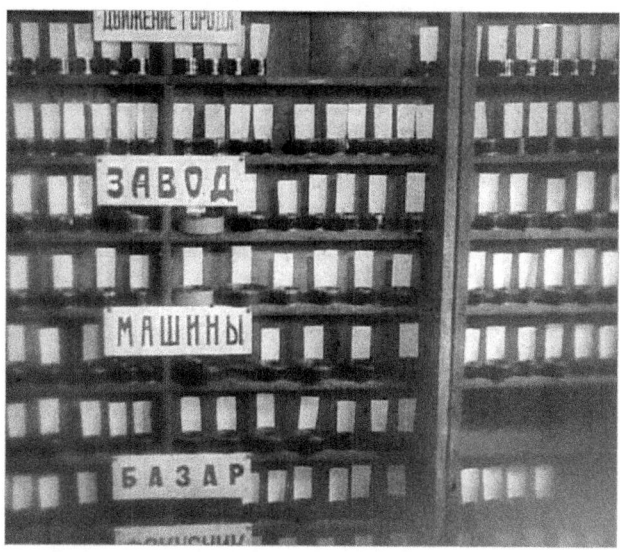

Fig. 63.
Filmed Subjects

Cinema's capacity to convey the dynamic is particularly evident in the images of the hydroelectric power station, where the shots of water surging over the dam evoke Vertov's Walt Whitman-inspired awe at the magical transformative force of electricity. Vertov's celebration of the camera's power also informs the dizzying display of filmic techniques in *Man with a Movie Camera*, its consistent exploration of the full gamut of stylistic possibilities available to cinema, including all kinds of tracking and hand-held camera shots, reverse motion, slow motion and speeded up action, stop-motion animation sequences, superimposed images or double-exposures, split frames in which the separate halves of the frame move in different directions, attempts to render sound through visual means, the interplay of still photography with the moving image, and experimentation with the pace of editing. Vertov's commitment to the significance of editing is evident not only in his practice but also in his writings, where the concept of the interval, as the editing together of movements, crops up repeatedly, beginning with his earliest published writings, "We: Variant of a Manifesto," believed to have been composed in 1918.[10]

---

[10]   Dziga Vertov, *Kino-Eye*, 8, in Further Reading.

Soviet avant-garde filmmakers of the 1920s as a whole stressed montage as the distinguishing feature of cinema: whereas movies borrowed many elements and insights from other arts, film's capacity to construct new meaning from the splicing together of disparate shots was famously declared by Lev Kuleshov in 1922 to be distinct and specific to the cinematic medium.[11] This emphasis upon montage in film echoed the general avant-garde preference for the fragment rather than the organic whole, and the Constructivist emphasis upon meaning as something made and re-ordered through conscious process rather than through mystical inspiration or the slavish recording of the world.[12] Such a vision of film is central to understanding *Man with a Movie Camera*, since, as its title and introductory intertitles suggest, this is a film about filmmaking.

Film about Film

The late 1920s witnessed the avant-garde's decline in all forms and with it the Soviet state's waning tolerance for avant-garde experiment in cinema, summed up by the influential slogan which emerged in 1928: "cinema for the millions."[13] Nevertheless, even in this climate Vertov was able to secure backing for *Man with a Movie Camera* as a production film about cinema, arguing that there were films about various industries and the making of all kinds of other goods, and there had not yet been one about cinema.[14] Seen in this light, the movie, framed by scenes of film exhibition in a cinema, demonstrates the filmmakers' interactions with the world and their capturing the dynamism of urban life from birth to death

[11] Lev Kuleshov, "Americanitis," in *The Film Factory: Russian and Soviet Cinema in Documents, 1896-1939,* ed. Ian Christie and Richard Taylor (Abingdon and New York: Routledge, 1994), 72-73.

[12] Peter Bürger, *Theory of the Avant-Garde* (Minneapolis: University of Minnesota Press, 1984), 104.

[13] *The Film Factory*, 212.

[14] Hicks, 62, 66.

on film, but also the process whereby this material is shaped and manipulated. While Vertov's cameraman throughout the 1920s, Mikhail Kaufman, plays the eponymous role of the cameraman, he is also filmed by an anonymous member of Vertov's Kino-Eye collective, whom he called the *kinoks* (a Futurist-style neologism also meaning "film-eyes").[15] Yet no less important a role in the film and in the *kinoks* is played by Vertov's wife, Elizaveta Svilova, whom we see editing the film, and it is her pale iris that comes to dominate the final images of the film. Here we confront issues with the translation of the title: the Russian word "chelovek,"which is translated by "man" would more accurately be translated as "person," and the word "kinoapparat," translated as "movie camera," more literally means "film apparatus," and might be seen as referring to the wider technology of the filmmaking process, and especially to editing. Certainly, one of the most influential readings of the film is that of Annette Michelson, who concentrates specifically on the scenes in which Svilova is shown to put pieces of film through the viewer on the editing suite: the still images of a woman wearing a headscarf, a crowd, and children watching a magician are seen on the editing table in Svilova's hands, and then come to life on the screen in front of us as a "systematic subversion of the certitudes of illusion."[16]

The scenes depicting the editing process are also central to a number of other debates about the film. One of these is the question of the representation of women. The episode showing a woman waking up and getting dressed has led to accusations that the film objectifies women or that it is voyeuristic.[17] However, if that depiction is seen as parodying the salacious fare of mainstream narrative film, and if we also consider the pivotal nature of the editing sequence, then the film appears to make women central to its vision of both cinema and society. Certainly, women's labor features

---

15   Roberts claims this was Petr Zotov: Roberts, 72.

16   Annette Michelson, "From Magician to Epistemologist: Vertov's *Man with a Movie Camera*," 111, in Further Reading.

17   Roberts, 50.

very centrally in the film, and repeatedly analogies are suggested between such work and the making of a film. In particular, *Man with a Movie Camera* edits together images of work carried out by and primarily for women, such as hairdressing, manicuring, beauty treatments and sewing, with the work of cutting and splicing bits of film, performed here by Svilova, and most often also done by women at this time in the USSR.

The resulting prominence that Svilova acquired both in the final film and in the trio who made the film, seems to have been one reason why cameraman Mikhail Kaufman broke with Vertov and Svilova, and never worked with them again. Kaufman also disagreed with the reflexive, experimental thrust of the film, and so made his own film using much of the same material, also celebrating dynamism and change, but stressing its biological analogues in love and in nature, hence its title: *In Spring* (*Vesnoi*, 1929). While Vertov and Svilova's approach alienated Kaufman, their exploration of a filmmaking practice in which man and woman play equal roles has been celebrated as a precursor to the emerging cyborg world in which distinctions between humanity and the machine, are, like gender differences, being elided.[18]

Similarly, *Man with a Movie Camera*'s distinct manner of reflecting on its own form and organizing its material, especially through editing, are central to the film's strong recent appeal as a rethinking of humanity's relation with machines and as a forerunner of digital forms. Lev Manovich in particular draws attention to Vertov's rethinking of vision, arguing that what we see in the film is from the perspective of "a computer, a cyborg, an automatic missile. It is a realistic representation of human vision in the future when it will be augmented by computer graphics and cleansed from noise. It is the vision of a digital grid."[19] Manovich considers Vertov the major "database filmmaker" of the twentieth century and *Man with*

---

[18]   http://project.cyberpunk.ru/idb/cyborg_futurist_past.html (accessed 8 March 2013).

[19]   Lev Manovich, *The Language of the New Media* (Cambridge, MA and London: MIT Press, 2002), xiv.

a Movie Camera as "perhaps the most important example of database imagination in modern media art."[20] In particular, the film's manner of organizing space and time is seen as breaking free from the habitual way in which films are organized and anticipating the new manner in which data texts are structured, the way in which computer users interact with data, the language of the interface, the "metamedium of the digital computer," in which different layers of reality are not seamlessly combined as in habitual editing, but made to retain their distinct identity.[21]

Social and Political Contexts

For all its relevance to the digital age and the idea of the cyborg, Vertov's film is also very much part of its time and can also be seen in the context of its analysis of Soviet society, and its exploration of the place of the artist in Soviet society during the ambiguous 1920s, when the tolerance for trade and private enterprise in the New Economic Policy period from 1921 was giving way to Stalin's brutal First Five-Year Plan in 1928. While Vertov thrived in the intellectually freer atmosphere of the 1920s, his utopian pathos is seen as more akin to the political tone of the Five-Year Plan. Be that as it may, *Man with a Movie Camera* gives us a snapshot of life in the Soviet Union as in flux, but also as still riven by social divisions and problems, alongside signs of the emerging new Soviet way of living, as Vertov saw it. The film dwells on and returns to a pair of well dressed, presumably well-off, women, accompanied by a man in a straw boater in a horse-drawn carriage. The fact they are in a horse-drawn carriage suggests their association with the old, bourgeois world, a link strengthened in the finale, when the same women are intercut with images of the Bolshoi Theatre, symbol of the old art loathed by the avant-garde. Moreover, their bags are carried by a barefooted servant and the next image, in which the cameraman

---

20   Ibid., xv.

21   Ibid., 33.

similarly carries his tripod over his shoulder, suggests sympathy with the downtrodden rather than the well-heeled.[22]

Vertov also explores contrasts between different kinds of labor, such as the daubing, by hand, of mortar onto buildings contrasted with a woman enjoying having make-up applied to her eyebrows: the implication seems to be that while the former form of labor is productive and active, the woman being made up is a passive consumer. The film also shows contrasts with images of a popular bar in which people drink a lot of beer, where point-of-view camera suggests drunkenness. This is juxtaposed with a worthy, well-appointed, Communist club in which a handful of people play chess, read papers and listen to the radio, enjoying the ennobling intoxication of music. The destitution of the 1920s USSR is further evident in the film's images of homeless street kids, a probable war veteran and a young woman, all of whom have been spending the night on park benches, and are awakened by the approach of the camera. The film's candor in representing the distance of the 1920s USSR from the ideals it set itself is something Vertov hoped to capture and, in part, this is a product of his distinctive approach to documentary filmmaking.

Man with a Movie Camera as Documentary

As a pioneer of the emerging documentary form, Vertov worked out his own approach to nonfiction film and dubbed this method "kino-eye," stressing documentary as central to film and as a form distinct from other arts. Central here was the notion of "life caught off-guard" (*zhizn' vrasplokh*), usually misleadingly translated as "life caught unaware." While this involved using hidden cameras or long-focus lenses enabling the camera operator to film subjects unaware they were being filmed, it also encompassed a number of techniques by which those filmed *were* aware of the camera, and these approaches have been adopted and extended by subsequent documentary filmmakers. Thus, "caught-off-guard" filming also

---

[22]   See Petrić, 107-09.

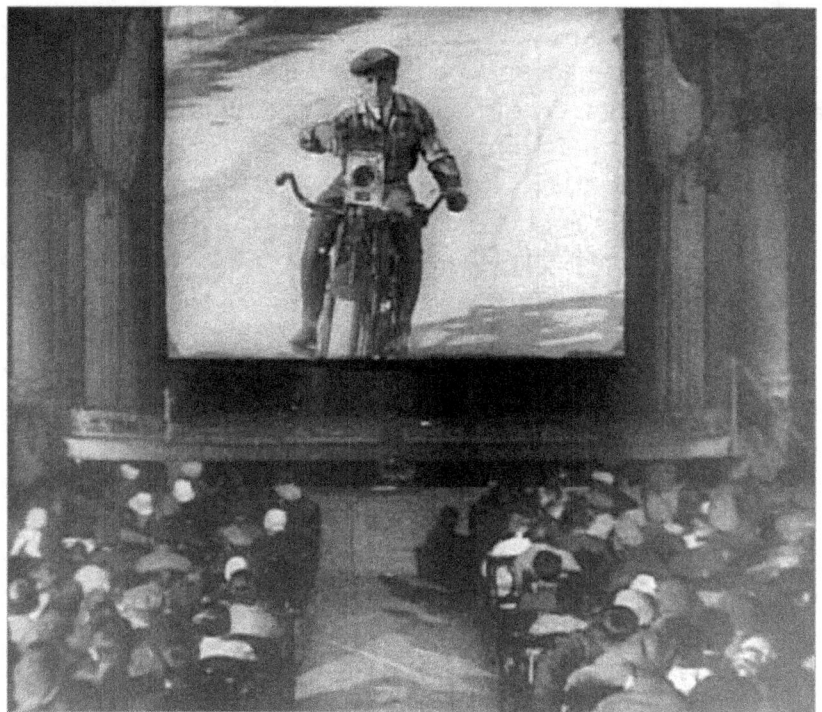

Fig. 64. Mikhail Kaufman Filmed by a Kinok

involved recording people while they were distracted by work, conversation, or familiarity, a technique that became central to 1960s observational or direct cinema, and is used at length in *Man with a Movie Camera*. The film employs another dimension of this technique by surprising people at unguarded moments and filming their reactions to being filmed, a technique that anticipated the alternative 1960s tendency of interactive *cinéma vérité*, which translated Vertov's term *"kino-pravda"* to signal a debt to Vertov.[23] The reactions of the many people caught off guard by Vertov and company, such as the street kid who laughs at being woken up, the woman who hurries off, or the divorcing couple, where the husband enjoys the attention and the mortified wife covers her face, are a fascinating aspect of the film and would be unobtainable by

---

[23]   Hicks, 133.

a purely hidden camera approach. They are also part of Vertov's strategy of drawing attention to the process of filming. Along with the many shots showing the camera operator filming what we have just seen or the editor editing it, these frequent reflexive reversals of perspective encourage the spectator to consider not just what is being shown, but also how. They demystify film and strip away the illusion of its unmediated reflection of reality, a radical gesture masked by the translation as "caught unawares."

By showing the cameraman filming, Vertov inevitably raises the question of performance in the film, since the cameraman being filmed, Kaufman, is not the one whose footage we are seeing at that moment: we see the footage of a second, uncredited, *kinok* (Fig. 64). Yet, while there is evidently an element of acting in filming someone conscious of the camera, Kaufman is at the same time just like the people shown while at work: he is himself working as a cameraman. Whereas the film repeatedly suggests analogies between women and the editor, it also does so between the male camera operator and other workers, such as the coal miners, whose hewing picks echo the cameraman's cranking of the camera, a comparison further suggested by the symmetrical composition of the shot where the two subjects are juxtaposed. The camera operator is shown everywhere, not just commenting on, observing, reflecting, but entirely forming part of life, which again echoes our own digital age in which the camera is ubiquitous. We even see the cameraman being warned to stand back in a steel works, after getting dangerously near the foundry. In this way, the film further elaborates on the analogy between filmmakers and workers in other industries, and thereby peels away further layers of mystique from the process of moviemaking: the filmmakers are workers like any others.

This process of interaction with life was very important to the kino-eye method of documentary and is part of the whole notion of "a film without a scenario" stated in the intertitles. In debates about the direction of documentary filmmaking, Vertov repeatedly insisted that "kino-eye" meant the rejection of the detailed written treatment as a starting point, since that promoted the primacy of the word over vision. Instead, Vertov advocated starting with a concept or theme and then conducting observations or reconnaissance, and only then revisiting the observed locations and shooting.[24] While some critics have associated Vertov's stance on the documentary with the misleading term "life as it is," Vertov's approach is more productively seen as a commitment to film as an analytical process.[25] This method meant that, rather than arranging shots and sequences that illustrated a preexisting narrative, Vertov's *kinoks* accumulated material according to categories, such as those seen in the editing suite sequence: "city traffic," "machines," "the factory," "the market," "the magician." While in earlier films such as *One Sixth of the Earth*, this tended to result in the structuring of material according to the list or inventory principle, which Vertov adopted from Whitman, here, by contrast, the various categories interact more freely, because the film cuts between them far more and they are not subordinated to a disambiguating verbal intertitle. One effect is to suggest and celebrate film's power to encompass all human life, very literally in the scenes of a baby's birth and of a young man's death in a traffic accident, as well as those of marriage and divorce. Above all, though, this approach suggests filmmaking as an attempt to grasp and make sense of the world, as an open-ended process, rather than the delivery of a predetermined message. This is reflected in spectators' experiences of watching the film: while they struggle to fix a meaning to the torrent of images, the effort required nevertheless means that the resulting interpretation is shared between filmmaker and spectators. This open-endedness, as we shall see, is key to the film's enduring appeal.

However, not all of the footage in the film was shot specifically for *Man with a Movie Camera*: Vertov had been planning the project of a film about film even before he left Moscow to take up a post in Ukraine's VUFKU studios in 1927, and appears to have used some of his earlier archive, including shots of Moscow's Bolshoi Theatre and the National Hotel. The film also borrows and builds from Vertov's ground-breaking 1924 film, *Kino-Eye*, in a number of ways, including

---

24   *Lines of Resistance*, 255, 337, in Further Reading.

25   Petrić, 4 and passim.

using footage of a Chinese magician entertaining children, but more profoundly in its attempt to set out programmatically a vision for cinema, and also a way of applying that vision through a method which a spectator might follow and enact. One key difference is that while Kino-Eye saw this process as an interaction with a growing movement of *kinoks* in the present, *Man with a Movie Camera* appears more consciously addressed to individuals and to posterity.

Reception and Afterlife

Despite the film's lukewarm initial reception in the USSR, where although its formal merits were sometimes acknowledged, its relative paucity of unambiguous Communist propaganda and its lack of clear characters, or a plot, meant it was not widely appreciated. As Soviet documentary moved ever further away from the experimental tendency in the 1930s and 1940s, Vertov's film became almost synonymous with the wrong way of making films.[26] Nevertheless, *Man with a Movie Camera* immediately made a profound impression when it was shown abroad, in Germany and the USA especially, but nevertheless occupied a unique and ambiguous position within documentary film history, because, as a film that stood so far above contemporaries, it did not fit into the categories and periodizations used to describe them. Bill Nichols, for example, has described documentary film in terms of modes, and the "expository" mode dominated from the 1920s: *Man with a Movie Camera*, however, belongs more to the "reflexive" mode that evolved in the 1960s.[27]

While it presented a challenge to scholarship, the film's untimely and unusual character has invited spectators to answer and extend its demystifying and democratizing creative magic. This accounts for *Man with a Movie Camera*'s appeal for filmmakers since the 1960s, and also to theorists of various kinds. This same openness has also

---

26   *Lines of Resistance*, 322; Hicks, 122.

27   Bill Nichols, *Representing Reality: Issues and Concepts in Documentary* (Bloomington and Indianapolis: Indiana University Press, 1991), 32-56.

made the film attractive to musicians as an alluring starting point for the creation of original and distinct soundtracks. These range from the Alloy Orchestra's version, which follows Vertov's own notes on the music and sounds he wanted to accompany performances of the film, to a much freer, substantially independent response to the film by composer Michael Nyman.[28] Perhaps the most compelling score of all is by British electric and jazz ensemble The Cinematic Orchestra, who place the exploration of the links between vision and sound at the center of their work.[29] Their accompaniment plays with silence, only starting when the film is projected in the prologue, before jazz, electronic sounds and percussion come to dominate intriguingly. The sense of free improvisation created seems to complement the film's own open-ended quality, and it was released as a stand-alone album in 2003.

As the digitization and democratization of filmic technology have transformed culture, *Man with a Movie Camera* has come to be seen as an analogue film with a kindred and contemporary sensibility in a way that has been theorized, as discussed above, by Manovich. Yet the sense that this is a film which teaches not only about film, but a universally accessible manual aimed at a global *kinok* movement, that demands the making of further films has been most vividly taken up by New York video artist Perry Bard's crowd-sourced *Man With a Movie Camera: The Global Remake*, centered around a website which invites people to upload footage remaking shots from Vertov's film in new settings. The effect is that "everyday a new version of the movie is built."[30] There can surely be no more eloquent tribute to the enduring spell of *Man With a Movie Camera*.

Jeremy Hicks

---

[28]   *Michael Nyman's Man with a Movie Camera*, BFI, 2008; *Man with a Movie Camera*, BFI, 2002 has the Alloy Orchestra accompaniment.

[29]   *Man with a Movie Camera*, The Cinematic Orchestra, Ninjatune, 2012.

[30]   http://dziga.perrybard.net (accessed 16 March 13).

Further Reading

Dziga Vertov's writings in English have long been available in *Kino-Eye*, a 1984 translation that uses the 1966 Russian edition, edited tendentiously by Sergei Drobashenko, suppressing, for example, mentions of Stalin and Trotsky, as well as any other politically sensitive issues. Recently, comprehensive editions of Vertov's works have appeared in Russian: *Iz naslediia* volume one is a collection of plans for films, rough working notes and ideas for musical accompaniment, and volume two is a collection of articles and other writings that is both more comprehensive than *Kino-Eye*, and unexpurgated. These have yet to be translated into English.

Vertov's Writings

Vertov, Dziga. *Iz naslediia*. Vol. 1: dramaturgicheskie opyty. Edited with a preface by Aleksandr Deriabin. Moscow: Eizenshtein-tsentr, 2004.

------. *Iz naslediia*. Vol. 2: Stat'i vystupleniia. Edited with a preface by Dar'ia Kruzhkova, notes by Dar'ia Kruzhkova and S. Ishevskaia. Moscow: Eizenshtein tsentr, 2008.

------. *Kino-Eye: The Writings of Dziga Vertov*. Edited by Annette Michelson, translated by Kevin O'Brien. Berkeley: University of California Press, 1984.

Secondary Criticism

Cook, Simon. "'Our Eyes, Spinning Like Propellers': Wheel of Life, Curve of Velocities, and Dziga Vertov's 'Theory of the Interval'." *October* 121 (Summer 2007): 79–91.

Hicks, Jeremy. *Dziga Vertov: Defining Documentary Film*. London and New York: I.B. Tauris, 2007.

McKay, John. *Dziga Vertov: Life and Work*. Bloomington and Indianapolis: Indiana University Press, forthcoming.

Michelson, Annette. "From Magician to Epistemologist: Vertov's *Man with a Movie Camera*." In *The Essential Cinema: Essays on Films in the Collection of Anthology Film Archives*, edited by P. Adams Sitney, 95-111. New York: New York University Press, 1975.

Petrić, Vlada. *Constructivism in Film — A Cinematic Analysis: The Man With the Movie Camera*. Cambridge: Cambridge University Press, 1993.

Roberts, Graham. *The Man with the Movie Camera*. London and New York: I.B. Tauris, 2000.

Tsivian, Yuri, ed. and introduction. *Lines of Resistance: Dziga Vertov and the Twenties*. Translated by Julian Graffy. Pordenone: Le Giornate del cinema muto, 2004.

Tsivian, Yuri. "*Man with a Movie Camera*: Reel One." *Film Studies* 2 (2000): 51-76.

EARTH

Zemlia

1930

89 minutes

Director: **Aleksandr Dovzhenko**

Screenplay: **Aleksandr Dovzhenko**

Cinematography: **Daniil Demutskii**

Art Design: **Vasilii Krichevskii**

Production Company: **VUFKU, Kiev**

Cast: **Stepan Shkurat (Opanas), Semen Svashenko (Vasyl'),
Iuliia Solntseva (Opanas' daughter), Elena Maksimova
(Natalka), Nikolai Nademskii (Grandfather Semen),
Petr Masokha (Khoma Belokon'), Ivan Franko (Khoma's father,
Arkhip), Vladimir Mikhailov (village priest)**

Earth was restored as a sound film in 1971 with music composed
by V. Ovchinnikov. A new score was composed by A. Popov in
1997. Dovzhenko's negative with the original Ukrainian titles
was lost during World War II; a circulation copy was used for the
restoration.

Aleksandr Petrovich Dovzhenko (1894-1956) was born into
a family of Ukrainian peasants with fourteen children, only two
of whom survived into adulthood. His childhood experiences
growing up in the Ukrainian countryside with its folk traditions,
agricultural way of life and natural rhythms of life and death were
the inspiration for his best films. After graduating from a teachers'
institute in 1914, Dovzhenko taught natural and social sciences
and physical education in Zhitomir and in Kiev. As a Ukrainian

nationalist sympathizer, he left Kiev with Petliura's troops in 1919 and fought against the Red Army. He spent the last four months of 1919 in a Cheka prison, but was saved from execution by political friends, now allied with the Communists.

In 1921-22 Dovzhenko served in Warsaw and Berlin as a diplomat representing the Soviet Ukrainian Republic and then studied art in Germany for a year. He learned to make films at the Odessa Studio where he directed three works, including *Love's Little Berry* (*Iagodka liubvi*, 1926) and the spy thriller *The Diplomatic Courier's Pouch* (*Sumka dipkur'era*, 1927). Dovzhenko came into his own as a filmmaker with his silent trilogy *Zvenigora* (1928), *Arsenal* (1929), and *Earth* (1930). The latter, now considered his masterpiece, was attacked at the time for its naturalism—depictions of urination, female nudity and childbirth—and the offending scenes were cut from the film. After the release of *Ivan* (1932), Dovzhenko's first sound film, which was in Ukrainian, party officials were confirmed in their suspicions of a hidden nationalist subtext in his work. He was eased out of his administrative position at the Kiev Film Studio and began to fear for his life during a wave of arrests. In order to survive, Dovzhenko moved to Moscow in 1933. He wrote a letter to Stalin, asking for his protection, and soon joined Mosfilm. With *Aerograd* (1935), a drama about saboteurs in the Far East, and *Shchors* (1939), the story of the "Ukrainian Chapaev," suggested by Stalin, and portraying Ukrainian resistance to the German intervention of 1918, the subsequent Polish invasion, and to Petliura's nationalist army during the Civil War, Dovzhenko rehabilitated himself politically. However, the remainder of his career became a series of soul-destroying compromises with an increasingly hostile regime. In 1944 Dovzhenko's screenplay *Ukraine in Flames*, describing the country's suffering during World War II, was banned by Stalin as narrow-mindedly nationalistic. Dovzhenko lost his official positions and was demoted to director third class. In the repressive post-World War II years directors turned to the "safe" historical genre of biopics of famous scientists and arts figures. After many revisions of the screenplay, Dovzhenko shot his last completed film, *Michiurin* (1948), an idealized biography of the famous horticulturist. His last project, the xenophobic *Goodbye, America* was closed down prema-

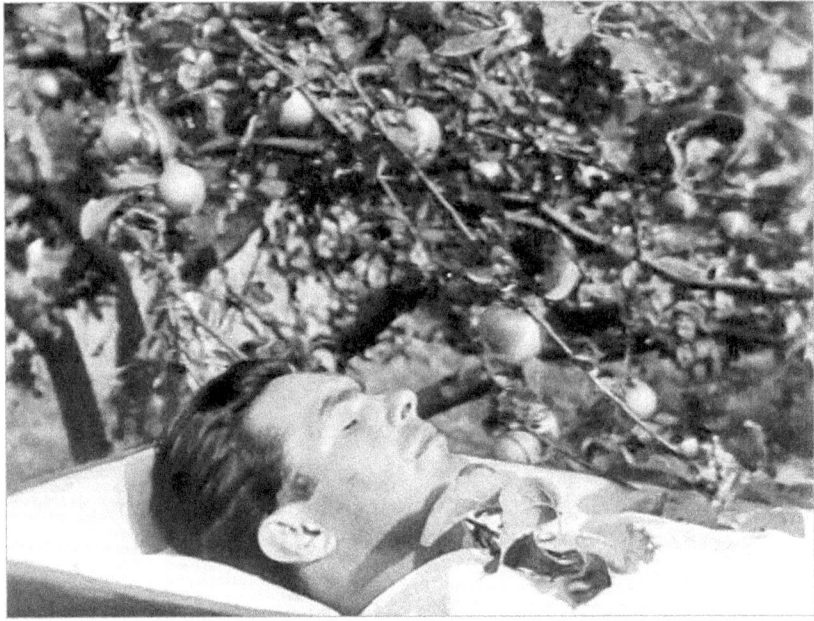

Fig. 65. The Funeral of Vasyl'

turely in 1951. Denied permission to return to his beloved Ukraine, Dovzhenko died and was buried in Moscow.

Although all Soviet directors working during the Stalin era were forced to make creative compromises with the regime, Dovzhenko bore the additional burdens of Ukrainian sympathies during an era of Great Russian cultural hegemony, as well as the stigma of a dubious political past. Throughout his life he struggled to reconcile his Ukrainian identity with his sincere belief in Communist internationalism. In explaining Dovzhenko's support of collectivization in *Earth*, critics have been at pains to point out that he conceived and filmed *Earth* during the early, voluntary stages of the process, before the outbreak of violence and brutality in the countryside. Dovzhenko initiated a lyrical line in Russian cinema, to be continued by his student, Andrei Tarkovsky,[1] and by Sergei Paradzhanov, whose films were strongly rooted in folk culture.

---

[1]   Tarkovsky admired Dovzhenko and the rain-drenched and scattered apples

Earth is a film-poem in which portrait, still-life and landscape shots are just as important as action sequences. The film opens with the death of Grandfather Semen in an apple orchard. He is surrounded by family and friends, including his son Opanas and grandson Vasyl', and Semen's old friend, Petr. Meanwhile, local kulaks (richer peasants) vow to resist the collectivization of farms in the area. Opanas is also dubious about the initiative, but Vasyl' and local activists support it, and bring the new collective its first tractor. The harvest is successful, thanks to the new tractor, but Vasyl' provokes kulak anger by plowing down their boundary fence. Returning home at night from an idyllic interlude with his betrothed, Natalka, and full of the joy of life, Vasyl' dances on the road where he is shot dead by the kulak Khoma. Inspired by his son's death, Opanas asks the collective to bury Vasyl' and leads the funeral procession that unites the village in support of collectivization. Apple branches brush Vasyl's face as his body is carried through the village (Fig. 65). During the funeral, Vasyl's mother gives birth to another child, and later Natalka finds a new love. Man thus continues the species in the same way apples form from blossoms which bear fruit that ripens and eventually dies, falling to the earth, decomposing and beginning the cycle of life and death anew.

Both the narrative and tempo of *Earth* define the film's two-part structure, which concludes with a circular coda. Part one begins slowly with the grandfather's stately death scene. The tempo of shots increases gradually as Vasyl' brings the new tractor, the villagers run to see it and Vasyl' plows energetically. The section culminates in the bread-making sequence which compresses time from harvest to baked loaves. Part two returns to a slow pace with the evening scenes of courting couples, older couples asleep in their beds, mist on the river and Vasyl's night walk, which develops into his ever more rapid dancing, broken by his sudden murder. The more rapid pace resumes in the intercutting of funeral scenes,

in Tarkovsky's early film, *Ivan's Childhood,* their roundness representing the harmony and regenerative powers of nature in Ivan's dream of the peaceful past, seem to have migrated from *Earth.*

Natalka's violent grief and breaking of an icon, Khoma's hysterical confession, the villagers' running to join the funeral procession, and the activist's speech, which culminates in the offscreen appearance of an airplane. The epilogue returns to a stately pace, returning to and recasting earlier archetypal scenes: the wind-blown fields, apples in the rain, and Natalka in the arms of her new lover.

EARTH

Vance Kepley, Jr.

As is his wont, Dovzhenko fashions a tale out of social conflict and then seeks a narrative strategy of resolution. *Earth* certainly draws from the record of social antagonism that marked collectivization: indeed, the central action of the narrative, Vasyl's murder, takes its historical source from the assassination by kulaks of a Soviet agent in Dovzhenko's home district.[1] In examining the tactic Dovzhenko employs to resolve the conflicts the film invokes, we will see that he creates a fictional "natural order" of life, death, and rebirth in the film's narrative and inserts collectivization into that cycle. Through juxtapositions that equate the processes of nature with human actions, the narrative of *Earth* seeks to "naturalize" collectivization, to represent it as predetermined and proper, deriving from an innate quality of nature rather than from the policies and practices of government [...].

To appreciate the problems addressed in this deceptively simple narrative, we must look briefly at the Soviet rural situation and the conflicts collectivization generated, conditions that Dovzhenko knew firsthand.[2] The roots of the issue lay in the nineteenth century and in the shortage of arable land to support the peasant population. With the emancipation of 1861 came the necessity to distribute land among landlords and ex-serfs, and this gave rise to the commune system, whereby groups of peasants shared blocks of land. This system proved somewhat inefficient, as it stifled individual peasant

---

1   Lazar Bodyk, *Dzherela velykogo kino* (Kiev: Radianskyi pys'mennyk, 1965), 66.

2   Except as otherwise noted, the following summary of the agricultural situation draws from Robinson, *Rural Russia*, chaps. 5-8; Moshe Lewin, *Russian Peasants and Soviet Power: A Study of Collectivization*, trans. Irene Nove (New York: Norton, 1975); and Alec Nove, *An Economic History of the U.S.S.R.* (Harmondsworth, England: Pelican Books, 1972), chap. 7.

initiative, and in 1906 the tsarist regime commenced a gradual set of reforms in which communal land was split into individual holdings. For the first time in much of the empire, peasants were permitted to own land, bequeath it to heirs, and experience a measure of economic independence. But the redistribution proved a slow, arduous process and often only increased the power of the kulaks. When the Bolsheviks came to power in 1917, they had to contend with an abiding desire among much of the peasantry to maintain family farms. Through the NEP period, the government tolerated private farming and the right of peasants to sell harvests at whatever price the market would bear. Formation of cooperative farms was encouraged under NEP but remained voluntary.

When Stalin initiated rapid industrialization of the Soviet economy in 1929, he called for consolidation of private holdings into large collective farms and an end to "rural capitalism." Serious grain shortages in the late 1920s, stemming in part from peasant work slowdowns and kulak manipulations of the market, prompted the timing of forced collectivization, but as important was Stalin's general recognition that if his industrialization plans were to succeed, the government would have to take control of the rural economy, reorganize and integrate agricultural production, and put an end to kulak authority in the villages. Predicting that kulaks would encourage resistance to such a plan, Stalin issued an ominous proclamation: "We must smash the kulaks, eliminate them as a class."[3] Collectivization would be accompanied by "dekulakization," and previous tactics encouraging voluntary enlistment in collectives would give way to force [...].

Such violence especially characterized the situation in Dovzhenko's native Ukraine, the setting for *Earth*. The Soviet government was particularly determined to enforce collectivization in this rich agricultural region, but the plan met much popular resistance in the Ukraine because Ukrainian peasants had long worked under a system of individual holdings, even during the era

---

[3]   Quoted in Isaac Deutscher, *Stalin: A Political Biography*, 2nd ed. (New York: Oxford University Press, 1966), 320.

of serfdom. With the emancipation, they retained their family plots and generally fared better than their Russian counterparts in the rural economy. Hence, Ukrainian peasants had a greater stake in the status quo and proved fiercely loyal to the tradition of private ownership, making Ukrainian collectivization especially difficult.[4] [...].

Dovzhenko in *Earth* appeals to the pastoral traditions which were part of his background and which he calculated were closest to his intended audience, the Soviet peasants who would be most affected by collectivization. *Earth* represents the most restrained and least oblique of Dovzhenko's major silent films. The narrative lacks the many disjunctive devices of *Zvenigora* and *Arsenal*, and its very simplicity has ideological significance. In the earlier films Dovzhenko dealt with the chaos of the Ukrainian revolution, and he sought to project that condition through narratives marked by sharp discontinuity and through his professed tactic of compressing the material of several films into one. The concern of *Earth*, however, is with cohesion and continuity as Dovzhenko creates an image of a world in repose and suggests that social revolution can still sustain order, an order that comes from the stability of nature. As indicated in the film's title, the natural terrain is the central concern, and in fact, the Ukrainian-Russian title, *Zemlia*, actually means soil, land, or ground. The soil—rich, stable, enduring—serves as the film's title character.

The film's rhetoric of naturalization suggests that the opponents of collectivization were somehow destined to pass out of existence as the seasons pass and that time and nature would heal social wounds. Dovzhenko represents social revolution as the equivalent of seasonal transition and endeavors thereby to provide a fictional reconciliation of the social conflicts that surfaced during the turmoil of collectivization. The specific strategies Dovzhenko employs to this end can be understood through a fuller discussion of the film's narrative.

---

4   W.E.D. Allen, *The Ukraine: A History* (Cambridge: Cambridge University Press, 1941), 324.

The sense of tranquility that dominates the narrative of *Earth* is made manifest at the very beginning of the film. Consider the opening scene and the resignation with which old Simon faces death. Dovzhenko has remarked of the scene that the old man seems simply to fall "from life like an apple from a tree."[5] The scene's mood suggests that the old man, having lived a full life, now faces death with complete equanimity. His death evokes a sense of unity between man and nature. After a series of dissolves among shots of apples on trees, Dovzhenko dissolves to the figure of Simon on the ground. The numerous graphic matches on the round shape of the apples culminate with a shot of the soft, round head and face of Simon, suggesting that he is as natural and innate a part of the terrain as the apples.

The connection between the grandfather and the fruit reappears in a series of associations that pertain to both life and death. Before Simon dies, he eats from a fresh apple. The crisp, clean fruit connotes health and vitality, especially since the infant children at Simon's side also munch on fresh apples. Simon's apple is offered to him in almost ceremonial fashion, as if he were partaking of communion. The granddaughter is then shown holding her bowl of apples at her stomach in a pose that is later matched by Opanas's pregnant wife holding her bulging stomach, thus linking apples with fertility. Surrounding Simon on the ground, however, are fallen, overripe apples. The fruit that lies on the ground, like the old man, is associated with death. These apples will never be eaten; they will decompose and enter back into the soil. But there they will replenish the ground and thus serve as a source of renewal. This opening scene is built around a series of associations of life, death, and regeneration, and these elements run throughout the film.

The notion that Simon, like the apples, returns to the earth to give rise to new life recurs later in the scene at Simon's grave. There the superstitious Peter attempts to communicate with the

---

5   Dovzhenko quoted in M.P. Vlasov, *Geroi A.P. Dovzhenko i traditsii fol'klora* (Moscow: VGIK, 1962), 29.

dead Simon to learn whether his friend can fulfill the promise to tell him of the experience of death. He kneels above the grave and asks, "Where are you, Simon?" He then puts his ear to the ground in the hope of hearing a response. Meanwhile, young children hiding behind a nearby grave tease the old man by making noises which he mistakes for Simon's answer from the grave. In addition, when Peter places his ear on the ground, Dovzhenko cuts to shots of Opanas plowing with oxen nearby, implying that Peter also hears that activity.

While this scene gently chides Peter's superstition on one level, on another level it subtly argues that there does indeed exist a form of life after death through biological renewal. The juxtaposition of the shots of the children, the plowing, and Peter at the grave provides a possible answer to the old man's question, "Where are you Simon?" In a way, the sounds Peter hears *are* Simon's response. If Simon is anywhere, he is one with the soil, the very soil Opanas tills. Moreover, he is, in a sense, reincarnated in his grandchildren who play nearby. The infinite possibility of replenishment is the ultimate lesson of Simon's death. The answer to Peter's question lies, the scene suggests, less in a religious or mystical definition of life after death than in a natural process of renewal.

The bond between man and his environment takes several forms in the film, including anthropomorphism. Frequently the natural environment seems to become animate and to interact with humans. When the family members stand together looking down at Simon in the opening scene, one shot shows an enormous sunflower bent in a position similar to that of the family members, seemingly gazing down at the old man. When Vasyl is carried off in the funeral procession, the branches and leaves of the trees gently brush against his face, as if they were reaching out to touch him one last time before he is taken to his grave. During moments of great excitement, horses react with the same fervor as the peasants. When village lookouts first spot the new tractor arriving in the distance, the horses turn their heads and glance down the road in eyeline matches which resemble those of humans, and when the villagers scurry to join the ranks of Vasyl's funeral, horses also lope toward the procession.

The most lyrical sequence suggesting the harmony between humans and nature occurs in the nocturnal passage that follows the harvest. The harvest had involved a dynamic ecstasy of labor, and the night scene shows the quiet satisfaction of rest. Various couples sit together under the summer moon in motionless rapture. The soft focus of the imagery and the summer mists of the landscape give the section a sense of peace. Some of the men have their hands on women's breasts, and the older couples lie in their marriage beds. This element of sex and fertility also relates to the lush, fertile landscapes of the evening and to the promise of health and life after the successful harvest.

Vasyl's hopak which concludes the scene, a dance traditionally associated with a successful harvest, seems the culmination of his satisfaction, stemming from his unity with the environment; even the dust he raises with his dance lingers in the air and graphically resembles the night mists shown earlier, further associating him with the natural setting.

Vasyl's death at the climax of this sequence seems tragic because it represents a disruption of this sense of order. Death per se is not defined as tragic in *Earth*; it remains part of the process of assuring rebirth, as we have seen in the scene of Simon's death. The grandfather's death is open and public; the entire family is present for his final moments, and they accept it with equanimity as something proper and natural. But Vasyl's death is abrupt, untimely, a crime in violation of what the narrative has represented as the proper sequence of events.

Yet even Vasyl's death has its purpose because, like the death of a god in spring fertility rites, Vasyl's martyrdom solidifies the peasants. In other Soviet films as well, martyrdom serves to confirm the resolve of the other members of the community. The deaths of the bull in *Old and New*, of the boy in *Bezhin Meadow*, and of the juvenile in Ekk's *Road to Life* inspire the followers. Vasyl's death leads to the "Song of New Life" sung by the young members of the collective in the final scenes. What is more, Vasyl's funeral is juxtaposed with several references to fertility: the young people of the procession carry bouquets and branches, and as the funeral is underway, Vasyl's mother goes through labor and gives birth. We sense from this that nature provides its own compensation for Vasyl's death.

This routine of life, death, and rebirth, Dovzhenko suggests, is as fundamental as the seasonal blooming and withering of foliage. The kulaks prove the villains of *Earth* precisely because they fail to recognize the inevitability of the order and attempt to disrupt it. The kulaks are associated with death—and not the death that promises renewal—but the death of sterility and obsolescence. The assassin Khoma's last name is Belokon, which translates roughly as "white horse," a traditional symbol of death. The kulaks, furthermore, engage in wanton destruction; Khoma's father would rather slaughter his horse than surrender it to the collective. Finally, when Khoma goes berserk with guilt near the end of the film, he dances an ugly parody of Vasyl's dance. Whereas Vasyl's hopak is a private, spontaneous celebration, Khoma's frenzied dance becomes a comic spectacle. Significantly, it is acted out in a graveyard, suggesting that Khoma and the kulaks are doomed to obsolescence. The idea carries over from the scene of the tractor's arrival. Dovzhenko cuts on a graphic match from three oxen to three kulaks, implying that if the tractor will remove the need for oxen the collective will do the same for the kulaks. The refusal of the collective to recognize the kulaks at the film's end assures the eventual demise of the class. Khoma is left to dance alone in the graveyard until he simply falls to the ground in exhaustion and frustration. Vasyl's death is compensated in the end when his mother gives birth to another child, but there are no signs of fertility among the kulak families.

One of the tragedies of the civil war represented in *Arsenal* is the turmoil that robs the land of its natural fecundity; and the misuse of technology proves a major factor in this. But in *Earth* people work in conjunction with technology to cultivate the land. The machines improve humans' ability to perform the traditional labor of tilling the earth. When machines break down in *Arsenal* they produce catastrophe; when the tractor stalls in *Earth* it provides only a brief dilemma and somewhat comic solution. The peasants repair it by urinating into the radiator, thereby blending the organic and mechanical realms. Machines, like humans, can work in harmony with nature in this film. At Vasyl's funeral, a Soviet speaker tells the villagers that Vasyl's fame will circle the globe. As a manifestation of this phenomenon, the orator does not seize on a mystical, ghostly image, but on a mechanical one; he compares Vasyl's spirit to a Soviet airplane that conveniently flies over the village at that instant. More important, the introduction of the tractor to the collective produces a work routine in which men, women, and machines operate in perfect unison. In the harvest sequence, Dovzhenko cuts between the work of the machines and the labors of the peasants, and the peasants develop an ecstatic rhythm as they work in synchronization with the machines.

The harvest sequence occupies a central position in the narrative and in Dovzhenko's effort to rationalize collectivization, and it is as important for what it omits as for what it includes. The sequence shows the stages of the growing and harvesting of the grain and the baking of bread. It begins with the initial plowing of the land. The sequence then proceeds to the cutting of the stalks with reapers. The stalks are promptly bundled and tied by hand. Machines shuck and separate the grain. The grain is then sorted, and we finally see the dough made from the flour kneaded, shaped into loaves, and baked. The sequence presumes to show the production of bread from the first planting of the seeds to the baking of the loaves.

One detail, however, remains conspicuously absent from the sequence. In the whole series of plowing, sowing, harvesting, and processing, the growing season is completely omitted. The entire operation seems to take place in one sunny afternoon in a single, labor-intensive effort. The crop is planted and harvested in a continuous process in the film, without an interval of growth or cultivation. In a sense, the role of nature is omitted in this sequence. The labor of men, women, and machines seems to take care of the entire operation. Nature's role is not so much denied as supplanted by labor and technology, the culmination of Dovzhenko's effort to link social organizations to natural processes.

One social organization of central importance to the film is the family, and in the final scenes, the entire definition of the family is broadened. At Simon's death, in the first scene, he is attended

by both his son and grandson; two generations are present to bid farewell to the patriarch. This sense of family cohesiveness dissolves when Vasyl splits with Opanas over the issue of whether to support the collective. Vasyl joins the other Komsomols in berating his own father when Opanas insists on maintaining a single farm. With this act, Vasyl shifts his primary loyalty from his family to the collective. After Vasyl's death, Opanas follows his son's path by appearing before the Komsomols, the same men who had previously criticized him, to ask that the young members of the collective bury Vasyl. Opanas has lost both a father and a son, but he realizes that such losses can be overcome through the communal spirit of the collective. The small family gathering at Simon's death, represented in a series of close-ups of individual faces, contrasts with the sea of faces seen in a single long shot at Vasyl's funeral. Collectivization is more than a matter of consolidating farm plots, introducing machinery, and improving harvests. It involves a reordering of social institutions and the substitution of the collective for the single family.

The revolutionary spirit in *Earth* does not involve violence. The true revolutionaries, Dovzhenko insists, are those who recognize the pervasiveness of the life cycle and who build a progressive system in conjunction with it. The rhetoric that runs through *Earth* is one of harmony: between man and nature, nature and technology, life and death.

In an attempt to naturalize the collectivization process, Dovzhenko presents an image of a countryside in harmony with itself. Naturalization is commonly understood to be an ideological tactic to defend the status quo, to make the existing social order seem to be the "natural order," one that cannot or should not be changed. Dovzhenko, however, employs the tactic to make a large-scale change appear spontaneous, practical, and palatable to a population resistant to collectivization [...].

Dovzhenko's film was caught in its own historical contradiction. Conceived in a period of voluntary collectivization, it appeared during the harshest phases of dekulakization. At a time when the Soviet press called for an all-out assault on kulaks in articles which sounded more like military communiqués than agricultural reports, Dovzhenko came forth with his most understated work. The appeal to nature and to pastoral traditions—not bellicosity—is the fundamental persuasive device of Dovzhenko's rhetoric.

Further Reading

Cavendish, Phil. "Zemlia/Earth." In *The Cinema of Russia and the Former Soviet Union*, edited by Birgit Beumers, 57-67. London and NY: Wallflower Press, 2007.

Kepley, Vance, Jr. "Dovzhenko and Montage: Issues of Style and Narration in Silent Films." *Journal of Ukrainian Studies* 19 (1994): 29-44.

Kepley, Vance, Jr. *In the Service of the State: The Cinema of Alexander Dovzhenko*. Madison, WI: University of Wisconsin Press, 1986.

Liber, George O. *Alexander Dovzhenko. A Life in Soviet Film*. London: BFI Publishing, 2002.

Nebesio, Bohdan Y. *Alexander Dovzhenko: A Guide to Published Sources*. Compiled and introduced by B. Nebesio. Edmonton: Canadian Institute of Ukrainian Studies, Univ. of Alberta, 1995.

Papazian, Elizabeth A. "Offscreen Dreams and Collective Synthesis in Dovzhenko's *Earth*." *The Russian Review* 62 (July 2003): 411-28.

Svashenko, S. "Tak rozhdalsia tanets." In *Dovzhenko v vospominaniiakh sovremennikov*, edited by Iu. Solntseva and L. Pazhitnova, 85-90. Moscow: Iskusstvo, 1982.

PART
THREE

STALINIST CINEMA 1928-1953

Lilya Kaganovsky

The Great Turning Point

By 1932, the Cultural Revolution had led to centralization of the arts and the formation of monolithic artistic unions (of writers, filmmakers, artists, composers, and the like). In 1930, Sovkino—the organization that since 1924 had been responsible for film production, distribution and importation, but whose authority had been limited to the Russian Federal Republic—was eliminated and Soiuzkino created in its place, headed by Boris Shumiatskii. Soiuzkino was given greater authority over the studios of the national republics, reflecting the new goals of centralization. It became the sole body to produce and control films made in the USSR.[1]

Reorganization and centralization of the film industry led not only to internal instability but also to the introduction of new bureaucratic administrative units in charge of censorship and review. Screenplays as well as finished films were now vetted by many different organizations, whose authority conflicted and overlapped. Depending on the year, scenarios had to be discussed by the studio's Party organization, members of the ODSK (Society of Friends of Soviet Cinema), ARRK (Association of Workers of Revolutionary Cinematography), the GUKF (Chief Directorate of the Film and Photo Industry), trade unions and the Komsomol before they could be approved for production. From 1934 onward almost every issue of the journal *Sovetskoe kino* (*Soviet Film*) included scenarios, published in order to encourage public discussion. In 1937 the authorities created special commissions, drawn from the

---

[1]   For a complete history of Stalinist cinema, see Kenez and Miller in Further Reading; Birgit Beumers, *A History of Russian Cinema* (Oxford: Berg, 2009).

representatives of the Party and of social organization. Sometimes workers or trade unions were also invited to participate in the discussion. The Komsomol demanded the evaluation and discussion of all scripts dealing with the problems of youth. This level of censorship was largely responsible for the severe script shortages that plagued the Soviet cinema industry in the thirties. It also meant that even those films approved at the script level might not make it through production, or having been completed, would not be released. A film like Ivan Pyr'ev's *The Conveyer Belt of Death* (*Konveier smerti*, 1933), for example, was remade fourteen times over a period of three years. Out of 130 planned films for 1935, only 45 were completed (46 out of 165 in 1936; and 24 out of 62 in 1937).[2] Moreover, scholars estimate that about a third of the completed films were never exhibited.[3]

The *perestroika* (as it was called at the time) and centralization of the film industry was only one of the major changes that marked the transition from the twenties to the thirties. The other two were the coming of sound and the imposition of the doctrine of Socialist Realism as the single method of all Soviet art.

It is not an exaggeration to say that the 1927 release of *The Jazz Singer* (Crosland, USA) radically altered the art of cinema. *The Jazz Singer*, as Douglas Gomery and others have noted, premiered in New York on 6 October 1927, to lukewarm reviews, but its four Vitaphone segments of Al Jolson's songs proved very popular, and by April 1928, "it had become clear that *The Jazz Singer* show had become the most popular entertainment offering of the 1927-1928 season."[4] Despite the many sounds (narrators, piano players, organs, etc.) that had been audible in the movie theater, the "silence" of silent film had been perceived as integral to the very art of cinematic

---

2   Richard Taylor, "Boris Shumyatsky and the Soviet Cinema in the 1930s: Ideology as mass entertainment," *Historical Journal of Film, Radio and Television* 6, no.1 (1986): 60.

3   For full account, see Kenez, 129-30.

4   Douglas Gomery, "The Coming of Sound: Technological Change in the American Film Industry" in *Film Sound: Theory and Practice*, ed. Elizabeth Weis and John Belton (New York: Columbia University Press, 1985), 14, 15.

expression, its distance from theater and literature in which the audible word predominated, its reliance on techniques of editing and montage, gestural language and the close-up. Everywhere, the coming of sound to cinema at the end of the twenties meant a thorough rethinking of cinematic technique, production and distribution. Everywhere, cinema industries had to be reorganized to convert the silent screen into "the talking pictures."

But in the Soviet Union the introduction of synch-sound technology also coincided with a cultural, political and ideological shift during the period known as the Great Turning Point. Stalin's First Five-Year Plan (1928-1932) began a massive industrialization campaign that led to a complete restructuring of the Soviet arts. Although the end result—that is to say, the sound cinema that was eventually produced in the USSR in the 1930s and beyond— came to look very much like that of the US and Europe (which is to say, synchronized sound and "talking pictures"), the ideological path taken by the Soviet film industry toward sound cinema was quite different from that taken by Hollywood, etc. In their debates over the nature of the coming of sound in the late twenties, Soviet filmmakers, theorists and ideologues emphasized a different set of issues from the ones that concerned the American film industry. One approach saw in sound cinema the possibility of continuing the practice of avant-garde revolutionary filmmaking and montage; the other saw the coming of sound as an opportunity to create a "cinema for the millions," a cinema that would directly address the masses.

The Coming of Sound

In "Sound film" ("*Tonfil'ma*"), an editorial for the prominent arts journal *Zhizn' iskusstva* (*The Life of Art*), the head of the Lenfilm script department Adrian Piotrovskii argued precisely for a revolutionary approach to the sound film. He began by describing Aleksandr Shorin's development of synch-sound technology in Leningrad and Pavel Tager's experiments in Moscow, and asked, now that Soviet cinema is very close to producing sound films, what kind of sound cinema should Soviet cinema be? Piotrovskii was specifically

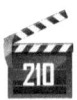

interested in the ways in which Soviet cinema must be different from American and European sound film, whose direction in 1929 was toward dialog and the reproduction of naturalistic sound effects. Specifically, he mentioned the unheard of and unprecedented sensation created by *The Jazz Singer* (which premiered in Moscow 4 November 1929) and Al Jolson's "cabaret" songs.

For Piotrovskii, this focus on "sensation" (singing and dancing) meant that sound cinema had abandoned the editing and optical techniques of its earlier, silent years. For the Soviet film industry, he argued, this kind of cinema would signal a return to its pre-revolutionary bourgeois roots; instead, we must think of sound in film as independent expressive material rather than naturalistic effects. This way, Soviet cinema would create what Piotrovskii calls "cinefied music" (*kinofitsirovannaia muzyka*)—a combination of sound, noise and "articulated intonations" requiring the same kinds of manipulation via montage as does the raw visual image. Piotrovskii particularly stressed that this way of making sound films would rely heavily on noise and other forms of disharmony that, as a result, would produce a sound track that was more expressive, with sounds that would be new to the ear. In second place in terms of its importance for sound film, Piotrovskii suggests putting music and song, and in third place, human speech (although he argues that even here, we should privilege non-speech—yelps, screams, sharp intonations over dialogue or any form of comprehensible speech).

Like Eisenstein, Pudovkin, and Aleksandrov's earlier "Statement on Sound" (1928), Piotrovskii argues specifically for contrast: non-parallel construction, confrontation, disjuncture. He advocates the dialectical possibilities of conflict, struggle and disagreement instead of having the sound track "passively" following the course set by the image track. This he believed would provide the new sound film with political and social value, as opposed to the merely aesthetic/naturalistic/reactionary forms of American and European sound cinema.

Sergei Eisenstein, Vsevolod Pudovkin and Grigorii Aleksandrov's 1928 "Statement on Sound" outlined the ways in which the coming of sound would liberate avant-garde cinema from a series of "blind alleys." In their "statement," the three directors dismissed "talking pictures" as those in which "the sound is recorded in a natural manner, synchronizing exactly with the movement on the screen and creating a certain 'illusion' of people talking, objects making noise, etc." They called this first period the period of "sensations," which, though innocent in itself, would lead to cinema's "unimaginative" use for "dramas of high culture" and other photographed presentations of a theatrical order. The "mere addition" of sound to image, they claimed, would equal subordination (of sound to image), a loss of independence, and the destruction of the "culture of montage." "Sharp discord," a "hammer and tongs" approach, "counterpoint" — these are the privileged terms of the "Statement's" argument. For Eisenstein, Pudovkin, and Aleksandrov, the history of silent cinema was a series of "blind alleys": the first of which was the use of intertitles, and the second, the reliance on explanatory sequences (long shots, for example). Sound, if treated "as a new element of montage" and moreover, as an "independent" variable combined with the visual image, will provide the "organic escape for cinema's cultural avant-garde" and preserve cinema's "world-wide viability."[5] Similarly, documentary filmmaker Esfir' Shub, in her short editorial "The Advent of Sound in Cinema," also argued for the non-passive use of sound: "For the moment we are certain only of the fact that sound film must not be a mere acoustical illustration, that it must be organic raw material just like the film footage, and that in this work a whole world of remarkable discoveries awaits us."[6]

Piotrovskii's theorizations of sound anticipate Dziga Vertov's sound use in his first sound documentary, *Enthusiasm — The Donbass Symphony* (*Entuziazm — Simfoniia Donbassa*, 1930). From the beginning, Vertov experimented with sound, and there was, in a sense, no time for him when image was privileged for its own sake, but rather, that

5   Sergei Eisenstein, Vsevolod Pudovkin, and Grigori Alexandrov, "Statement on Sound," in *The Film Factory: Russian and Soviet Cinema in Documents 1896-1939*, ed. Richard Taylor and Ian Christie (London and New York: Routledge, 1994), 234-35. First published as "Zaiavka," *Zhizn' iskusstva*, 5 August 1928.

6   Esfir Shub, "The Advent of Sound in Cinema," in *The Film Factory*, 271. First published as "K prikhodu zvuka v kinematograf," *Kino*, 1929.

sound-on-film technology had not yet caught up to what Vertov had always imagined cinema to be. In 1925, he proposed the notions of *"kinopravda"* and *"radiopravda,"* suggesting that, "we must now talk about recording audible facts." "Technology is moving swiftly ahead," he wrote, "A method for broadcasting images by radio has already been invented. In addition, a method for recording auditory phenomena on film tape has been discovered. In the near future man will be able to broadcast to the entire world the visual and auditory phenomena recorded by the radio-movie camera."[7] Vertov wanted direct, "live" sound to go with his "live" images, and this is what we see in his 1930 *Enthusiasm*: the production of live recorded sound (not necessarily synch-sound, but sound recorded directly at the source, not recreated in the studio), of sound and image as two equal elements of cinema. In *Enthusiasm*, sound is both "live" (produced by the machines and recorded on the spot) and post-synchronized, which is to say, added to the image or used along with the image as part of the elements of montage:

> Th[e] final, decisive month of our sound shooting took place in a setting of din and clanging, amidst fire and iron, among factory workshops vibrating from the sound. Penetrating into the mines deep beneath the earth and shooting from the roofs of speeding trains, we abolished, once and for all, the fixity of sound equipment and *for the first time in history* recorded, in documentary fashion, the basic sounds of an industrial region (the sound of mines, factories, trains, etc.). Herein lies the … special significance of the sound documentary, *Enthusiasm*.[8]

Vertov's approach to sound differed from that of most filmmakers, including fellow "montage" enthusiasts such as Sergei Eisenstein and Vsevolod Pudovkin, who worried about how sound was going to do away with the primacy of montage, immobilizing the camera and substituting the freedom of editing with the limits of

---

[7]   *Kino-eye: The Writings of Dziga Vertov*, trans. Kevin O'Brien (Berkeley: University of California Press, 1985), 56.

[8]   Dziga Vertov, "Let's Discuss Ukrainfilm's First Sound Film: *Symphony of the Donbas* (the author on his film)," in *Kino-eye: The Writings of Dziga Vertov*, 109.

synchronization. However, because of the numerous difficulties involved with both initially obtaining and then working with brand new, Soviet sound equipment, the stratification of the sound levels of the film did not come through.[9]

Contemporary critics referred to *Enthusiasm* as a cacophony (a charge that Vertov greatly resented) in large part because in this film the distinction between the different kinds of recorded sounds was not given any clear hierarchy: radio, speeches, music, church bells, factories—all spoke with the same urgency, failing to prioritize human and non-human "voices." "Vertov fetishizes the machine and its sounds," wrote Petr Sazhin in the journal *Kino-front* (March 1930), "Vertov has not given us a socialist Donbass Symphony. He has given us a cacophony of machines, he has given us crashing noise, din, hell."[10]

In his editorials on sound cinema, Piotrovskii calls for the best, most radical film directors, and the best, youngest, most talented composers that, together, would create a revolutionary sound cinema. He wants to continue the path of a radical cinema whose revolutionary form reflects its revolutionary content—but the time for such radicalism had passed. While Piotrovskii's position was clearly in line with the kinds of cinema envisioned (and produced) by Eisenstein, Vertov, Shub, etc., it was directly at odds with the other discussions taking place on the same pages of Soviet film journals, where the call for "cinema for the millions" was beginning to be voiced.

Cinema for the Millions

Already by 1929 the pages of *Zhizn' iskusstva* are filled with talk of the "crisis in Soviet cinema" and Soviet films' apparent inability to

---

[9]   John MacKay reads this description in terms of the linkage of different spaces through "sonic" as well as "visual" montage. See John MacKay, "Disorganized Noise: Enthusiasm and the Ear of the Collective," *KinoKultura* 7 (January 2005). http://www.kinokultura.com/articles/jan05-mackay.html (accessed 27 June 2013)

[10]   *Kino-front* (March 1930), RGALI, f. 2091/1/91, l. 99.

be "intelligible to the masses." "We call our cinema Soviet," writes Leningrad director Pavel Petrov-Bytov, in another editorial in *Zhizn' iskusstva*, "Do we have the right to call it that at present? In my view, we do not." "*We have no workers' and peasants' cinema,*" he stresses. There is no cinema that speaks to the everyday life of the masses, and the masses answer by leaving the theater: "What do we have to offer the peasant woman, thinking with her ponderous and sluggish brain about her husband who has gone to make a living in the town, about the cow that is sick in the dirty cowshed with tuberculosis of the lungs, about the starving horse that has broken its leg, about the child that is stirring in her womb? 'What have you done for me?' the worker asks. 'For goodness sake: *October, New Babylon, The Happy Canary*,' we answer familiarly. He does not say a word but swings his fist and slugs us."[11] He continues: "For peasants we have to make straightforward realistic films with a simple story and plot. We must talk in his own sincere language about the cow that is sick with tuberculosis, about the dirty cowshed that must be transformed into one that is clean and bright, about the child that is stirring in the peasant woman's womb, about crèches for the child, about rural hooligans, the kolkhoz, and so on." "*Every film must be useful, intelligible and familiar to the millions,*" Petrov-Bytov stresses. "We are surrounded by such obscenity, such dirt, poverty, coarseness, and thickheadedness."[12] Soviet cinema must sift through this "vile filth" on the "dung hill of everyday life" to uncover the "beautiful life" hidden deep within. As Richard Taylor and Ian Christie point out, we can already "detect the kernel of the later doctrine of Socialist Realism" that informs this way of thinking.[13]

The First Congress of Soviet Writers took place in Moscow in August 1934, in which countless delegations of kolkhoz members, workers, pioneers, soldiers and readers' clubs surged in to make

---

[11]   Pavel Petrov-Bytov, "We Have No Soviet Cinema," in *The Film Factory*, 261; originally published as "U nas net sovetskoi kinomatografii," *Zhizn' iskusstva* (21 April 1929): 8.

[12]   "We Have No Soviet Cinema," *The Film Factory*, 261-62.

[13]   *The Film Factory*, 247.

statements, read messages of friendship, state their demands, or issue orders on literary and aesthetic matters. The 1,500 members of the new Union of Soviet Writers represented the literatures of fifty-two Soviet nationalities, but the dominant figures at the Congress were unquestionably Maksim Gorky, who presided, and Andrei A. Zhdanov, secretary of the Central Committee, along with Nikolai Bukharin and Karl Radek. The Congress established Socialist Realism as the official method of all Soviet art, stressing specifically that artistic works should display the socialist idea (*ideinost'*), national character (*narodnost'*) and Party loyalty (*partiinost'*). As Zhdanov defined it, Socialist Realism demands of the artist "the truthful, historically concrete representation of reality in its revolutionary development"—that is to say, not life as it is, but as it should and will be. The film that perhaps came to best exemplify the spirit and the letter of Socialist Realism was the 1934 *Chapaev* (directed by the Vasil'ev "Brothers"), which was watched by millions of viewers and has since become a cult film, generating hundreds of references, popular quotations and jokes. "The Whole Country is Watching *Chapaev*," declared the headline of the newspaper *Pravda* on 21 November 1934. Stalin watched the film repeatedly, remarking each time on its topicality. Audiences came to the theaters again and again, many hoping that this time, the Red Army commander would survive the final attack and emerge alive at the end of the film.

In 1935, the All-Union Creative Conference on Cinema Affairs adopted the principles of Socialist Realism as set out for literature. Indeed, for the Soviet film industry, the first shift in ideology can be traced back to the 1928 All-Union Party Conference on Cinema, which decreed that Soviet cinema "must furnish a 'form that is intelligible to the millions'."[14] From this point forward, Soviet films had to be entertaining first and foremost: unlike their avant-garde predecessors, they needed to have a simple plot and be organized around a coherent storyline. Moreover, as the new head of the

---

14   B.S. Ol'khovyi, ed. *Puti kino. Pervoe Vsesoiuznoe partiinoe soveshchanie po kinematografii* (Moscow, 1929), 429-44.

centralized film industry, Boris Shumiatskii wrote in 1933: "We need genres that are infused with optimism, with the mobilizing emotions, with cheerfulness, *joie-de-vivre* and laughter. Genres that provide us with the maximum opportunity to demonstrate the best Bolshevik traditions: an implacable attitude to opportunism, with tenacity, initiative, skill and a Bolshevik scale of work."[15] "The victorious class wants to laugh with joy," he argued, "That is its right and Soviet cinema must provide its audiences with this joyful Soviet laughter."[16] Shumiatskii urged a concentration on three genres: drama, comedy and fairy tales. Of the 308 films produced in the 1930s, fifty-four were made for children, and of the musical comedies, twelve were set in factories and seventeen took place on collective farms: one strongly got the impression, as Richard Taylor wrote, "that the countryside was a round of never-ending dancing and singing."[17]

In his notes from Kremlin screenings a year later, Shumiatskii reported that Stalin was particularly interested in "light" films, noting specifically that: "The audience needs joy, cheerfulness and laughter. They want to see themselves on the screen." Shumiatskii spends a long time accounting for the lack of humor in current Soviet cinema, before assuring Stalin that the next films coming up—*Veselye rebiata* (*Jolly Fellows*, Aleksandrov, 1934), *Entuziasty* (*The Enthusiasts*, Simonov and Lukashevich, 1934), and *Garmon'* (*The Accordion*, Savchenko, 1934) —would be "refreshingly comical, cheerful and joyful."[18]

The Stalinist musical comedy was born precisely out of this desire for light, joyous movies in which the audience would be

---

15   Boris Shumiatskii, "Tvorcheskie zadachi templana," *Sovetskoe kino* 12 (December 1933): 1.

16   Shumiatskii, *Kinematografiia millionov. Opyt analiza* (Moscow, 1935), 249.

17   For a full account, see Taylor, "Boris Shumyatsky and the Soviet Cinema in the 1930s."

18   "A driani podobno *Garmon'* bol'she ne stavite?.." Zapisi besed B. Z. Shumiatskogo s I.V. Stalinym posle kinoprosmotrov. 1934 g. (Publikatsiia i kommentarii A. S. Troshina), *Kinovedcheskie zapiski* 61: 281-346.

able to recognize themselves on the screen.[19] Like the Hollywood musical that gets its reputation as an "escapist" genre from the musicals produced in the early 1930s—the image of tuxedoed Fred Astaire and high-heeled Ginger Rogers dancing their way through the Great Depression—the Stalinist musical was also a tool for the affirmation of a collective utopia. In a typical Hollywood musical of the 1930s, each person was shown to be part of an interdependent group. Elaborate musical numbers choreographed by Busby Berkeley, in which scantily clad rows of girls kicked together or formed pyramids on enormously spectacular sets, symbolized the importance of social cohesion and harmony, while reaffirming the American dream of unity and social cohesion at a time of strife and social unrest. (We see a similar conceit in Grigorii Aleksandrov's 1936 *Tsirk* [*Circus*], which borrows from these earlier American musicals.)

For Soviet cinema and its new search for a "cinema for the millions," Igor' Savchenko's *The Accordion* (Fig. 66) and Aleksandrov's *Jolly Fellows* similarly represented the birth of the new genre of musical comedy, while rejecting the designation "musical" because of its association with bourgeois culture (both Savchenko and Shumiatskii, for example, called *The Accordion* the "first attempt at musical [film] operetta"). Coming on the heels of the adoption of Socialist Realism as the official method of all Soviet art, Stalinist musical comedies became a way to link the notion of "reality in its revolutionary development" to the "feeling of utopia" generated by

---

[19] On Soviet musicals in the 1930s, see in particular: Richard Taylor, "Singing on the Steppes for Stalin: Ivan Pyr'ev and the Kolkhoz Musical in Soviet Cinema," *Slavic Review* 58, no. 1 (Spring 1999): 143-59; Taylor, "K topografii utopii v stalinskom m'iuzikle" and Katerina Clark, "'Chtoby tak pet,' dvadtsat' let uchit'sia nuzhno: Sluchai *Volgi-Volgi*," both in *Sovetskoe bogatstvo. Stat'i o kul'ture, literature i kino*, ed. Marina Balina, Evgenii Dobrenko and Yurii Murashov (St. Petersburg: Akademicheskii proekt, 2002), 358-70 and 371-90 respectively; David C. Gillespie, "The Sounds of Music: Soundtrack and Song in Soviet Film," *Slavic Review* 62, no. 3 (Autumn 2003): 473-90; and Rimgaila Salys, *The Musical Comedy Films of Grigorii Aleksandrov: Laughing Matters* (Bristol: Intellect, 2009).

Fig. 66.
The Accordion

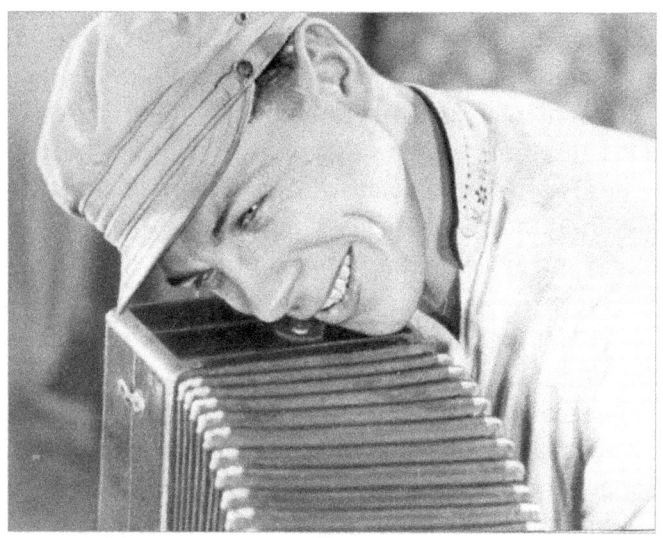

the musical. It was the main genre that helped create the dream of mass utopia, once sound cinema had arrived.[20]

For Soviet cinema, the two leading figures in the production of Soviet musicals were Grigorii Aleksandrov and Ivan Pyr'ev. When Eisenstein and Aleksandrov returned from Mexico in May 1932, Shumiatskii asked Eisenstein to make a musical comedy (as part of Shumiatskii's dream of a "Soviet Hollywood"). Eisenstein refused, but Aleksandrov accepted and the new genre of the Stalinist musical comedy was born. Most notably, in close collaboration with Isaak Dunaevskii, who composed the score, and Vasilii Lebedev-Kumach, who wrote the lyrics, Aleksandrov produced *Jolly Fellows* (1934), *Circus* (1936), *Volga-Volga* (1938—one of Stalin's favorite films, which he famously sent to President Roosevelt as a present in 1942), and *The Radiant Path* (*Svetlyi put'*, 1941), films that are considered the epitome of the genre to this day. They specifically reflected the cultural mandate to "turn fairy tales into reality," ideology *plus* entertainment, and the creation of an ideal Soviet space filled with singing and dancing.

---

[20]   Richard Taylor, "Singing on the Steppes for Stalin," 145.

The films all starred Aleksandrov's wife, Liubov' Orlova, in Soviet versions of a rags-to-riches Cinderella story, in which a peasant woman from the countryside, possessed of talent and determination, makes it to Moscow where she becomes a sensation — either for her singing or for her industry. *Jolly Fellows* opened with the announcement, "This film does not star Buster Keaton, Harry Lloyd and Charlie Chaplin," pointing out the fact that Soviet cinema no longer needed American imports. *Circus* similarly underscored the Soviet Union's superiority over the United States, living up to the slogan of the age to "catch up and overtake America." At the end of *Circus*, the American circus star Marion Dixon (Orlova), now called Masha, joins the Soviet collective as they march through Red Square for the May Day Parade. Together they sing the "Song of the Motherland" (composed by Dunaevsky), a song that celebrated the freedoms of the new Stalin constitution and which became an unofficial Soviet anthem, until the official version was introduced in 1944.

A prolific film director, decorated with two Orders of Lenin and four Orders of the Red Banner, Ivan Pyr'ev had a forty-year career in cinema that started with his first black comedy *The Foreign Woman* (*Postoronniaia zhenshchina*, 1928) and ended with the screen adaptation of *The Brothers Karamazov* (*Brat'ia Karamazovy*, 1968). Yet during the Stalin period, Pyr'ev was known best for his "tractor musicals," which all took place on collective farms. Pyr'ev's musical comedies—*The Country Bride* (*Bogataia nevesta*, 1938), set on a communal farm in Ukraine; *The Tractor Drivers* (*Traktoristy*, 1939), also set on a communal farm in Ukraine; *The Pig Farmer and the Shepherd* (*Svinarka i pastukh*, 1941), set on communal farms in Belorussia and Georgia; and *Cossacks of the Kuban'* (*Kubanksie kazaki*, 1949), set on a communal farm in Kuban' — all starred Pyr'ev's wife Marina Ladynina, who drove a tractor, danced with pigs and was always willing to sacrifice her own happiness for the happiness of the collective. These comedies showed the prosperity of the great Soviet state through well-choreographed musical numbers, depicting the joys of industrialized farming.

But while the Soviet musical comedy celebrated the joy of communist labor and the successes of the Soviet Union, taking its

cue from Stalin's famous 1935 pronouncement, "Life has gotten better, comrades, life has become more joyous,"[21] a different film genre—political melodrama—expressed the threat to living in this collective utopia.

The Great Terror

On 5 December 1936 Stalin unveiled his plan for a new constitution that guaranteed equal rights to women, as well as "freedom of speech, press, assembly and meeting, the right to unite in public organizations, inviolability of person, inviolability of domicile and privacy of correspondence, the right of asylum for foreign citizens persecuted for defending the interests of the working people or for their scientific activities, or for their struggle for national liberation."[22] The new Stalinist constitution that went into effect on 5 December 1936 proclaimed the Soviet citizen the most free on earth and celebrated the success of the new socialist state. Cinema and soccer formed two poles of "socialist" popular culture and in the summer happy citizens were said to "frolic" in the shadow of various life-size statues of Stakhanovite workers, Soviet aviators and Soviet leaders. The press was full of stories of Soviet achievement on the labor front: work on the construction of the Moscow metro began in 1932; in the Don Basin in 1935, the miner Aleksei Stakhanovite extracted 102 tons of coal in six hours, setting a record that earned him the title "Hero of Socialist Labor," and triggered the call for Stakhanovite (or "shock-worker") performances in all areas of industry; and in 1937, the pilot Valerii Chkalov flew nonstop from Moscow to Portland, Oregon, setting the record for the farthest long-distance flight.

At the same time, the 1930s were marked by terror, fear, arrests and executions. Forced collectivization and "dekulakization,"

---

[21]   Stalin's speech on 17 November 1935 to the workers-Stakhanovites: *"zhit' stalo luchshe, tovarishchi, zhit' stalo veselee."*

[22]   *The History of the All-Union Communist Party of the Bolsheviks, A Short Course* (Moscow: OGIZ, 1945); see in particular, Chapter 12, section 3, "Eighth Congress of Soviets. Adoption of the new constitution of the U.S.S.R."

begun in 1929-1930 (and which continued in fits and starts until 1940), led to famine in the Ukraine (Kholodomor, 1932-1933). The price of collectivization was so high that the 2 March 1930 issue of *Pravda* contained Stalin's speech, "Dizzy with Success," in which he called for a temporary halt to the process: "It is a fact that by February 20 of this year 50 percent of the peasant farms throughout the U.S.S.R. had been collectivized. That means that by February 20, 1930, we had overfulfilled the five-year plan of collectivization by more than 100 per cent.... some of our comrades have become dizzy with success and for the moment have lost clearness of mind and sobriety of vision."[23] After the publication of the article, the pressure for collectivization temporarily abated and peasants started leaving collective farms. But soon collectivization was intensified again, and by 1936, about 90% of Soviet agriculture was collectivized.

The assassination on 1 December 1934 of Politburo member, head of the Leningrad party organization and Stalin's main political rival, Sergei Kirov, signaled that the country was indeed in danger of enemy attack both from within and from without.[24] The ascension to power in Germany of Adolf Hitler in 1933, the revelation of a "Leningrad Center" responsible for Kirov's assassination, followed shortly by the discovery of a "Moscow Center" that had ties to White Guard organizations, and the trials and death sentences for the accused, brought the rhetoric of "vigilance" to a fever pitch. The initial purges of the Central Committee (1933-1936) were aimed at reducing the number of members of the Communist Party. Since 1931, Party membership had reached unprecedented numbers: during the collectivization and industrialization campaigns of the First Five Year Plan (1929-1932) it had grown by 1.4 million members.[25] The 1933 *chistka* (purge), the 1935 *proverka* (verification),

23   J. V. Stalin, "Dizzy with Success: Concerning Questions of the Collective-Farm Movement," *Pravda* 60 (March 2, 1930); trans. Foreign Languages Publishing House, in Stalin, *Works*, Vol. 12 (Moscow: Foreign Languages Publishing House, 1955), 197-205.

24   Stephen Kotkin, *Magnetic Mountain: Stalinism as a Civilization* (Berkeley: University of California Press, 1995), 303.

25   J. Arch Getty, *Origins of the Great Purges: The Soviet Communist Party*

and the 1936 *obmen* (party card exchange) were all meant to rid the party of the thousands of politically illiterate, "alien," "parasitic," "unreliable" and "unsteadfast" persons who had entered the party.[26] The show trials held between 1935 and 1938 likewise targeted high-ranking Party officials who were accused of espionage, sabotage and conspiracy. For the cinema industry, the purges affected studio heads, artists, consultants, technicians—in particular those with foreign connections, who were seen as potential enemies of the people.

The years 1935-1937 thus marked a period of particular uncertainty for both films and filmmakers. At the All-Union Creative Conference on Cinema Matters in January 1935, Sergei Eisenstein was subjected to severe criticism for not having produced any new films since his return to the USSR. In response, Eisenstein, along with a number of other directors, delivered a half-hearted apology for cinematic formalism and intellectual montage—for everything, in other words, which had made Soviet avant-garde cinema famous the world over. Some of the avant-garde film directors quit, others adapted, and still others came to take their place. Eisenstein spent the beginning of the decade in Hollywood and Mexico (returning home without a completed film) and the middle of the decade making *Bezhin Meadow* in an increasingly hostile environment. His only fully finished film of the decade, the 1938 *Alexander Nevsky*, has been generally considered a compromise by film scholars. The film is nevertheless a masterpiece both in terms of its cinematography and in its use of contrapuntal sound, advocated earlier by Eisenstein, Aleksandrov and Pudovkin in their 1928 "Statement on Sound." Dziga Vertov's *Three Songs of Lenin* (1934) briefly brought the director national and international fame, but the film was quickly pulled from Soviet screens. Vertov's final attempt to make sophisticated documentary films was the 1937 *Lullaby* (*Kolybel'naia*) that, despite its open glorification of Stalin, was not well received.

Reconsidered, 1933-1938 (New York: Cambridge University Press, 1985), 48.

[26]   Getty, 48.

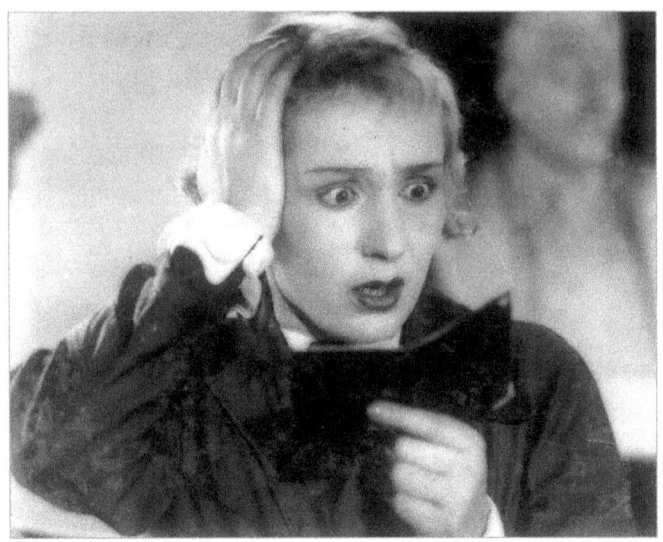

Fig. 67.
Anna in Shock

Aleksandr Dovzhenko, on the other hand, successfully negotiated the transition from the twenties to the thirties, mostly due to Stalin's personal involvement. After *Aerograd* (1935), Dovzhenko was given explicit orders to make a "Ukrainian *Chapaev*." *Shchors* (1939) was based on the life of Mykola Shchors (played by Evgenii Samoilov) who fought against the German intervention of 1918 and the Polish invasion of 1919, and who, like Chapaev, perished in battle. Dovzhenko, however, infused the film with personal memory, with images of death and devastation that seemed out of step with the tenets of Socialist Realism that demanded optimism and utopian visions of the bright future yet to come. More successful in terms of socialist realist conventions was the so-called "Maxim trilogy," made by former FEKS (Factory of the Eccentric Actor) directors Grigorii Kozintsev and Leonid Trauberg. The three films— *The Youth of Maxim* (*Iunost' Maksima*, 1934), *The Return of Maxim* (*Vozvrashchenie Maksima*, 1937), and *The Vyborg Side* (*Vyborgskaia storona*, 1938)—told the story of a young worker who, seeing the injustices of tsarist Russia, joins the Revolutionary movement. Like *Chapaev*, the trilogy was a model socialist realist text that chronicled the hero's evolution from "spontaneity" to "consciousness," always guided by the firm hand of the Party. And, like Chapaev, Maksim was both ideologically correct and charming and funny—

satisfying both the ideological conventions and the need for entertainment.

Similarly, Fridrikh Ermler went on to make films that tapped into the spirit of the decade. His 1932 *Counterplan* (*Vstrechnyi*) dealt with the First Five-Year Plan; his 1934 *Peasants* (*Krest'iane*) was set during collectivization and showed the struggle of the regime against the old guard of kulaks and saboteurs; and his best-known film, *The Great Citizen* (*Velikii grazhdanin*, 1938-39), showed the progress of industrialization, the danger of foreign sabotage and provided cinematic justification for the show trials.

The question of internal enemies preoccupied both the newspapers and the cinema. Of the eighty-five films made between 1933-1939, fifty-two dealt with the struggle against saboteurs, many of whom turned out to be family members—spouses, parents and best friends. One such film is Ivan Pyr'ev's 1936 *The Party Card* (*Partiinyi bilet*), a high melodrama about the dangers of trusting your husband (Fig. 67). *The Party Card* is in every way the reverse of Pyr'ev's communal farm musicals. While the tractor musicals brought us the happy and successful life of the countryside, Pyr'ev's urban melodrama showed the need for "Bolshevik vigilance" to preserve that happy life. In the film, Anna Kulikova (Ada Voitsik), a good communist from solid proletarian stock, marries Pavel Kuganov (Andrei Abrikosov), a newcomer from Siberia who seems to have all the credentials of Soviet heroism, but who turns out instead to be an unreformed kulak, murderer and traitor. Because of Anna's blind trust, Pavel is able to join the plant where she works, move into her apartment in Moscow, get himself elected to the Communist Party, and to make plans for a work-transfer to a high-security military plant. He is also able to steal Anna's party card—that "precious symbol of communist membership dear to the heart of every Bolshevik"—and to deliver it into the hands of Soviet enemies.[27]

---

27   As Julie Cassiday notes, "Pyr'ev's film taught that ordinary paper cards issued to party members were no less sacred than membership itself." See Cassiday, 182, in Further Reading.

The theft allows "the enemy" (unnamed traitors who have infiltrated the USSR) to freely move about Moscow, and leads to Anna's expulsion from the Communist Party for the negligent loss of her party card. When Iasha (Igor' Maleev), Anna's true love and the "positive hero" of this film, comes back to Moscow, he discovers Anna's tragedy and dishonor. The film ends with Iasha, Fedor Ivanovich (the head of the local party cell, played by Anatolii Goriunov) and the NKVD bursting into the couple's apartment to find the brave Anna holding her villainous husband at gunpoint. As Soviet film reviewers in 1936 were fond of repeating, *The Party Card* showed the enemy's new methods of operation and demonstrated the ease with which a class enemy could pass himself off as a loyal Soviet citizen.

After the signing of the non-aggression pact in 1939, Soviet propaganda briefly engaged in pro-German rhetoric, and films that had been aimed specifically against Germany, such as Eisenstein's *Alexander Nevsky* (1938) that celebrated Russian victory over the Teutonic knights in the thirteenth century, were pulled from the theaters. When the Germans invaded the Soviet Union on 22 June 1941, however, all that had been feared in the thirties had come to pass. For the next four years the Soviet Union suffered the greatest losses of any nation during the Second World War, over twenty million people.

In the autumn of 1941, the Lenfilm and Mosfilm studios were evacuated to Alma-Ata in Central Asia, where the newly formed Central United Film Studios made war chronicles and feature films, largely about the war. Most notably, however, Sergei Eisenstein filmed *Ivan the Terrible* (*Ivan Groznyi*, 1945, 1946/1958) while in Alma-Ata, a film originally commissioned by Stalin and in which the leadership of the sixteenth century tsar was meant as an allegory for Stalin's Russia.

The Cult of Personality

In 1949 the Soviet Union prepared to celebrate Stalin's seventieth birthday. The nation had just emerged victorious from World War II and history was quickly being rewritten to reflect Stalin's role

in the Great Patriotic War. Though the war brought the Soviet people together in the defense of their homeland, it nevertheless shook the foundation on which belief in the Party and the socialist dream rested. Thus, in the late forties the commitment to Stalin and Soviet Russia had to be actively renewed. The dominant fiction of the Soviet Union as the most prosperous and happiest nation on earth, with Stalin at its head as the great and loving father, had to be reinscribed, and cinema became the privileged medium by which this was accomplished.

The pre-war fear of "enemies of the people" returned in full force as soldiers and prisoners of war came back from the western front and were now perceived as potential saboteurs and spies by the increasingly paranoid Stalinist regime. Andrei Zhdanov's "anti-cosmopolitan campaign" of 1946-1948 was a result of this return to xenophobia: Zhdanov, the new head of culture and ideology, launched attacks on poets and writers (most famously, the poet Anna Akhmatova and the writer Mikhail Zoshchenko, who were subsequently excluded from the Writers' Union), as well as on the journals that published them. He classified jazz music as "hysterical and cacophonous," and ordered the arrests of jazz musicians, such as Eddie Rosner and Leonid Piatigorskii, as well as the "arrests" of saxophones.[28] His "Resolution on Cinema" (4 September 1946) attacked Eisenstein's *Ivan the Terrible* (Part II, 1946), Pudovkin's *Admiral Nakhimov* (1946/47), and Kozintsev and Trauberg's *Simple Folk* (*Prostye liudi*, 1945). In 1948, a campaign targeting Jews began. The "anti-cosmopolitan campaign" attacked Jewish writers and art critics, leading to expulsions, arrests and the murder of the great Jewish theater actor Solomon Mikhoels. Vertov was one of a number of filmmakers accused of "cosmopolitanism" during the "Open Party Session of the Central Studio of Documentary Films" on 14-15 March 1949, with 200 people in attendance.[29]

Immediately after the war, in March 1946, the Directorate of Cinema acquired ministerial status (becoming the Ministry of

---

[28]   Beumers, 107.

[29]   See Protokol n. 11 in *Iskusstvo kino* 12 (1997): 128-33.

Cinema) and Ivan Bol'shakov was appointed as its head. Shumiatskii, who had overseen the cinema industry through the thirties, had been arrested on 8 January 1938 and denounced in *Pravda*, *Kino* and *Iskusstvo kino* as a "fascist cur" and a member of the "Trotskyite-Bukharinite-Rykovite fascist band." He was executed on 29 July 1938. Shumiatskii's replacement, Semen Dukel'skii, lasted just over a year (he was appointed on 23 March 1938 but removed on 4 June 1939), to be replaced by Bol'shakov—who, as Leonid Trauberg had put it, "had as much connection with cinema as a policeman on point-duty."[30]

Post-war xenophobia, paranoia and the start of the Cold War all led to a precipitous drop in film production, which, alongside the bans on films, produced the so-called "film famine" or "anemia" (*malokartin'e*) of the late 1940s. In the 1930s, production had been around fifty feature films per year, but it would drop to under ten by 1951 (a number particularly striking when compared to the yearly output of 400-500 films produced in Hollywood or the 200-300 films a year made in India or Japan during the same period).[31] After the war, it became increasingly difficult to find a "safe" topic for films, and filmmakers turned to the production of biopics about heroic leaders. None were as popular as films about the Great Leader himself, Stalin.

Beginning in 1946, with the release of Ermler's *The Great Turning Point* (*Velikii perelom*, 1946), the Soviet people witnessed the birth of films dedicated to Stalin. Though the practice of dramatizing recent historic events—such as the Revolution, the Civil War, collectivization and industrialization—was nothing new to Soviet cinema, this was the first time that films were made which centered their diegesis on an actually living leader. When, in 1927, Sergei Eisenstein filmed *October* (*Oktiabr'*), his desire to cast an actor in the role of Lenin was seen as almost sacrilegious. A decade later,

---

30   Richard Taylor, "Ideology as mass entertainment: Boris Shumyatsky and Soviet cinema in the 1930s," in *Inside the Film Factory*, 193-216; 216.

31   Beumers, 109; Kenez, 188.

Mikhail Romm made *Lenin in October* (*Lenin v oktiabre*, 1937), casting Boris Shchukin in the role of Lenin and Semen Gol'dshtab in the role of Stalin. The success of this film effectively put an end to the avant-garde debate over whether a communist leader could be represented in cinema.[32] Romm's film began the *Kinoleniniana*— films about Lenin—but it also opened the way for the possibility of films about Stalin. Though Stalin plays a secondary role in the films of the *Kinoleniniana*, he is shown frequently, standing by as Lenin's right hand man and his obvious successor.[33] On his own, that is to say, in films that did not feature Lenin, Stalin appeared in the thirties mostly as an off-screen presence—the elusive *vozhd'* (leader) in whose name and under whose portrait events take place. Ermler's *Peasants* originally contained an animated dream sequence showing Varvara (the positive hero of the film) with her child and Stalin, which had to be deleted, as it was not deemed suitable for the leader to appear in animated form. Aleksandrov's *Radiant Path*, on the other hand, depicted the heroine Tania Morozova (Orlova) receiving her award for Stakhanovite labor from an invisible source, Stalin himself.[34] In the thirties, Stalin's name became synonymous with the Party, with Moscow and with the Kremlin, and protagonists often referred to Moscow as "the place where Stalin lives."[35]

---

[32]   See Maya Turovskaya, "The 1930s and 1940s: Cinema in Context," in *Stalinism and Soviet Cinema*, 34-53, in Further Reading.

[33]   For example, *Lenin in October, Lenin in 1918* and *The Vyborg Side* all feature Stalin in their original, uncut versions. Many other thirties films contained references to Stalin (including song lyrics) that were systematically reedited after 1956 to remove all traces of Stalin.

[34]   Stalin never gave out the Stalin prizes himself; rather, they were given out by Mikhail Kalinin, Chairman of the Presidium of the Supreme Soviet of the Soviet Union and nominal head of state, and this episode has its source in the photo of Orlova receiving the prize from Kalinin. However, the film plays up the divine invisible source that overwhelms Tania, a source that points to Stalin, without naming him directly.

[35]   One such example is Aleksandr Medvedkin's 1938 *New Moscow* (*Novaia Moskva*) in which the hero, Alesha, sings a song about beautiful Moscow where Stalin lives.

As Ian Christie has noted, "after 1939, when Mikhail Gelovani took over the role of Stalin … it became customary to include scenes involving Stalin whenever possible and these soon became climactic. In 1946, Stalin became a—perhaps *the*—central subject of Soviet cinema."[36] After World War II, Stalin took his "rightful place" in cinema; indeed, never is the cult of personality so glaring as in these post-war years. Stalin's participation in World War II, his unique (portrayed as single-handed) role in bringing about the fall of Hitler and the extension of Soviet rule throughout Europe, is central to such films as Ermler's *The Great Turning Point* (1946), Mikhail Chiaureli's *The Vow* (*Kliatva*, 1946) and his *The Fall of Berlin* (*Padenie Berlina*, 1949). In all of these films, Stalin's commitment to Russia and his presence at the site of greatest conflict are underscored.[37] But in Chiaureli's films in particular Stalin is given the central role: nothing in the country happens without his direct knowledge and involvement. In *The Vow*, Stalin's oath given at the site of his last meeting with Lenin inspires common men and women to defend their homeland against the German invader. In *The Fall of Berlin*, Stalin's expert command of the Russian army leads the nation to victory and the destruction of Nazi Germany. The triumphant soldiers raise the red Soviet flag on the Reichstag and Stalin descends from the sky in a white airplane to greet the victorious and thankful masses.

In 1956, three years after Stalin's death, in a special report to the closed session of the Twentieth Party Congress, Nikita Khrushchev addressed the problem of Stalin's cult of personality and its "harmful consequences" for the Soviet nation. After Stalin's death, Khrushchev suggested, the Central Committee of the Party began to implement a policy of "explaining concisely and consistently that it is impermissible and foreign to the spirit of Marxism-Leninism to

---

[36]   Ian Christie, "Canons and Careers: The Director in Soviet Cinema," in *Stalinism and Soviet Cinema*, 163.

[37]   This is particularly ironic since, according to Nikita Khrushchev, "during the whole Patriotic War, [Stalin] never visited any section of the front or any liberated city." Nikita Khrushchev, *The Crimes of the Stalin Era: Special Report to the 20th Congress of the Communist Party of the Soviet Union*, annotated by Boris Nikolaevsky (New York: New Leader, 1956), S40.

elevate one person, to transform him into a superman possessing supernatural characteristics, akin to those of a god. Such a man supposedly knows everything, sees everything, thinks for everyone, can do anything, is infallible in his behavior."[38] Speaking directly of such films as *The Vow* and *The Fall of Berlin,* Khrushchev denounced Stalin's cinematic image as one example of his cult of personality. He also stressed Stalin's isolation and his "reluctance to consider life's realities," claiming that Stalin never traveled anywhere, and knew the country and agriculture "only from films." And these films, Khrushchev noted, "dressed up and beautified the existing situation in agriculture. Many films pictured kolkhoz life such that (farmhouse) tables groaned from the weight of turkeys and geese. Evidently, Stalin thought that it was actually so."[39]

In his "Secret Speech," Khrushchev restated what French film critic Andrei Bazin had argued six years earlier.[40] The cult of personality of a political leader had very much come to resemble the cult of a film star. And this was achieved, at least in part, by turning the leader *into* a film star—by creating a superhuman, omnipotent and omniscient cinematic version of Stalin. Unlike the films of the *Kinoleniniana*, which were reedited after 1956 to remove all traces of Stalin and had continued to be shown until the Soviet Union's collapse, *The Vow* and *The Fall of Berlin* were withdrawn from circulation altogether.[41] Thus, it was not until *The Fall of Berlin* was screened at the Ciné-Mémoire festival in Paris in October 1991 that audiences had the chance to see the film that most directly represented the Stalin cult in Soviet cinema.

---

[38] Khrushchev, *The Crimes of the Stalin Era,* S7.

[39] Khrushchev, *The Crimes of the Stalin Era,* S58.

[40] André Bazin makes a point of contrasting fictional films such as *The Vow* to documentaries such as Leni Riefenstahl's *Triumph of the Will* (1934). See André Bazin, "The Stalin Myth in Soviet Cinema," trans. Georgia Gurrieri, *Film Criticism* 3, no. 1 (Fall 1978): 17-26; originally published as "Le mythe de Staline dans le cinéma soviétique."

[41] For details, see Alexander Sesonske, "Re-editing history: *Lenin in October,*" *Sight & Sound* 53, no 1 (Winter 1983-4): 56-58.

Conclusion

For the Soviet film industry in the 1930s and beyond, Socialist Realism largely displaced the genre system as developed by Hollywood. Terms such as "melodrama" and "musical" became *verboten* because of their bourgeois associations, and were replaced by *"templany"* — that is, "thematic planning" that mixed genre and themes indiscriminately. For each year, the thematic plan would designate a particular quantity of films that should be made and provide the industry with a series of particular themes that had to be covered.[42] Thus, for example, for 1934, the *templan* called for films about: "socialist construction," "collective farms and political divisions," "the Red Army and Civil War," "children's films," "comedies," "various themes," and "the classics" (*sotsialisticheskoe stroitel'stvo, kolkhozy i politotdely, Krasnaia armiia i grazhdanskaia voina, detskie kartiny, komedii, raznye temy, klassiki*). *Templan* was another form of a planned economy, intended in part as a means of quality control, and as an assurance that the Soviet cinema industry would produce both the quantity and the quality of films expected of it. But, despite these intentions, during the Stalin era the industry continued to be underfunded and poorly equipped, with poorly organized production (as compared to the American studio system) and an underdeveloped distribution network, constantly derailed by the changing political winds. Indeed, it was not until after the death of Stalin and the Twentieth Party Congress that the Soviet cinema industry began to recover, producing, for the first time since the 1920s, films and film directors that could once again rejoin the canon of world cinema.

---

[42]   For a full account, see Miller, 91-104, in Further Reading.

Further Reading

Bagrov, Peter. "Ermler, Stalin, and Animation: On the Film *The Peasants* (1934)." Translated by Vladimir Padunov. *KinoKultura* 15 (January 2007). http://www.kinokultura.com/2007/15-bagrov.shtml (accessed 20 January 2013).

Cassiday, Julie A. *The Enemy on Trial: Early Soviet Courts on Stage and Screen*. DeKalb, IL: Northern Illinois University Press, 2000.

Christie, Ian. "Canons and Careers: The Director in Soviet Cinema." In *Stalinism and Soviet Cinema*. Edited by Richard Taylor and Derek Spring. London: Routledge, 1993.

Clark, Katerina. *The Soviet Novel: History as Ritual*. Chicago: Chicago University Press, 1981.

Dobrenko, Evgeny. *Political Economy of Socialist Realism*. New Haven: Yale University Press, 2007.

------. *Stalinist Cinema and the Production of History: Museum of the Revolution*. Edinburgh: Edinburgh University Press; New Haven: Yale University Press, 2008.

Dobrenko, Evgeny, and Eric Naiman, eds. *The Landscape of Stalinism: the Art and Ideology of Soviet Space*. Seattle: University of Washington Press, 2003.

Dobrenko, Evgeny, with Katerina Clark, Andrei Artizov and Oleg Naumov, eds. *Soviet Culture and Power. A History in Documents, 1917-1953*. New Haven: Yale University Press, 2007.

Fitzpatrick, Sheila. *Everyday Stalinism: Ordinary Life in Extraordinary Times: Soviet Russia in the 1930s*. Oxford: Oxford University Press, 1999.

Garros, Véronique, Natalia Korenevskaya and Thomas Lahusen, eds. *Intimacy and Terror*. Translated by Carol A. Flath. New York: The New Press, 1995.

Groys, Boris. *The Total Art of Stalinism: Avant-Garde, Aesthetic Dictatorship, and Beyond*. Translated by Charles Rougle. Princeton: Princeton University Press, 1992.

Günther, Hans. "Wise Father Stalin and His Family in Soviet Cinema." In *Socialist Realism Without Shores*, edited by Thomas Lahusen and Evgeny Dobrenko, 178-90. Durham: Duke University Press, 1997.

Gutkin, Irina. *The Cultural Origins of the Socialist Realist Aesthetic, 1890-1934*. Evanston, IL: Northwestern University Press, 1999.

Haynes, John. *New Soviet Man: Gender and Masculinity in Stalinist Soviet Cinema*. Manchester, UK: Manchester University Press, 2003.

Kaganovsky, Lilya. "Visual Pleasure in Stalinist Cinema: Ivan Pyr'ev's *The Party Card*." In *Everyday Life in Early Soviet Russia: Taking the Revolution Inside*, edited by Christina Kiaer and Eric Naiman, 35-60. Bloomington: Indiana University Press, 2006.

------. *How the Soviet Man Was Unmade: Cultural Fantasy and Male Subjectivity Under Stalin*. Pittsburgh: University of Pittsburgh Press, 2008.

Kenez, Peter. *Cinema and Soviet Society: From the Revolution to the Death of Stalin*. London: I.B. Tauris, 2001.

Miller, Jamie. "The Purges of Soviet Cinema, 1929-38." *Studies in Russian and Soviet Cinema* 1, no. 1 (2007): 5-26.

------. *Soviet Cinema: Politics and Persuasion under Stalin*. London: I.B. Tauris, 2010.

Petrone, Karen. *Life Has Become More Joyous, Comrades: Celebrations in the Time of Stalin*. Bloomington: Indiana University Press, 2000.

Robin, Régine. *Socialist Realism: An Impossible Aesthetic*. Translated by Catherine Porter. Stanford: Stanford University Press, 1992.

Taylor, Richard, and Derek Spring, eds. *Stalinism and Soviet Cinema*. New York: Routledge, 1993.

Youngblood, Denise, and Tony Shaw, eds. *Cinematic Cold War: The American and Soviet Struggle for Hearts and Minds*. Lawrence: University Press of Kansas, 2010.

Yurchak, Aleksei. *Everything Was Forever, Until It Was No More: The Last Soviet Generation*. Princeton: Princeton University Press, 2005.

Zubkova, Elena. *Russia After the War: Hopes, Illusions, and Disappointments, 1945-1957*. Translated and edited by Hugh Ragsdale. Armonk, NY: M.E. Sharpe, 1998.

CHAPAEV

1934 (restored 1963, 2005)

95 minutes

Director: **The Vasil'ev Brothers**

Co-director: **Iurii Muzykant**

Screenplay: **The Vasil'ev Brothers**

Cinematography: **Aleksandr Sigaev, Aleksandr Ksenofontov**

Art Design: **Isaak Makhlis**

Composer: **Gavriil Popov**

Sound: **Aleksandr Bekker**

Production Company: **Lenfilm**

Cast: **Boris Babochkin (Chapaev), Leonid Kmit (Pet'ka), Varvara Miasnikova (An'ka), Boris Blinov (Furmanov), Illarion Pevtsov (White Army Colonel Borozdin), Stepan Shkurat (Potapych, Borozdin's orderly), Boris Chirkov (bearded peasant), Viacheslav Volkov (Elan'), Nikolai Simonov (Zhikharev), Georgii Vasil'ev (White Army lieutenant)**

The directors Georgii and Sergei Vasil'ev (1899-1946 and 1900-1959) were unrelated, but lifelong collaborators who styled themselves the Vasil'ev brothers. For both Vasil'evs, years of reediting foreign films laid the foundation for their craftsmanship as directors and, during the late twenties, they also studied in Eisenstein's film workshop. In 1928 they edited the documentary film *Heroic Deed in the Ice (Podvig vo l'dakh)* about the rescue of Umberto Nobile's airship by Soviet icebreakers. Its success helped them obtain their first directing assignments, *Sleeping Beauty* (1930) and *Personnel File* (or *A Personal Matter, Lichnoe delo,* 1932). In 1934 they shot *Chapaev*, which received a Grand Prix at the 1937 Paris Exhibition and was recognized as the iconic film of Socialist Realism, their only lasting contribution to the history of Russian cinema. The Vasil'evs' subsequent films were conventional monumental battlefield conflicts. After Georgii Vasil'ev's death, Sergei Vasil'ev, then executive director of Lenfilm Studio, directed a solo film, *Heroes of Shipka* (*Geroi Shipki*, 1954), which won him best director at Cannes.

Chapaev

A Red Army division commanded by Vasilii Chapaev is fighting White Army troops, led by Colonel Borozdin, in a region near the Urals. When political commissar Furmanov is sent to the division, he is initially greeted with mistrust by the hot-tempered peasant commander but gradually earns his respect. The story of Chapaev's adjutant Pet'ka and the machine-gunner An'ka provides the love interest of the film. Chapaev's men turn back White Army troops who attempt a "psychological attack," but the following autumn Chapaev's headquarters are attacked at night by Borozdin's men and the mortally wounded Chapaev disappears in the Ural River—a force of nature returns to its source. Chapaev's brigade commander, Elan', leads a counterattack which defeats the Whites. Chapaev's death is avenged by the second ending, a resounding explosion that victoriously eradicates the enemy troops.

The film is structured in two parts, separated by the climactic attack of White officers (the Kappelevtsy), An'ka's heroic stand and the Red victory. The first half of the film is concerned with psychological conflicts which develop strategically—along a positive vector for Chapaev and Furmanov, and spiraling downward for their enemy, Colonel Borozdin. Chapaev is initially dominant—ironic toward Furmanov (their first conversation on the bridge), an able strategist and brave commander (the potato scene). But his weaknesses soon emerge—a hot temper, ignorance, physical violence and unmilitary dress: Chapaev cannot understand why a peasant veterinarian cannot be automatically certified as a medical doctor, almost throws a chair at Furmanov, and is scolded by him for sloppy dress which sets a poor example for the troops. The conflict between Chapaev and Furmanov peaks as the commissar forbids looting food from the peasants and orders the arrest of

Zhikharev, one of Chapaev's commanders. When a peasant comes to thank him for returning the stolen animals, Chapaev sees the light and converts to Furmanov's position. Further (comic) testing of political knowledge by a peasant and Furmanov reveals Chapaev's ignorance, but he still triumphs through native intelligence, and even scolds Pet'ka for his careless dress. By the end of part one, Furmanov and Chapaev are firm allies and both are confident in their respective abilities: with the masculine swagger of a coat thrown over his shoulders, Furmanov, who was formerly shaky on military strategy, can now deal with sentries and answer Chapaev's "What does the commissar think?" When Pet'ka asks Chapaev about his abilities, Chapaev acknowledges that he is capable of commanding regional and even national armies. An'ka and Pet'ka's initial screwball comedy sparring develops into his ritual testing by entering enemy territory to capture a "tongue" and her initiation in battle, both of which resolve themselves successfully in harmonious love at the end of part one as Pet'ka offers An'ka an egg, the promise of their future life together.

Colonel Borozdin first appears as a sympathetic, fatherly figure in his affection for his orderly, Potapych, who repays him with complete loyalty: Borozdin has no need to watch his back in battles. But the Colonel shows himself to be a false father when, for appearance's sake, he is unable to bring himself to save Potapych's brother in the presence of another official. Borozdin is completely discredited by the end of part one: he plays the "Moonlight Sonata" with feeling, while Potapych, grieving over his dead brother, waxes the floor. The film now uses diegetic sound symbolically: Potapych "shoots" the Colonel in the back through the sound of a falling brush, while Borozdin shoots back by banging down the lid of the piano.

Furmanov's departure at the beginning of part two, accompanied by a folk song about a son's suicide, signals the downward momentum of Chapaev's life. In a fatal mistake he ignores the new commissar's advice to post additional sentries, which allows the Whites to successfully carry out a night attack. A melancholy folk song ("Chernyi voron," "The Black Raven") enters the film before the first battle; additional melodies in the same register

pervade the second half of the film, as it moves toward a tragic ending.

As ideologically correct action film with snappy dialogue and folksy humor, *Chapaev* soon became the iconic socialist realist cinematic work that also appealed to a broad audience, including even the anti-Soviet poet Osip Mandel'shtam and the unsocialist director Andrei Tarkovsky.[1] *Chapaev* also reintroduced the individual hero to Russian cinema—another factor in its popularity with audiences— initiating a counter-tradition to the masses as hero, familiar from 1920s Soviet films, such as Eisenstein's *Potemkin*.[2] Impulsive, temperamental, yet naturally gifted, Vasilii Chapaev embodies the socialist realist paradigm as he develops from spontaneity to Bolshevik consciousness under the guidance of his party mentor, Furmanov. Socialist Realism is also strongly future-oriented: before the final battle Chapaev talks to Pet'ka and An'ka about the happiness awaiting them, a life such that no one will want to die. Although Chapaev does die, the demise of a socialist realist hero serves only to inspire others.

The Vasil'ev Brothers also constructed Chapaev as an epic folk hero of the *bylina* tales: brave, generous, resourceful and somewhat infantile. As a character, Chapaev is alternately heroic and comic. While dedicated to Soviet power, he is nevertheless something of a subversive hero, another possible source of his popularity. Like the cunning peasant who outwits his master, Chapaev may be defeated in argument, surpassed in book knowledge or scolded by the commissar, but always saves face through his native wit. Initially Chapaev is distressed that he knows nothing about Alexander the Great as a great military leader. But in response to Furmanov's criticism of his unmilitary dress, Chapaev parries good-naturedly:

---

[1]   Julian Graffy, *Chapaev* (London-New York: I.B. Tauris, 2010), 79-81, 93-4. On Socialist Realism, see Evgeny Dobrenko, "Socialist Realism," in Evgeny Dobrenko and Marina Balina, eds., *The Cambridge Companion to Twentieth-Century Russian Literature* (Cambridge: Cambridge University Press, 2011), 97-113.

[2]   Evgeny Dobrenko, "Creation Myth and Myth Creation in Stalinist Cinema," *Studies in Russian and Soviet Cinema* 1, no. 3 (2007): 242-43.

"So Alexander the Great fought in white gloves—eh?" Furmanov responds that Alexander didn't walk around looking like a bum, but Chapaev counters: "And how do you know? Two thousand years ago…" When the commissar, obviously feeling superior, jokingly tests Chapaev by asking whether he is for the Second or Third International, Chapaev (who does not know the difference) inquires: "Which one was Lenin in?" "The Third," answers Furmanov. "Well then, I'm for the Third too!"[3]

---

[3] Evgeny Dobrenko points out that the cinematic—and legendary—Chapaev appeared at the time the history of the Civil War was being rewritten to exclude its heroes, such as Tukhachevskii, Egorov and Uborevich, who were being replaced by popular heroes, "natural talents" who had never graduated from a military academy: "Strictly speaking, there was no legend [of Chapaev] before the fantastic success of the film (although there was an ideological demand for it). Even the creators of the film themselves spoke of this: "The hero of the picture is the legendary Chapaev. Few people know about him. What he was like in actual fact almost nobody knows." (Brat'ia Vasil'evy, "'Chapaev' Furmanova i 'Chapaev' na ekrane," 139, in *Sobranie sochinenii v 3 tomakh*, ed. V.E. Baskakov et al., vol. 2 [Moscow: Iskusstvo, 1982]). […] Meanwhile, "historical reality" was the most important constituent part of the film. It is precisely *Chapaev* that is linked with the famous episode that sheds light on Stalin's conception of "historical truth" (and, generally speaking, of truth in Socialist Realism): when the film was shown to members of Chapaev's family and his comrades-in-arms, they expressed their disapproval and declared that nothing in the film really happened like that, and that Chapaev had borne no resemblance to how he was depicted. However, when Stalin saw the film, having been given the views of Chapaev's comrades and family, he replied with the sacramental phrase: "They're lying, like eyewitnesses." An entire aesthetic programme was derived from this. "Similitude" became one of the main problems in biographical films, because the main question here concerned the limits of historical myth. The directors had to emphasize the "truthfulness of the picture": "having rejected narrow biography [biografichnost'], we were brought to a more complete realization of the true features of Chapaev through an entire artistic process. His son and daughter, having watched the film, recognized their father in it—only after several viewings!" (G. and S. Vasil'evy, "Zametki k postanovke," 59, in *Chapaev* [Moscow: Kinofotoizdat, 1935]). (Dobrenko, 247-48).

CHAPAEV

Steven Hutchings

Chapaev is perhaps the most famous, and certainly one of the most influential, films of the Soviet period. Like its hero—whose reputation owes much to the film—it achieved a cult status soon after it was released that it has never really lost. Images from the film such as Chapaev on his white horse, and Chapaev demonstrating battle tactics using potatoes, are now imprinted in Russian cultural memory. Generations of Soviet children played at "Chapaev" just as American children played at "Cowboys and Indians." […]

Chapaev is based on Dmitrii Furmanov's (1891-1926) autobiographical novel, set in the period of the Civil War which raged in Russia between 1919 and 1921. Furmanov draws heavily on the diary that he kept whilst serving as a political commissar for the Communist Party, amongst relatively undisciplined, peasant-led elements of the Red Army. Furmanov gives himself the name Fedor Klychkov to signal the pseudo-documentary status of his text, but Chapaev himself, who actually existed and whose historical role was not dissimilar to that attributed to him by Furmanov, appears under his own name. As one might expect of a text based on diary entries, Furmanov's novel is highly episodic in nature, lacks a clear plot line and is punctuated with extracts from factual documents. The plot, such as it is, tells of Klychkov's initial awe and fascination before the legendary ataman and his gradual assertion of party authority and values over the recalcitrant Chapaev, whose outbursts of spontaneous voluntarism (*stikhiinost'*) diminish as the novel wears on. Klychkov's enchantment decreases as his function as a literate observer, consciously organising what he sees, increases. The narrative degenerates into a series of sketches, ever more reliant on the use of hindsight—the enwrapping of Chapaev's image as a figure from the past in the light of his significance for the post-Civil War present. […]

The film traces a more definitive path than the novel from Chapaev as unenlightened, impulsive peasant leader to Chapaev as disciplined Bolshevik commander, and by the end of the film the Vasil'evs portray the peasant commander more or less uncritically as an (albeit still unsophisticated) hero of mythic proportions — precisely the attitude that Furmanov set out to question. [...]

In reinforcing the Party's role (the film's task is not just to adapt Furmanov's novel, but to "adopt" it into the socialist realist canon), the Vasil'ev brothers depict Furmanov (Klychkov) rather than Chapaev solving the looting crisis. This sequence is emblematic of the ideological work carried out by the film as a whole and repays closer attention. It begins with shots of a bemused peasant who, having been robbed of his livestock by marauding Chapaev soldiers, complains that the Reds and the Whites are all the same. The leader of the looters (one of Chapaev's most trusted men) is subsequently arrested by a suitably stern and authoritative Furmanov, who orders the looted goods to be returned. When he learns of the arrest of his trusted lieutenant, Chapaev explodes with anger, accusing Furmanov of being a bureaucratic Party paper-pusher, to which Furmanov retorts by reminding Chapaev that he, too, is a servant of the Party. Chapaev remains stubbornly resistant to the notion of Party discipline and to acknowledging the impropriety of his mens' actions until a small group of peasants come to him and mistakenly thank him instead of Furmanov for righting the wrong done to them. At this point Chapaev undergoes a radical and permanent transformation conveyed dramatically through a facial close-up highlighting his "moment of truth." [...] Chapaev immediately calls all his men to a meeting and gives his admonitory speech (lifted word for word from the novel), in which he describes the looters as "a disgrace to the Red Army." He is shot admiringly from below, with Furmanov sitting silently and inconspicuously in the audience, rather than actively interpreting the event through his verbal narration. Visual gesture becomes the outer manifestation of the inner Party truth, which remains unseen, silent, but forever present. Rather than contradicting inner truth, visual surface, with all its excesses, becomes that truth's ideal expression.

This filmic desire for a coincidence of inner truth and outer gesture is apparent also in the rendition of Furmanov's depiction of the peasantry's long "coming to knowledge," compressed here into sudden revelations. The decision of the White servant to switch allegiance is identified with the precise moment when he realises that the General bears responsibility for his brother's fate. The camera once again focuses on the peasant's face to capture the moment of inner truth made available for public scrutiny. The very impulsiveness critiqued by Furmanov in his novel provides the mechanism by which its cinematic representation is achieved. In another transformative gesture with ideological consequences, the novelistic hindsight framing Chapaev's death is translated into a musical soundtrack dominated by the mournful tones of the "Black Raven" folksong. The enwrapping of emotive image by rational word is replaced by a mystic fusion of word and image in which Chapaev becomes a fated, mythic figure. Far from undermining the Party's underlying truth, Chapaev's folksy eccentricities confirm that truth and, contrary to the novel's intention, remove him from time. The "Black Raven" theme also confirms that the film is an embodiment of the official folklore that accumulated around Chapaev following the publication of Furmanov's novel, assimilating novel to legend and allowing the portrayal of Furmanov besides the fictionalised figures of Pet'ka and An'ka. [...]

No discussion of *Chapaev* can be left without reference to the enduring fate of its intrepid hero beyond the year of its release. The film served initially to cement and augment the hero's cult status. Buildings, streets, battleships and even small towns were renamed after Chapaev. He became an object of reverence within the artificially manufactured Stalinist folklore documented by Frank Miller. World War Two even saw the release of a short film sequel: *Chapaev s nami* (*Chapaev is with Us*, 1941), directed by Vladimir Petrov, in which Chapaev makes it to the other side of the Ural river and returns to aid the Soviet war effort. But it was, ironically, the very public visibility and mythic abstraction of the hero dominating the 1934 film which generated the hero's subversive, post-Stalinist hypostasis. This subversion was the price to be paid by Stalinist ideology for the constructing of such inflated abstractions. Much of the cinematic Chapaev's humour is directed against the lack of practical know-how characteristic of the much-derided bureaucratic intellectual. In the context of Stalinist efforts to undermine the status of the *intelligent*, the presence of such humour in the Vasil'ev brothers' film is understandable. (The fact that it sits uneasily with their counter emphasis on the principles of Party-mindedness is one of many tensions with which viewers must engage.) In the political jokes *(anekdoty)* which circulated in the 1960s and 1970s, the humour is inverted since the addressee of the typical Chapaev joke is precisely the knowing intellectual (by now replete with dissident tendencies) who mocks the naïve beliefs and impossible feats of the unwitting socialist hero. In a post-Soviet twist to the Chapaev story, and to his peregrinations from text to oral culture to film and back, the anecdotes provided the basis for Viktor Pelevin's novel *Chapaev i Pustota (Chapaev and Pustota,* 1996) in which the characters of the anecdotes find themselves entangled in a web of absurd plot lines involving post-Soviet businessmen, eastern mystics, western popular icons, as well as the heroes of the 1934 version of *Chapaev.* [...]

Chapaev lives on, too, thanks to the nostalgic Soviet "retro-culture" which has insinuated itself into post-Soviet society at a number of levels; newly published books of Chapaev jokes coexist with websites devoted to (sometimes scatalogically, sometimes affectionately) humorous visual and verbal caricatures of the legendary hero and his two eternal sidekicks, Pet'ka and An'ka. And there now even exists a web-based computer game based around the comic exploits of the Chapaev and Pet'ka of the anecdote genre: "Pet'ka and VICH Save the Galaxy." Chapaev, it would seem, is as much a man for all media as he is a man for all seasons.

REFERENCES

Crofts, S. (1977). "Ideology and Form: Soviet Socialist Realism and *Chapaev.*" *Essays in Poetics* 2, no. 1, 43-57.

Ferro, M. (1976). "The Fiction Film and Historical Analysis," in P. Smith (ed.), *The Historian and Film*, 80-95. Cambridge: Cambridge University Press.

Furmanov, D. (1966). *Chapaev.* Moscow: Detskaia literatura.

Hicks, J. (2005). "Educating Chapaev: From Document to Myth," in S. Hutchings and A. Vernitski (eds) *Russian and Soviet Film Adaptations of Literature, 1900-2001: Screening the Word*, 43-58. London: RoutledgeCurzon.

Leyda, J. (1960). *Kino: A History of the Russian and Soviet Film.* Princeton: Princeton University Press.

Shumiatskii, B. (1988 [1935]). "A Cinema for the Millions (extracts)," in R. Taylor and I. Christie (eds) *Inside the Film Factory: Russian and Soviet Cinema in Documents 1896-1939*, 358-69. London and New York: Routledge.

Zorkaya, N. (1991). *The Illustrated History of Soviet Cinema.* New York: Hippocrene Books.

THE ELEMENTS AND CONSCIOUSNESS: THE COMMANDER AND THE COMMISSAR

Oksana Bulgakova

Chapaev belongs among the "folkloric," "vulgar" heroes and his bodily manifestations, as well as his language and way of dressing, are topics in this Civil War film. In several scenes he knows how to use the correct oratorical gestures of the sovereign (the right hand extended forward or raised upward), but in most scenes he violates the "correct" code of behavior and is educated by his commissar Furmanov who, although a civilian (a worker-communist), is given a more severe military bearing than the White officers of the film.

Chapaev acts in seventeen episodes of the film, four of which are battle scenes, three are his speeches addressed to his men, the peasants and the rebellious anarchists, and the rest are scenes with Furmanov (six episodes) and four with his adjutant, Pet'ka. It is already clear from the numerical distribution that the story of Furmanov and Chapaev's relations is at the center of the film. Their confrontation may be represented not only in the ordinary opposition "the elements vs. consciousness," but also as a confrontation of the masculine (discipline, state, notions of law, history, culture, hierarchy, ideology) and the feminine (biological, anarchic, nature, emotions etc.). The masses of unorganized fighters represent the feminine, hysterical element; their leader — the masculine element. Chapaev is the hero-mediator between the masculine and feminine, culture-nature, order-anarchy and so on. In scenes with the fighters, peasants and Pet'ka, he represents the masculine element of order and discipline; in scenes with Furmanov (the representative of higher knowledge—ideology and the Party, the higher form of organization), he emerges as the feminine element. Here he is provided with all the characteristics of the hysterical, spontaneous, biological hero. This fluctuation between the masculine and feminine, anarchy and order, is underscored by his clothing and bodily costume. In scenes with

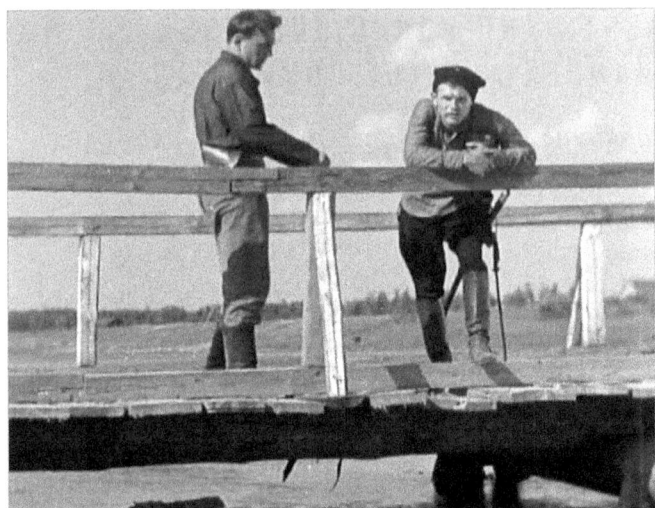

Fig. 68.
Furmanov
and Chapaev

the fighters, Chapaev appears in a military uniform. In the scenes with Furmanov, he is in his underwear, without a belt. During his hysterical fit (the argument with Furmanov about the arrested fighter), he begins to undress. The peasants don't recognize him as the commander, leading Furmanov to suggest he pay attention to his clothing. In the death scene Chapaev combines feminine (white underclothes) and masculine attributes (field pants, black boots) in his costume. In the scenes with his men, he dominates over the elemental "savages" as the masculine element of order and law; in the scenes with Furmanov, he is neurotic and submits to a stronger masculine will. In the first battle scene, when he stops the panicking deserters and in the scene of the anarchists' rebellion, Chapaev enters from the upper right edge of the frame moving from right to left and rising above the disorderly crowd moving in the lower left area of the frame, which corresponds to the accepted iconography (right is masculine, left—feminine; the upper part is divine, the lower—biological).[1]

---

[1]   These oppositions are analyzed in detail by Sergei Dobrotvorskii, who inscribes them into the Freudian paradigm of the male leader and female, neurotic crowd (Sergei Dobrotvorskii, "Fil'm 'Chapaev': opyt strukturirovaniia total'nogo realizma," *Iskusstvo kino* 11 [1992]: 22-28).

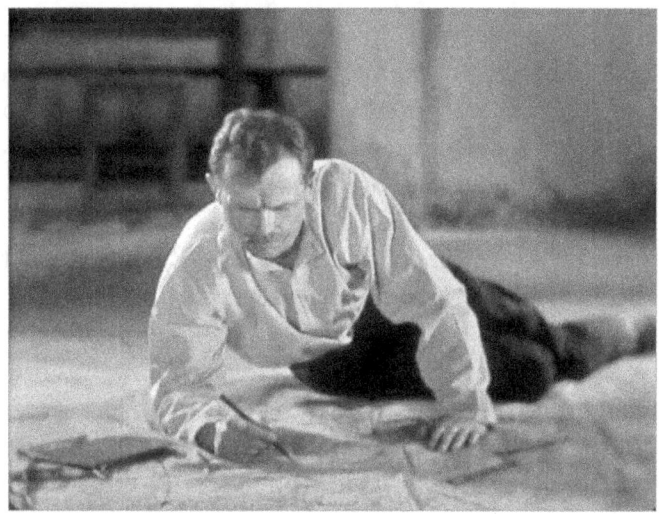

Fig. 69.
Chapaev
Plans Strategy

As the vitalist hero of the twenties, Chapaev moves impetuously, and stands and sits in an overly free and easy way. Already in the second scene of the film—right after the suppression of the deserters—he does not stand like a military man, but instead lounges, leaning on the railings of the bridge with one leg in front (Fig. 68). The commander's careless pose contrasts with the military bearing of the civilian Furmanov who is embarrassed by his "formality" and immediately imitates Chapaev's pose in order to establish contact with him.

In most scenes Chapaev is either lying down or sits in a half prone position (twice before the attack, twice in conversation with Pet'ka, Fig. 69). But unlike the immobile sovereign or the "Buddhist" Kutuzov, he is hysterical, like the proletarian (decadent) hero of the early twenties. He is even more high-strung than the hysterical intelligentsia doctors, who produce an unbelievable number of chaotic gestures. He bangs his fist on the table, crashes a stool against the floor, tears his shirt, undresses and throws his hat and sword on the floor, and grabs for his revolver in a fit of anger. The same hysterics characterize his army's warriors: in the scene of the psychological attack, one tears his striped sailor shirt and Anka rips off her hat and tears her hair.

247

Chapaev is physiologically vulgar, like the naturalistic hero, the hero from the common people, like an ill-mannered peasant. He munches noisily, throws gnawed scraps of food on the floor, drinks tea from a saucer, scratches the back of his head, his stomach or chest, touches his body, fidgets with his hand, waves his arms, insists on body contact, and claps a woman on the shoulder as he would one of his men. In his first speech, directed at the peasants, he gestures with his left hand, shakes his finger, pounds his chest, and straightens his back only toward the end of the speech (and here he uses the lifted right hand) that is, demonstrates the body language of an orator from the common people who lacks a sense of the norm. But the spontaneous manifestations of temperament are subjugated to discipline, and the oratorical gestures of the commander change. In the speech to the rebellious anarchists, where Chapaev resurrects the old concepts of retribution, blood revenge and patriotism, he does not violate the established oratorical code (straight back, shoulders thrown back, immobile torso, and gestures with the right hand only, which doesn't rise above shoulder level), while his antithesis, the anarchist, uses the gestures of a bourgeois hysteric with hands spread wide in an arc. [...]

The most disciplined and civilized figure in the partisan army is the civilian communist. Commissar Furmanov's gestures are extremely restrained: he smokes a pipe that restricts the movements of his hands (and truncates gesticulation, like Peter the Great's or Stalin's). He stands with a military greatcoat thrown over one shoulder, which fetters shoulder and back movement. Consequently, he makes no motions, but the position he occupies within the frame is significant. If Chapaev sits (on a map, chair, stool etc.), the commissar stands; if Chapaev half-reclines, he sits. When Chapaev sits down, he stands up. He is always ensured spatial "superiority" and domination over the hero, who is placed lower or seated. The civilian commander teaches the partisan commander military bearing, frontline discipline and self-control.

FURTHER READING

Dobrotvorskii, Sergei. "Fil'm 'Chapaev': opyt strukturirovaniia total'nogo realizma." *Iskusstvo kino* 11 (1992): 22-28.

Ferro, Marc. See above, Hutchings, "Chapaev," References.

Furmanov, Dmitrii. *Chapayev.* Translated by George Kittell and Jeanette Kittel. Moscow: Foreign Languages Publishing House, n. d.

Graffy, Julian. *Chapaev.* London-NY: I.B. Tauris, 2010. [This is the most comprehensive book on the film.]

Haynes, John. *New Soviet Man: Gender and Masculinity in Stalinist Soviet Cinema.* Manchester: Manchester University Press, 2003.

Hicks, Jeremy. See above, Hutchings, "*Chapaev*," References.

Pliukhanova, Mariia. "'Chapaev' v svete estetiki protiazhnykh pesen." In *Ot slov k telu*, edited by Aleksandr Lavrov et al., 260-72. Moscow: NLO, 2010.

Vasil'ev, Sergei. "Beseda v Gosudarstvennom institute kinematografii." In Brat'ia Vasil'evy, *Sobranie sochinenii v 3 tomakh*, edited by V.E. Baskakov et al., 143-63. Moscow: Iskusstvo, 1982.

CIRCUS

Tsirk

1936 (restored 1970)

94 minutes

Director: **Grigorii Aleksandrov**

Screenplay: **Grigorii Aleksandrov with Il'ia Il'f, Evgenii Petrov, Valentin Kataev**

Cinematography: **Vladimir Nil'sen, Boris Petrov, Boris Aretskii**

Art Design: **Georgii Grivtsov**

Composer: **Isaak Dunaevskii**

Lyricist: **Vasilii Lebedev-Kumach**

Sound: **Nikolai Timartsev**

Production Company: **Mosfilm**

Cast: **Liubov' Orlova (Marion Dixon), Sergei Stoliarov (Ivan Martynov), Pavel Massal'skii (Franz von Kneischitz), Vladimir Volodin (Liudvig Osipovich, the circus director), Evgeniia Mel'nikova (Raechka), Aleksandr Komissarov (Skameikin), James Patterson (Jimmy), Solomon Mikhoels, Lev Sverdlin, Pavel Geraga, Robert Ross in the "International Lullaby" episode**

Grigorii Aleksandrov (born Mormonenko, 1903-83) began his Moscow career acting in Eisenstein's theatrical productions and moved with him into cinema, becoming the most important member of the "Iron Five," Eisenstein's group of assistants. Aleksandrov helped with the scripts of *Strike* and *Potemkin*, in which he played Lt. Giliarovskii, and co-directed *October* and *The Old and the New*. He travelled abroad with Eisenstein and Eduard

Tisse during 1929-32, primarily studying American filmmaking, and assisted Eisenstein with his ill-fated *Que Viva México!* Upon returning to Russia in 1932, Aleksandrov felt the need to build a career separate from Eisenstein and accepted an offer from Boris Shumiatskii, the head of the Soviet film industry, to make a musical comedy film. The enormously popular *Happy Guys* (*Veselye rebiata*, also known as *Jolly Fellows*, 1934), which starred Aleksandrov's second wife, Liubov' Orlova, and marked the beginning of his collaboration with the masters of Soviet mass song, Isaak Dunaevskii and Vasilii Lebedev-Kumach, was followed by *Circus* (1936), *Volga-Volga* (1938), *The Radiant Path* (*Svetlyi put'*, 1940), and *Spring* (*Vesna*, 1947), making him one of the most successful Soviet directors. *Meeting on the Elbe* (*Vstrecha na El'be*, 1949), a Cold War spy flick, starring Orlova as an American agent, was his last moderately successful feature film. In spite of his gift for musical comedy, his technical expertise and organizational talents, Aleksandrov was so thoroughly a conformist product of the Stalin era that he was never able to adjust to the new themes and approaches of the 1960s-70s, and his cinematic career went into decline. Two attempted comebacks, the comedy *Russian Souvenir* (*Russkii suvenir*, 1960) and the spy tale *Starling and Lyre* (*Skvorets i Lira*, completed in 1974 but not released at the time) failed completely. Aleksandrov taught at the State Film Institute from 1950-57 and in the Literature and Art Department of the Central Committee's Academy of Social Sciences beginning in 1955, also serving on various committees for friendship with foreign countries, enabling him and Orlova to travel abroad regularly as representatives of the Soviet film establishment. Aleksandrov died several months after completing his last project, the script for the documentary film *Liubov' Orlova* (1983).

CIRCUS: THE SPECTACLE OF IDEOLOGY

Rimgaila Salys

The plot of *Circus* is based on Il'f and Petrov's play *Under the Big Top* (*Pod kupolom tsirka*), which Aleksandrov saw at the Moscow Music Hall, quickly deciding on a film adaptation as his next project. The director transformed Il'f and Petrov's comedy about Soviet circus life, which satirized the political fashions of the day, into a musical comedy film with elements of melodrama, embodying the core myths of High Stalinism and the ideals of the new Stalinist constitution: the Soviet New Man, the Great Family, the spontaneity–consciousness paradigm of Socialist Realism, the archetype of the Leader, racial equality, international solidarity of workers, state support for mothers and children. *Circus* was the director's most stylistically imaginative and tightly structured film, largely due to his collaboration with Vladimir Nil'sen, who had just returned from the US with a thorough understanding of American production practices and technology.

In the film Marion Dixon, an American star performing at the Moscow circus, falls in love with Russian performer Ivan Martynov, who introduces her to the values of Soviet society. Franz von Kneischitz, Dixon's abusive manager, tries to foil the romance by implying, through an intercepted letter, that Marion loves the amateur inventor Skameikin, and ultimately attempts to ruin Dixon by revealing her secret: she has an illegitimate mulatto child. However, the Russian circus audience welcomes the child without prejudice, Kneischitz is disgraced and possibly arrested, and Skameikin is reunited with his true love, the circus director's daughter Raechka. Dixon remains in the land of the Soviets, marching with Martynov and the other circus performers in the May Day parade on Red Square.

The circus plot overlays the syntax of the show musical in the film, and combines with elements of the folk musical in its Stalinist iteration. Making a show (the development of the Soviet

circus act "Flight to the Stratosphere") parallels the making of a couple identified with differing cultural and ideological values: the American artiste Marion Dixon and the Soviet performer Ivan Martynov. The secondary couple, one of whom is a rival to the hero or heroine, is also present in Skameikin and Raechka, who both provide comic relief and function as temporary impediments to the successful making of the show (Raechka's weight gain causes the failure of the Soviet act in rehearsal) and the successful outcome of the primary love affair (Skameikin's infatuation with Dixon). Liudvig Osipovich, the circus director and Raechka's father, fulfills the traditional senex role—the crusty but well-meaning establishment figure who is initially hostile to the primary romantic couple for financial reasons. Elements of the folk musical, in which the making of the couple parallels the formation of a community at the local and national levels, enter the plot as Martynov teaches Marion the "Song of the Motherland," realizing through a song rather than a kiss both the couple's declaration of love and patriotic devotion to the USSR. The musical's traditional dual focus on the male and female leads is diminished in *Circus* because Liubov' Orlova, the preeminent movie star of the Stalin era, is the narrative focus of the film. Nevertheless, the dual focus manifests itself in secondary oppositions: the homegrown hero vs a foreign heroine; communist vs. capitalist ideologies; Martynov's ethic of socialist collectivity vs. Dixon's focus on individual life experiences; social stability and order vs. chaotic passions and deviation from conventional norms of morality (Dixon's past). The American folk musical paradigm of the wandering male who is tamed by the civilizing female and endows the community with his energy and spirit is reversed as Marion Dixon abandons her peripatetic ways and endows the concluding communal celebration, the May Day parade, with *her* energy. Like the American folk musical, *Circus* concludes with the reconciliation of the opposing values attached to the primary couple through their successful union, accompanied by the reaffirmation of patriotism and community.[1]

---

[1]   Critics have pointed to Ernst Lubitsch's *Ninochka* (1939), in which a Soviet

[…] The circus as a metaphor/microcosm of the world has a long pedigree in cinema, including Chaplin's *The Circus* (1927) and Tod Browning's *Freaks* (1932), through Fellini's circus films and Wim Wenders' *Wings of Desire*. Aleksandrov borrowed the enslaved heroine motif from Chaplin's film, in which the father is the villain, as well as several comic routines. In one of these, Charlie enters the lion cage by mistake; to impress the girl, he later braves another lion, but is then frightened by a kitten. Skameikin finds himself in the lions' cage by mistake, but the new lion tamer later faints at the barking of the Captain's terrier. Charlie knocks out a rival and kicks sawdust all over him. Skameikin pistol-whips the lions with a bouquet of roses and then shows dominance by kicking sawdust at them. Aleksandrov actualizes the circus-world metaphor at the beginning of the film through the emblem of the Southern Railway car on which Marion escapes the Sunnyville lynch mob. The globe displaying the United States spins to reveal the landmass of the USSR and then descends to a Soviet circus arena to enter the performance: a seal balances the globe on its nose, a bear balances on a barrel with the same image, Durov family performers throw the globe to performing dogs and a clown. The change to playful circus music at this point defines the Soviet world as happier and more carefree than the violent American South.

The backstage plot alternates with circus acts, songs, and other performances (Fig. 70) which, through parallel editing, not only guarantee a brisk tempo but just as importantly, mirror and comment on the peripeties of the plot. Marion Dixon's "Flight to the Moon" act[2]—the song and dance on the cannon that propels her

---

KGB agent chooses to remain in Paris after she falls in love with a French aristocrat, as the western response to *Circus*.
(M.Turovskaia, www.svoboda.org/programs/Cicles/Cinema/Circus.asp. [Accessed 7 May 2005]).

[2]   Such acts were popular as far back as Jules Verne's novel *De La Terre à la Lune* (1865) in which the Baltimore Gun Club builds a gigantic cannon which shoots a projectile carrying three men to the moon. In 1902, George Méliès made the first science fiction film, *Le Voyage dans la Lune*, based on the Verne novel and H. G. Wells's *First Men in the Moon* (1901). In the fourteen-minute Méliès feature, astronomers, housed in a giant shell, are launched from

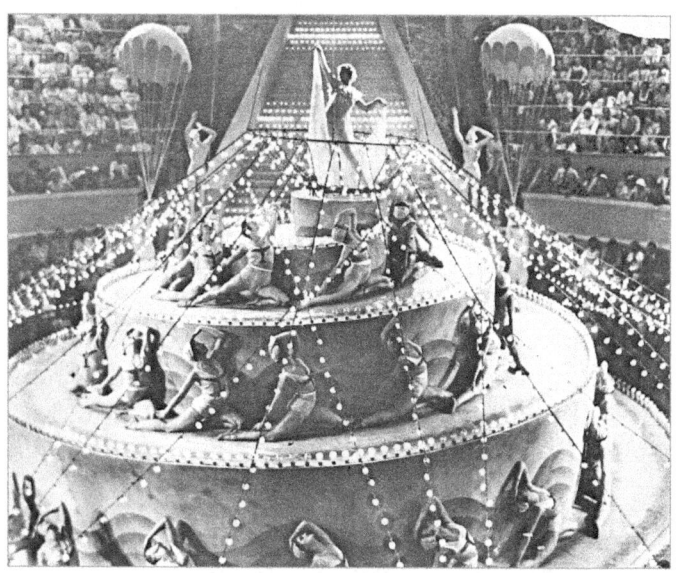

Fig. 70.
Circus
Performance

to the moon, the lyrical "Moon Waltz," and flight around the arena on a trapeze controlled by ropes from the ground—metaphorically rehearses her predicament as objectified female, sexualized and enslaved by patriarchal western culture. Marion-Mary's frenetic jazz song and Charleston atop the cannon appropriate the jerky rhythms of a marionette and, in fact, puppet master Kneischitz not only supervises Marion's circus act—she is announced as performing "under his direction" ("pod rukovodstvom")—but also literally controls the ropes of her trapeze swing throughout the performance. The phallic cannon of sexual transcendence propels Mary to the moon, where she sings a dream of escape from earthly travail and oppression. It is only after the performance that both Marion and Kneischitz reveal their true selves: the fragile, vulnerable blonde under the black vamp wig and the physical weakling and degenerate, screened by a pneumatic chest.[3] At the moment Martynov becomes

---

a cannon to the moon. The film includes a scene of a goddess sitting on the crescent moon.

[3]   According to Rina Zelenaia, she provided the idea for the vest. Zelenaia had used an inflatable bust in a 1920s cabaret act, which she afterward deflated and put in her pocket, to the amusement of fellow actors. Zelenaia related

conscious of his love for Dixon he sprouts cartoon Cupid's wings, and his flying is similarly a metaphor for sexual transcendence. When Fred Astaire teaches Ginger Rogers a set of dance steps, he also teaches her to love and falls in love himself. When Martynov teaches Marion Dixon "Song of the Motherland," he enacts the same paradigm. [...]

The success of the show "Flight to the Stratosphere" parallels the now successful love of the couple, whose cultural values—domestic and foreign, capitalist and communist—have been reconciled. The sexual transcendence of flight is now melded with national transcendence, just as Martynov's cupid wings have been replaced by the wings of Icarus. Dixon and Martynov make their entrance as equals, dressed in unisex aviators' jumpsuits, capes and Flash Gordon helmets, and descend the grand staircase to the rhythm of "Song of the Motherland." Symbols of Soviet air power abound, from propellers on the showgirls' tank tops to their imitation of whirring blades in front of a triangular bank of propellers to the stratospheric rocket itself. The glorification of military might is paradigmatic for the folk musical, as in Busby Berkeley's synchronized marching and flag waving in *Footlight Parade* (1933) and the battleship number of *Born to Dance* (1936). In the Soviet instance, feats of aviation, such as the rescue of the Cheliuskin crew, also signify communication and unity between the center and the marginal areas of the Motherland. [...]

Circus concludes with typical Aleksandrovian multiple finales: the conclusion to the romantic plot with the reunion of Dixon and Martynov, the conclusion to the social narrative in the acceptance of Dixon's black baby by the circus audience, and the conclusion that opens out into the greater (and real) Soviet world of the May Day parade on Red Square. The "International Lullaby" of the second ending, in which Russians, Ukrainians, Jews, an Uzbek, a Georgian, and a black American expatriate participate, is typical

---

the story to Orlova, thereby giving Aleksandrov the idea for the pneumatic vest (G. Skorokhodov, *V poiskakh utrachennogo* [Moscow: Rutena, 2000], 135–36).

of the folk musical's passed- around song that creates community in the localized space of the circus.[4]

Rick Altman argues that the folk musical typically displays a more genuinely evil villain than the show musical, providing a touch of melodrama, along with the reassurance that evil can be overcome.[5] With his racist views on miscegenation (paralleling and alluding to the rise of National Socialism in Germany) and abusive relationship with Dixon, Kneischitz embodies the sociopolitical evils of the bourgeois world. Evil is overcome as his blackmailing of Dixon fails, and he is followed out of the circus by two Soviet policemen. Altman notes that the tragic syntax of the first wave of American musicals (1928–30), initiated by Jolson's *The Singing Fool*, was often expressed by a plot highlighting "the plight of the child caught between quarrelling parents or abandoned by a dissolute mother."[6] In *Circus*, Jimmy is both illegitimate and the victim of racial prejudice: Kneischitz reproaches Dixon with Jimmy's kinky hair, thick lips and flattened nose, and he frightens the child to tears. To Aleksandrov, who could easily have seen the early tragic musicals during his stay in Hollywood, the melodrama of the early scenes of *Circus* may therefore not have seemed as contrary to the laws of the genre as it did to Russian critics of the film.

Aleksandrov's dramatic prologue was intended to justify Dixon's fear of exposure by Kneischitz: Dixon and her black baby barely escape a Southern lynch mob by clambering onto a passing

---

4   The lullaby was performed by Aleksandra Panova, Pavel Geraga, Lev Sverdlin, Solomon Mikhoels, and the American actor Wayland Rudd of the Kamernyi Theatre. Rudd was the most famous African-American actor of the Stalin era. After the assassination of Mikhoels in 1948, his Yiddish lullaby was cut from the film. In 1966, in preparation for the thirtieth anniversary of the release of *Circus*, Aleksandrov located an early print of *Circus* in Czechoslovakia and restored the scene to the film (A.M. Saraeva-Bondar', *Siluety vremeni* [SPb: Lenizdat, 1993], 204).

5   Rick Altman, *The American Film Musical* (Bloomington, IN: Indiana University Press, 1989), 289.

6   Altman, 210.

train.[7] Although she fears the dangers of the "Flight to the Moon" act (illustrated by her use of the ingenious religious makeup kit), Dixon dreads the revelations about her past even more. However, within the body of the film, melodrama turns into farce after Dixon's first conversation with Martynov in the dressing room, and melodramatic motifs are consistently undermined by ironic-comedic treatments.

The animated materialization of Martynov's frosty gaze on the window as he stares angrily at the eavesdropping Kneischitz is a highly aestheticized and not fully serious treatment of the men's rivalry. Warmth pervades Martynov's dressing room, but Martynov's gaze freezes Kneischitz out, excluding him from the space Martynov shares with Dixon. As the window frost melts, the warmth of Martynov's room translates to mild spring weather on Red Square. With his dark hair and mustache, black top hat, long cloak and intense gaze, Kneischitz is as much an inflated image of the melodramatic villain as his pneumatic vest. After setting the intrigue in motion by giving Skameikin Mary's letter, Kneischitz dramatically wraps himself up in his cloak and dissolves into thin air—a parodic comment on the conventional figuration of the cinematic villain. The "performance" of Skameikin's floor fight with Kneischitz over the revolver alternates with circus performance—the pandus production numbers. Moreover, the struggle resolves itself comically as a monkey named "Sniper" shoots off the coveted gun. During the fight, Jimmy stands watching from a corner, but his supposed distress is undermined by the comic pose of the circus animal behind him: a dog sitting upright on its haunches with a rifle over its shoulder. Throughout the film, melodramatic action is repeatedly contravened by secondary images that tell us not to take any of this seriously.

The Chaplin clown in *Circus* functions as both slapstick performer and servant. As a diminished Charlie, he provides only simple physical humor throughout the film (pratfalls, clowning

---

7   The diagonal overhead shot of the running crowd is an Eisensteinian treatment.

with the audience, and cane tricks during the circus act; a collision with a pole when leaping off the train) and serves both Kneischitz and Dixon offstage, pumping up the manager's vest and bringing Dixon her makeup kit. Aleksandrov had met Charlie Chaplin during the early thirties in Hollywood and remained friends with him throughout Chaplin's life, visiting him regularly in Europe during his and Orlova's trips abroad. Throughout his career, Chaplin had struggled with studios over creative and financial control of his work. The Chaplin figure in *Circus* thus embodies Aleksandrov's view of genius in bondage to capitalist society: the timid, quiet Little Tramp of *Circus* is Chaplin himself, the humiliated artist forced to serve the almighty dollar. The diminished Chaplin figure stands in the same economic relation to Kneischitz as Dixon, and the cinematic Little Tramp evokes the same pathos offstage as the abused American circus star. [...]

In *Circus*, the film's composer, Isaak Dunaevskii, formulated the musical model which was to govern his work in cinema for the rest of his career: a central song to be elaborated throughout the film, one that would be popular outside the movie theatre; musical leitmotifs for major characters; extensive use of illustrative music to convey central plot peripeties to the viewer. The musical centerpiece of the film, "Song of the Motherland," with its memorable melody and patriotic message quickly became a second Russian national an-them. During World War II the song preceded announcements of official orders and later, the call sign with which Radio Moscow began its morning broadcasts was the first line of "Song of the Motherland." Aleksandrov's first musical, *Happy Guys*, began with a brilliant jazz overture rather than its famous march. In *Circus* Dunaevskii systematically engraves the central song in audience memory, beginning with the overture. As the movie poster for *Happy Guys* is pasted over with the *Circus* poster, the Mexican-sounding introductory phrase of the "March of the Happy Guys" slips into an instrumental rendering of the line "Where man breathes as freely" ("Tak vol'no dyshit chelovek") from "Song of the Motherland," fol-lowed by a choral rendition of the song accompanying the intro-ductory credits of the film. Although the musical bridge implies continuity between the two projects, the effacing of the visual image

underscores Aleksandrov's abandonment of foreign slapstick comedy for a more serious musical genre in a national register. [...]

Initially, "Song of the Motherland" defines Martynov's happy situation as a Soviet citizen and later comes to represent the same for Marion Dixon. As Martynov faces down—or rather, freezes out—Kneischitz through the window, the "Moon Waltz" modulates into "Song of the Motherland," as sung by Martynov to Mary, signaling the change in her situation from capitalist subservience to Soviet independence ("Man passes as the master," "Chelovek prokhodit, kak khozain"). In the following piano scene, individual love is parsed through love of country, again mediated by the central song. This movement is reinforced visually: as we hear Martynov singing the patriotic song, the camera slowly pulls back from Red Square (the metonymical representation of Motherland) on which three trucks spell out "Mai" in white letters for the May 1 holiday and the same letters appear on the roof of a building near Dixon's hotel. The pattern is repeated as Marion writes her love letter to Martynov while a choral rendition of the first quatrain plays on the soundtrack. "Song of the Motherland" in march tempo accompanies the performers' grand entrance in the Stratosphere act because of the significance of aviation to the State. In the first ending of the film, after Liudvig Osipovich's declaration of welcome for children of all stripes in the USSR, the instrumental "baiu-baiu" of Mary's lullaby on the soundtrack passes into her exalted rendition of "Song of the Motherland," thereby resolving Jimmy's situation by relocating him musically to the Soviet family. As Marion removes her dark wrap to reveal a white sports outfit, a cymbal clap signals (in the manner of a magic show) her transformation to Soviet citizen, and the tempo of "Song of the Motherland," now performed chorally, shifts to that of a military march, which continues to the end of the film.

Circus is also ideological in its conscious construction of masculinity and femininity. While decrying racism, the color significations of the film reinforce white, Northern European stereotypes. The rise of modern European nationalism and notions of bourgeois respectability at the turn of the 18th and 19th centuries was accompanied and complemented by a Greek revival. Like

European masculinities, that of the Stalinist hero derives from the classic ideal of Greek beauty described by J. J. Winckelmann in his *Geshichte der kunst des Altertums* (1774). Supple, muscular and harmonious figures became the symbols of masculinity, the nation and its youth. Like the flag, the national anthem and the official coat of arms, the ideal of classical beauty was co-opted by European nationalisms in an attempt to provide masculine and feminine national stereotypes.[8] According to Winckelmann, a restrained and calm masculinity was naturally connected to national defense: "The quiet and repose of the body reveals the lofty and harmonious spirit of him who braves the greatest dangers for the sake of justice, who provides for his country's defense and brings peace to its subjects."[9] Like the newly rediscovered sculpture of Laocoon, the masculine hero was expected to display calm in the face of unbearable pain.[10]

In *Circus*, Ivan Martynov is figured as precisely this Aryan physical type—tall, muscular, square-jawed and blonde. His first appearance in the film confirms his recent military service and unerring marksmanship. When not performing, he wears uniform garb, a Stalin-style jacket with cavalry trousers and high boots. Whether in public or private space, whether marching in a parade, sitting in a circus loge, or at the piano, Martynov's bearing is military, a return to the pre-revolutionary officer's body language: straight back, expanded chest, and erect torso that does not bend, even when seated.[11] Martynov is calm, self-controlled and a man of few words, all characteristic of the socialist realist hero who has achieved consciousness. His first greeting to the perpetually harried and angry circus director is, "Hello, and let's not be upset." As a circus performer and athlete, his physical prowess is a given. Martynov's profession also serves to underscore his courage: the circus poster Dixon finds on the floor of his former dressing room advertises him

---

8   George L. Mosse, *Nationalism and Sexuality: Respectability and Abnormal Sexuality in Modern Europe* (NY: Howard Fertig, 1985), 16.

9   Wolfgang Lepmann, *Winckelmann*, qtd. in Mosse, 14.

10   Mosse, 14.

11   O. Bulgakova, *Fabrika zhestov* (Moscow: NLO, 2005), 208.

as "the pinnacle of human bravery and courage," and he refuses a safety rope during the rehearsal for the Stratosphere act. His stoic denial of pain and trauma after his fall is yet another demonstration of virility.

The native template for Martynov's masculinity is, of course, the folkloric Russian knight or *bogatyr'*—the super-sized human specimen, protector of the innocent and oppressed, and guardian of the nation's borders who serves to legitimize the Soviet government through historical continuity. Sergei Stoliarov embodied the type so successfully that, as the Stalinist hero merged with the traditional fairy tale hero, he subsequently spent most of his film career as literal *bogatyr'* in the films *Vasilisa the Beautiful* (*Vasilisa prekrasnaia*, 1939), *Kashchei the Immortal* (*Kashchei bessmertnyi*, 1944), *Sadko* (1952), and *Il'ia Muromets* (1956). The swarthy Kneischitz is Martynov's opposite in iconic masculinity: he is physically underdeveloped, nervous, temperamental, and generally out of control, as shown by his shouting and physical abuse of Dixon. These traits in the *German* entrepreneur-villain are precisely those—physical weakness, nervousness, lack of self control—attributed by the National Socialists to Jews and homosexuals.[12]

In the role of Marion Dixon, Liubov' Orlova was able to merge European standards of feminine beauty and glamour (her vaunted resemblance to Marlene Dietrich) with the ideal Soviet heroine. At the beginning of the film, the vamp is Dixon's stage persona and a reminder of her dark past. Offstage and in street clothes, she is an elegant, fashionably dressed and cultured woman—much like period photos of Orlova herself. The sophistication of Orlova's heroine is acceptable not only in a foreigner, but more importantly, as the personification of the ideals of an emerging middle class in Stalinist Russia. Clothes make the (wo)man in *Circus*, for Dixon's transformation into Soviet citizen is marked by changes of costume. In the hotel room episode, Kneischitz throws at Marion, covering

---

12   Mosse, 173. On the foreign "other," see Josephine Woll, "Under the Big Top: America Goes to the Circus," in *Insiders and Outsiders in Russian Cinema*, ed. Stephen Norris and Zara Torlone (Bloomington: Indiana University Press, 2008), 68–80.

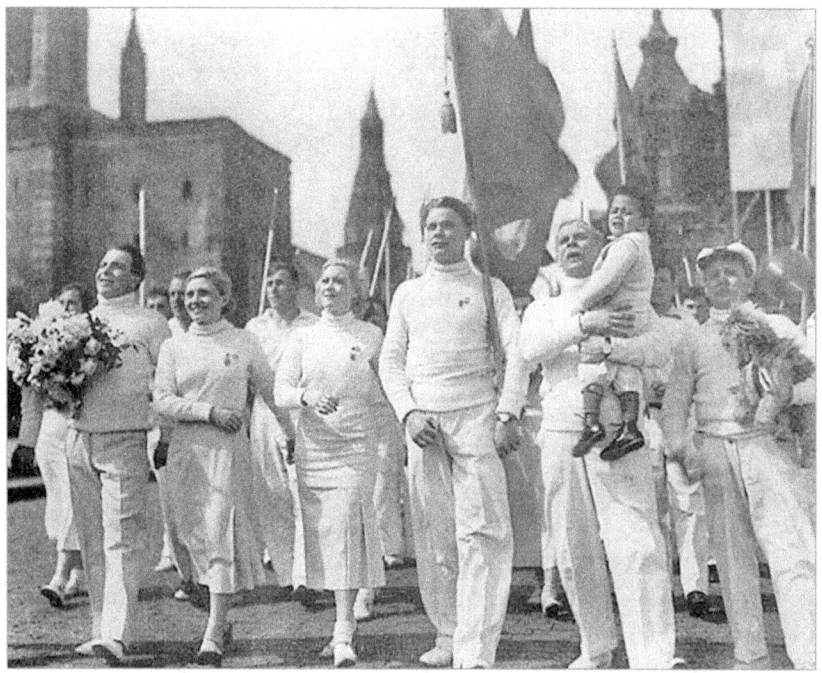

Fig. 71. May Day Parade

her, the expensive gowns and furs with which he has bought her professional cooperation and, most likely, sexual acquiescence. Her transformation begins as she throws off the extravagant clothing exclaiming, "The Mary you knew is no more!" And the bridge between the first finale, which confirms Dixon's place in the Soviet circus family, and the Red Square ending, which confirms her place in the Soviet social hierarchy, is marked by her change into the sports attire of a May Day participant (Fig. 71).

From the outset, in her offstage persona Dixon, as a "good" foreigner, displays some of the traits of the impulsive, straightforward and slightly naïve 1930s Soviet heroine. By nature, she is a kind and sincere woman who generously advises Raechka on the fine points of performance. With Martynov at the piano, she earnestly tries to sing the difficult foreign words of "Song of the Motherland" and later writes a love letter to him on impulse. During her final circus performance she cannot hide her despair at losing him, but naïvely takes no action. Instead, it is the cunning

Raechka who devises the scheme of escaping Kneischitz's clutches. Because Dixon must ultimately become part of the Soviet Great Family, her metamorphosis is mediated through a subcategory of the *femina sovietica*: she is transformed into an energetic, confident *fizkul'turnitsa* (woman athlete).

The body language of foreigner vs. Soviet citizen is contrasted in Dixon's two circus performances. The sinuous body movements, flirtatious blowing of kisses, throwing a rose to an admirer and coquettish hand waving are replaced in the Soviet act by the upraised arm of a military commander or orator, a military salute and synchronized marching down the circus staircase. Marching in the Red Square parade, the body language of both Dixon and Martynov—erect bearing, head thrown back, arms held at the side—displays the restraint of the thirties hero, ultimately modeled on the gravity of the Leader himself.

Kissing, like fanny-slapping, is reserved for the comedic lines of the narrative. The spotlight catches Raechka and Skameikin in the act at the beginning of the film because the plot will chronicle the peripeties of their subsequent misunderstandings. During the piano scene, Martynov pulls away and runs to another room instead of kissing Dixon. When Dixon saves the day by stepping in for Raechka during the performance, the circus director kisses her— but only as part of a standing joke begun earlier with Martynov: "on behalf of the management, on behalf of the *mestkom*, on behalf of the Ministry of Finance." Angry at his daughter's lateness for the premiere of the stratosphere act, the circus director swats Dixon, dressed in Raechka's clothes, on the rear. After Marion's decision to remain in Russia and replace Raechka in the new act, she loosens up and mimics the peasant-vulgarian as *she* swats Liudvig Osipovich in return to get his attention.

For Aleksandrov, the transition from the pomp, pageantry and pathos of the Hollywood musical to the Stalinist grand style and spectacle was a natural one. The successful musical—and especially the folk musical—expresses the ritual values of a society that coincide with the ideological values of the producer, in this case the Soviet State, so that Stalinist myths and their visual elaborations enter *Circus* naturally as a function of the genre. Aleksandrov's

musical was perhaps the first Soviet film to give full and direct expression to the core myths of high Stalinism. Like many socialist realist heroes, Dixon undergoes a painful rite of passage as part of her path to consciousness and incorporation into Soviet society. Her arrival in the Soviet Union may be seen as separation; learning about Soviet society in Moscow under Martynov's tutelage expresses the transition. Dixon suffers initiation, regression into chaos and symbolic death via Kneischitz's public revelations regarding her illicit past. At one point he tells Dixon, "This city has driven you mad!" Madness is not excluded from the near-death experience of the initiate. Traumatized by the public exposure of her past, Dixon runs away from the circus arena and literally faints from shame and horror. By forming a proper family with Martynov, she transforms her formerly illicit and dark sexuality into a healthy, wholesome femininity, figured by the white sweater and skirt of the *fizkul'turnitsa*. She is resurrected into the great Soviet family in the Red Square finale of the film. Her sexual "spontaneity" is first stabilized and made passive within the family unit and then transformed into consciousness and subsumed to the state patriarchy during the second finale.

In a scene intercut with the International Lullaby, Martynov finds Dixon offstage, prostrate in a pile of straw intended for the circus animals (an elephant stands nearby), and carries her back to the arena, cradling her passive figure in his arms. In the first ending, the formation of the private family is simultaneous with acceptance into the multi-ethnic family of the circus audience. Personal integration is then superseded by incorporation into the great Soviet family in the finale as Dixon enters the sacred space of Red Square and participates in a May Day parade. But sacred space is simultaneously real-world space. Through the use of documentary footage, Aleksandrov signals our departure from the fictional world of the musical out into the actual space of the USSR. In formal terms, the device is laid bare through the differing grain of film stock. As a parade participant, Dixon is subsumed to the collective body of the State as figured in the marching masses and choreographed locomotives, Palace of Soviets towers and other human bio-constructs of May Day parades.

In totalitarian societies, both sexual love and its energy (libido) and the incest taboo (mother) are typically sublimated into love of country, which must be protected. During the Red Square finale, the film enacts this paradigm through the figure of Dixon, who is both private mother and lover, as well as the foreigner who has been assimilated to Mother Russia and towards whom Martynov turns as he sings, "We love our Homeland like a bride,/ We protect her like a tender mother." Both visually and melodically, the Red Square finale brings to the foreground the connection between sports and military preparedness. Dressed in athletes' garb, the actors end the film marching and singing, "But our brows will contract in a stern frown/ If any enemy tries to break us." By 1936, the Soviet government was promoting physical culture programs for women, and one of the functions of sports in the Soviet Union was physical fitness for military preparedness.[13]

The repeating comic motif of understanding vs. not understanding, present from the early scenes of the film, is similarly recalibrated as it reaches resolution on Red Square. In the early dressing room scene of *Circus*, Dixon tells Martynov in broken Russian that she doesn't understand the language. He responds that it doesn't matter ("eto nichego"), which will ultimately prove to be true: linguistic incompetence is not an obstacle to esoteric understanding. Subsequently the motif is varied in the personal spheres of work and love relations. As Dixon shows Raechka how to hold herself during a performance, chin up, back straight, she asks: "Do you understand?" When the jealous Raechka repeatedly slaps Skameikin after reading Mary's note, he exclaims, "Raechka, I don't understand—for what?" She slaps him again, asking, "Now do you understand?" and he finally does. During her visit to Dixon's hotel room, Raechka affirms Martynov's love for Dixon: "You are everything, absolutely everything to Martynov, do you understand?" Marion responds ungrammatically in the negative,

---

13   Hoffmann, David L. "Bodies of Knowledge: Physical Culture and the New Soviet Man," in Igal Halfin, *Language and Revolution: Making Modern Political Identities* (London: F. Cass, 2002), 280.

"Ne ponimaesh." Raechka continues, "He loves you, do you understand? Stay, do you understand?" Finally, during the parade on Red Square, Raechka glances up and nods toward the mausoleum as she asks Dixon, "Now do you understand?" Dixon answers in the affirmative, albeit ungrammatically ("Teper' ponimaesh'"), but her linguistic incompetence does not impede true understanding. The motif has been recalibrated from individual apprehension of everyday reality (language and human relations) to a higher, metaphysical level—the understanding of Stalinist discourse by the now ideologically conscious heroine. The leader-godhead toward whom Raechka's words and nod are directed remains unseen, for he preserves sacred status by limiting access to his person in the semi-profane medium of cinema and frivolous musical comedy genre.[14] During the May Day reenactment of revolutionary events in the film, the dead leaders Lenin and Marx are resurrected through their images on flags; Stalin, the living leader, and Klim Voroshilov, People's Commissar for Defense, appear on parade posters, but not in person.

ПЕСНЯ О РОДИНЕ	SONG OF THE MOTHERLAND
От Москвы до самых до окраин,	From Moscow to the very borderlands,
С южных гор до северных морей	From the southern mountains to the northern seas,
Человек проходит как хозяин	Man passes as the master
Необъятной родины своей.	Through his boundless Motherland.
Всюду жизнь и вольно и широко,	Everywhere life flows freely and broadly,
Точно Волга полная, течет.	Like the brimming Volga.
Молодым — везде у нас дорога,	All roads are open here to the young,
Старикам — везде у нас почет,	Everywhere the old are honored.
Припев:	*Refrain:*
Широка страна моя родная,	Broad is my Motherland.
Много в ней лесов, полей и рек.	It has many forests, fields and streams.
Я другой такой страны не знаю,	I know of no other country like it,
Где так вольно дышит человек!	Where man breathes as freely.

---

14   In reality, the May Day demonstration was one of the few public events at which privileged Soviet citizens were able to see and be seen by Stalin and the political elite.

Наши нивы глазом не обшаришь,
Не упомнишь наших городов,
Наше слово гордое — товарищ —
Нам дороже всех красивых слов.
С этим словом мы повсюду дома,
Нет для нас ни черных, ни цветных,
Это слово каждому знакомо,
С ним везде находим мы родных.

Над страной весенний ветер веет,
С каждым днем все радостнее жить,
И никто на свете не умеет
Лучше нас смеяться и любить.
Но сурово брови мы насупим,
Если враг захочет нас сломать, —
Как невесту, Родину мы любим,
Бережем, как ласковую мать.[15]

Your eyes can't take in all our fields,
You can't recall all our cities,
Our proud word—"comrade"
Is dearer to us than any beautiful words.
We're at home everywhere with this word,
For us there are no black or colored races,
This word is familiar to each of us,
With it everywhere we find our own.

A spring wind blows over the land,
With every day life becomes more joyous,
And no one in the world knows how
To laugh and love better than we do.
But our brows we'll contract in a stern frown
If an enemy tries to break us.
We love our homeland like a bride,
We protect her like a tender mother.

FURTHER READING

Dobrotvorskaia, Karina. "'Tsirk' G.V. Aleksandrova." *Iskusstvo kino* 11 (1992): 28-33.

Haynes, John. *New Soviet Man: Gender and Masculinity in Stalinist Soviet Cinema*. Manchester, UK: Manchester University Press, 2003.

Holmgren, Beth. "*The Blue Angel* and Blackface: Redeeming Entertainment in Aleksandrov's *Circus*." *The Russian Review* 66, no. 1 (2007): 5-22.

Salys, Rimgaila. *The Musical Comedy Films of Grigorii Aleksandrov: Laughing Matters*. Bristol, UK: Intellect, 2009.

Taylor, Richard. "The Illusion of Happiness and Happiness of Illusion: Grigorii Aleksandrov's *The Circus*." *Slavonic and East European Review* 74, no. 4 (1996): 601-20.

---

[15]   After the release of *Circus*, Lebedev-Kumach wrote a stanza praising the new Stalin constitution (not included here).

IVAN THE TERRIBLE

Ivan Groznyi

Part I completed 1944, released 1945; Part II completed 1946,
released 1958; Part III, unfinished

Part I: 99 mins

Part II: 85 mins

Director, Screenplay: **Sergei Eisenstein**

Cinematography: **Andrei Moskvin and Eduard Tisse**

Art Design: **Sergei Eisenstein with Isaac Shpinel' (sets), Lidiia
Naumova (costumes), Vasilii Goriunov (makeup), Rostislav
Zakharov (choreography)**

Score: **Sergei Prokofiev**

Sound: **Boris Vol'skii**

Editor: **Sergei Eisenstein with Esfir' Tobak**

Production Company: **Mosfilm**

Cast: **Nikolai Cherkasov (Ivan the Terrible),
Liudmila Tselikovskaia (Anastasiia Romanova, Ivan's wife),
Serafima Birman (Efrosin'ia Staritskaia, Ivan's aunt),
Pavel Kadochnikov (Vladimir Staritskii, Ivan's cousin),
Mikhail Nazvanov (Andrei Kurbskii), Andrei Abrikosov
(Fedor Kolychev, later Filipp, Metropolitan of Moscow),
Aleksandr Mgebrov (Pimen, Metropolitan of Moscow, later
Archbishop of Novgorod), Vladimir Balashev (Petr Volynets),
Mikhail Zharov (Maliuta Skuratov), Amvrosii Buchma
(Aleksei Basmanov), Mikhail Kuznetsov (Fedor Basmanov),
Semen Timoshenko (Livonian ambassador),
Vsevolod Pudovkin (The Holy Fool, Nikola), Erik Pyr'ev
(Ivan as a child), Pavel Massal'skii (King Sigismund
of Poland), Ada Voitsik (Elena Glinskaia)**

Ivan the Terrible is a strange, complex, and haunting film; a difficult film made in difficult times. It has been controversial since even before it was released and its meanings have long been contested. Eisenstein was commissioned to make the film on Stalin's direct orders and it was widely understood that such a film should glorify Stalin in the guise of Ivan and justify the violent terror of both regimes. Eisenstein, however, had a more complicated project in mind. From the very beginning of his preparation for the film he saw Ivan as a complex man subject to contradictory impulses for both violence and remorse. And although his portrait of Ivan is based partly on Stalin, it isn't *always* about Stalin or *only* about Stalin. The film contains a critique of absolute power and mass violence, but Eisenstein's primary goal was to understand the kind of power hunger that leads rulers to subject their own people to reigns of violence. It is undoubtedly informed by the history Eisenstein lived through—the degeneration of the idealistic revolution into a cult of personality and mass terror—but it is not always easy to see where his present shapes his view of the past.

Eisenstein made the film difficult to read for three reasons: to convey the contradictions in human nature, to defeat censorship, and to defy the conventions of Socialist Realism by raising hard questions without clear answers. Writing about *Ivan the Terrible*, therefore, poses several difficulties. First, the film was never completed; it was butchered by censorship and some scenes that were removed have been lost. We have the complete screenplay, which Eisenstein wrote in 1941 and published in the literary journal *Novyi mir* (*New World*) in 1943/44. However, Parts I and II depart in significant ways from the published screenplay, so it provides only the roughest guide to the director's intent for the unfinished Part III.

Second, the film's plot is intentionally deceptive. Both to evade censorship and to explore a variety of themes, Eisenstein depicts the events in Ivan's life in ways that simultaneously seem to praise Ivan as a visionary leader, to damn him as a brutal tyrant, and to sympathize with him as a tragic, divided, and lonely man. Understanding the relationships among these thematic threads is one of the challenges this film poses.

Third, any attempt to understand the plot is complicated by a similar degree of ambiguity in regard to each of the film's characters. Ivan himself is difficult to pin down. At various times, Eisenstein identified Ivan with Stalin, with his own father, and even with himself and he saw all of these characters (including himself) as deeply divided figures, torn between contradictory desires. In any given scene it is difficult to determine which Ivan (or Ivans) we are meant to see.

Fourth, in *Ivan the Terrible* Eisenstein experimented with much more than narrative and identity. The film contains the director's current thinking about individual psychology, artistic creativity and spectatorship, and the ways cinema might trigger feeling and thoughts, and enable transcendence, or what he called *ekstasis* (ecstasy). Dense networks of repeated and inverted images, imitations of animation, strange and exaggerated gestures, masks and disguises, cross-dressing and character substitutions work together (or against each other) to form a shifting, layered series of episodes that comment on *all* of these subjects at the same time. Understanding this unusual structure and distinguishing the film's various conceptual strands is another of the puzzles *Ivan the Terrible* presents.

Finally, writing about *Ivan* is complicated by the contradictory reception it received in the 1940s when it was produced and by the mistaken assumptions people routinely make about artistic production under Stalin's regime. Because Part I of *Ivan the Terrible* received the Stalin Prize (a kind of combination Academy Award and Presidential Medal of Honor), and Part II was banned only a few months later, many people have assumed that the two parts of the film differ radically in their portrait of the all-powerful leader, but this assumption is false.

Difficulties such as these give the reader some indication of the almost infinite complexities involved in this remarkable film, but I have not introduced them here to scare you away. I offer contradiction and ambiguity as an invitation to appreciate this great director's powerful imagination and to enter the rich world of the film as he wanted us to: with more questions than answers and with curiosity about the complexities of art, power, violence, and human experience.

Such a complex film is also difficult to summarize, but here is a short synopsis of the plot. Eisenstein's *Ivan the Terrible* follows the tsar from his traumatic childhood through his efforts to establish a modern, secure and unified state in the face of opposition from the established aristocracy—the boyars—the Orthodox Church, and hostile neighboring states. Eisenstein selected incidents from Ivan's life to explain both his achievements and his violent methods. This approach challenges the audience to consider whether the ends (national unification and imperial expansion) justify the means (intimidation, demagoguery, deception and terror). A lifelong distrust of the boyars is rooted in childhood experiences: their poisoning of his mother and their greedy exploitation of international treaties to line their own pockets. When he is crowned as tsar, he announces that he will make Russia strong as a nation by weakening the powers of the aristocracy and the church and by challenging foreign domination of Russia. The boyars respond by trying to unseat him when he is ill and then to unnerve him by poisoning his wife, Anastasiia. After his friend and leading general Andrei Kurbskii turns traitor, Ivan turns to new friends for advice: Maliuta Skuratov and Aleksei and Fedor Basmanov. They advise him to form a new army, loyal only to Ivan, an ominous band of brothers called oprichniki. When the church, represented by another close friend, Filipp, opposes him, Ivan has Filipp's family executed. When the boyars, led by Ivan's aunt and nephew, Efrosin'ia and Vladimir Staritskii, threaten to assassinate him, Ivan tricks them into murdering Vladimir instead. And when (in Part III) the oprichnik leaders, the Basmanovs, are found to be stealing from the state, Ivan has the son Fedor kill his father Aleksei. The only individual Ivan can trust is his spy and executioner Maliuta Skuratov. By the end of Part III, Ivan defeats all his domestic and foreign enemies and reaches the Baltic Sea. He is at the height of his powers but he is utterly alone and Russia is in ruins, everything sacrificed for the Great Russian State.

Background

In January 1941, Eisenstein received a visit from Andrei Zhdanov, a senior Party official and head of the Politburo's Cinema Commission. Zhdanov brought Stalin's request that Eisenstein make a film about the sixteen-century tsar, Ivan the Terrible.[1] This commission was part of a campaign to polish the reputation of prerevolutionary Russian rulers and to justify the centralization of power under Joseph Stalin. With the centralization of power in the 1930s, Stalin's government sought legitimacy in historical precedents that had been rejected during the revolution period. Soviet historians developed new histories of tsarist leaders that lauded their efforts at modernizing Russia, centralizing its government and expanding its power. By the early 1940s, historians of Ivan's reign (1533-84) went so far as to justify the terror he unleashed, during the period known as the oprichnina. Mass violence was viewed as necessary for establishing the modern centralized state against the opposition of the reactionary aristocratic elites—the boyars—and the Orthodox Church, and for securing its borders against its predatory neighbors.[2] This was the storyline Eisenstein was expected to follow.

Ivan the Terrible as a Whole

Eisenstein could have made a relatively simple film glorifying the Russian ruler and confining his creative energy to aesthetic elements of the film. But as he put it in April 1941, when he confessed in his diary that he was tempted to write a realistic, conventional script,

---

[1] *Kremlevskii kinoteatr, 1928-1953. Dokumenty* (Moscow: Rosspen, 2005), 690.

[2] On the Stalinist historiography of Ivan the Terrible see Maureen Perrie, *The Cult of Ivan the Terrible in Stalin's Russia* (Basingstoke: I.B. Tauris, 2001); Kevin Platt and David Brandenberger, "Terribly Pragmatic: Rewriting the History of Ivan IV's Reign," and "Internal Debate within the Party Hierarchy about the Rehabilitation of Ivan the Terrible," in Platt and Brandenberger, eds., *Epic Revisionism* (Madison: University of Wisconsin Press, 2006); Bernd Uhlenbruch, "The Annexation of History: Eisenstein and the Ivan Grozny Cult of the 1940s," in Hans Günther, ed., *The Culture of the Stalin Period* (NY: St. Martin's Press, 1990).

he resisted because of "the guilt of not sticking one's neck out!"[3] He chose instead the more difficult task of trying to neither damn nor glorify Stalinist tyranny in the image of Ivan, but to explain how Ivan became the kind of ruler he became. That he managed to create a film of great cinematic innovation, intellectual depth, *and* political critique is a testament to Eisenstein's brilliance as a filmmaker and his insight into the ravages of Stalinism on his country and on himself.

In both published articles and private notes, Eisenstein wrote that he wanted to "humanize" the tsar, to look beyond his one-sided reputation for brutality in order to understand what motivated him: "Not to whitewash," as he put it, "but to explain."[4] Eisenstein seems to have approved of Ivan's campaign to expand Russia's empire and centralize power in the hands of the tsar at the expense of the boyars, so he was driven to understand how a talented and committed leader could become a brutal tyrant, a demagogue and a mass murderer. Early in his research he reported his wish to understand "the process of becoming such a character as he became."[5] Eisenstein was well aware that a film with such a conception of Ivan would require a special strategy to evade criticism. "The most effective way of hiding something is to put it on display," he wrote.[6] In *Ivan the Terrible*, Eisenstein used several forms of subterfuge. He put "on display" a surface narrative that was politically acceptable. Then he proceeded to undermine that surface with diversionary tactics.

The surface narrative of *Ivan the Terrible* is the story that made the screenplay unobjectionable. Many viewers have accepted it as the primary narrative meaning of *Ivan the Terrible* in part because it corresponds to a common socialist realist plot. The hero sets off

---

3   RGALI (Russian State Archive of Literature and Art), 1923/2/1165/4 [4 April 1941].

4   S.M. Eisenstein, "*Ivan the Terrible*: A Film about the Sixteenth-Century Russian Renaissance," in *Writings*, 4 vols.: vol. 3, 191 (London: British Film Institute, 1988-96).

5   RGALI, 1923/1/552/55 (in English in the original, spelling corrected).

6   Eisenstein, *Beyond the Stars*, in *Writings*, vol. 4, 453.

on a quest, the hero is challenged, the hero overcomes obstacles, and at last, the hero triumphs. In this case, Ivan's goals are the establishment of the Great Russian State unified in the name of the people and the reclamation of Russia's ancient lands for imperial glory and security against external enemies. Ivan triumphs over boyars, the church and foreign enemies as well as over his own internal doubts to persevere in his efforts to build the Great Russian State. The tsar repeatedly justifies violence as necessary to protect the Great Cause for the people, and against traitors. In the end, he defeats his enemies, establishes a unified state and expands the state's authority over new territories in the east by defeating Kazan', and in the west with victory over Livonia on the Baltic Sea.

Eisenstein undermines this acceptable narrative in several ways. First, the actual plot departs significantly from the stated plot. Eisenstein plays to the expectations of his audience—that a film about the all-powerful ruler of the sixteenth century will reflect positively on both his own historical role and the role of the all-powerful ruler of the twentieth century—and then he defies those expectations.

The titles that introduce the film tell us exactly what we are to expect:

> This film is about the man
> Who in the XVIth century first united our country.
> About the Grand Prince of Muscovy
> Who out of separate discordant and autonomous principalities
> Created a mighty and unified state.

These lines frame our image of the tsar as bold, victorious, majestic, a Russian national hero. But the plot quickly takes a turn away from these themes. Instead of unification, and in the midst of military glory, attention is focused not on heroism and achievement but on conflict, betrayal, accusations, illicit flirtation, treason, murder, conspiracy, terror and violent annihilation. As early as Part I, the state is not only *not* united, it is torn apart. And its tragedy is not due exclusively to the opposition of discordant, reactionary, selfish boyars, but also to Ivan's own ruthless pursuit of power and his chosen methods for dealing with boyar resistance.

Part I, which takes us up to the founding of Ivan's personal guard (the oprichniki) and private fiefdom (the oprichnina), and to the tsar's retreat from Moscow, shows Ivan to be a man who resolves to trick his people into submission if they do not choose him to rule over them and a man who creates his own army of inhuman sons without mothers or fathers to terrorize his political enemies. By Parts II and III, it has become the story of the man willing to destroy every living thing in his country in the name of an abstraction, the Great Russian State.

Further, the stated plot of the screenplay is undermined by the visual universe of the film. The heroic elements of the surface narrative were able to dominate perceptions of the written screenplay, precisely because it was presented textually, rather than visually. Themes connected with Ivan's conscience were less pronounced in the absence of the cathedral settings and religious objects that surround much of the action. The ubiquitous conspiracies and counter-conspiracies were less apparent to the first official readers of the script, without the repeated close-ups of sinister facial expressions and without the claustrophobia of the palace chambers where most of the action takes place. It is easier to believe in the goals of imperial power and state building before one has seen the bizarre movements and poses, the glaring and shifting eyes, the highly stylized and melodramatic mode of the acting, and the strangely disproportionate structures of the interior spaces. In other words, the surface narrative is powerfully challenged in a contest between words and images. The acceptable socialist realist plot unfolds within a visual universe composed of distortions, mirrors, historical falsifications, grotesque folk motifs, unsettling gender reversals, menacing icons, enormous, ubiquitous eyes, and a myriad of other images which destabilize meaning and leave us wondering what to believe.

Throughout the completed Parts I and II and into the unfinished Part III, the acceptable surface narrative and its challenging mirror images contest one another with increasing visibility and intensity. The confrontation escalates steadily from beginning to end. In Part I, the acceptable surface just retains its primacy; elements of heroism and self-sacrifice in the name of the Great Russian State still have the power to contain (though not to justify) the elements of vengeance and violence. In Part II they do equal battle as the contest between worthy ends and brutal means comes to a crescendo. In Part III, demagoguery, manipulation, violent annihilation, tragic loneliness and self-doubt negate the original appeal of the cause. Individual examples of disloyalty, treachery, deviousness and political maneuvering follow a similar trajectory through the three parts of the film. Consequences of treason, for example, become increasingly more serious and Ivan's strategies for dealing with his enemies become increasingly more convoluted and cruel.

This incremental process, by which the surface narrative is overwhelmed and destroyed, is set in motion by Eisenstein from the very beginning of his reading, thinking, and sketching out of ideas in early 1941. There was no decisive break between Parts I and II, no change of horses midstream, as is commonly thought. The structures of meaning, the mirrors and contradictions, the surface and the underground, the intensification of repeated motifs and actions, were all in place at the outset and although Eisenstein continued to refine his conceptualization of the film throughout (and after) production, the historical and political critique of tyranny in Russian history was in place well before shooting began. The critique is not presented directly. Instead, each step Ivan takes towards achieving his goal, each decision he makes, each reaction to opposition is shown to have increasingly disastrous consequences. The surface narrative (and the introductory titles) state that the boyars' opposition was rooted in their selfish and reactionary attempts to hold on to power in contrast to Ivan's unselfish purpose to create a Great State for the good of the people. Though this "positive" and "progressive" Ivan remains throughout the film, his own battle to retain power will erode his moral high ground, revealing the dangers of autocratic power. Ivan's choices and reactions illustrate the ways in which power and the desire for power corrupt its holders and destroy them as individuals whether they are from the people or the elite and whether their goals are "progressive" or "reactionary." As such, *Ivan* becomes a devastating critique of tyranny and a brilliant challenge to the conventions of Socialist Realism.

Ivan the Terrible: Part I

Let's examine some representative scenes to see how Eisenstein constructs this multi-layered narrative. Part I opens with a long, slow scene depicting Ivan's coronation and introducing most of the characters who will become his opponents. After crowning himself, Ivan makes a speech announcing his plan to unify the Russian lands at the expense of the power of the boyars and the wealth of the Church. The announcement establishes two contradictory narrative paths. On the one hand, it initiates a classic socialist realist parable about a great hero, facing and overcoming terrible obstacles to achieve a worthy goal. On the other hand, it shows Ivan as a fearful, manipulative tyrant who will carry out an unpopular policy, no matter what the cost to his people, because he deems it the right path. In this scene we are introduced to most of the major characters and their faces are all stamped with fear, uncertainty, hatred and paranoia. The only exceptions are some of the women in the audience, including Ivan's future wife Anastasiia, who eye Ivan admiringly with the kind of gaze offered up to Stalin in posters, paintings and films on display throughout the Soviet Union at that time.

The fate of the Great Russian State depends on Ivan's ability to retain the loyalty of his subjects. The major turning points in Part I come when Ivan tests his subjects and distinguishes the loyal from the disloyal. Much of Part I is taken up by tests of loyalty, displays of disloyalty, and the tsar's responses to each. Until Anastasiia's poisoning, he holds out hope that he can achieve his goal with the willing support of his people, including some of the boyars. The crisis at Anastasiia's coffin, where disillusion threatens to undo him, instead leads him to embrace demagoguery, coercion and violence. But even before that point, he uses political manipulation both to test those around him and to coerce their support. After the Coronation, the next three major sequences (the wedding, the popular revolt and the battle at Kazan') are all apparent displays of power, challenged by acts of betrayal.

The first direct challenge to Ivan's rule comes from a "dark mob" which floods into the palace, interrupting his wedding. The tsar easily subdues the rabble, but what makes this scene interesting are the various constructions of tsarist authority and the rhetoric that accompanies them. Under the leadership of Maliuta Skuratov, the crowd rushes into the palace to attack the tsar. Ivan pushes away his guards and Kurbskii intercepts Maliuta, who is suddenly overcome with awe, as is the crowd behind him when they see "the Tsar!" Ivan's legitimacy (questioned elsewhere in the film) is confirmed in the eyes of the people—with one exception. Nikola, the Holy Fool, remains defiantly on his feet and accuses the tsar and his boyar relatives of using witchcraft to murder people, squeeze blood from their hearts, and destroy their homes.[7] Maliuta chimes in with the claim that bewitched church bells were falling from their steeples.

Now Ivan steps up to the challenge. Ignoring the Holy Fool's claim to social justice, he turns the accusation of witchcraft into a joke—at Maliuta's expense. "A head that believes in witchcraft is itself like a bell...empty!" Then he abruptly shifts direction (not for the last time) and turns the joke into a sinister threat. "And a head can fall off all by itself? No, it has to be cut off." Next, he equates tsarist authority with coercive violence. Those who disobey the tsar's orders "will have their own heads cut off." Then, the threat of violence is directed specifically at treasonous boyars and finally emerges as a general principle or rule: "A tsar can only rule if he holds the reins. A state without reins is as uncontrollable as a horse without a bridle." The crowd is in his hands by the time the scene is interrupted by the ambassador from Kazan, with the same single exception, the Holy Fool Nikola. Nikola's image has multiple resonances here. A defiant voice of the people, holy fools often said what others were afraid to say. The Pskov Chronicles reported that a Holy Fool named Nikola shamed Ivan the Terrible into sparing Pskov (after Ivan had annihilated Novgorod) by appealing to his

---

7   Holy Fools were well-known but vaguely defined characters in pre-modern Russian culture. Often considered to have a special spiritual sensibility and moral authority by virtue of their eccentric or otherworldly demeanor and their outsider status, they defied social and political norms for reasons ranging from political opposition to some form of mental incapacity.

conscience. Eisenstein's Nikola, on the contrary, is humiliated by Ivan and he alone remains unpersuaded by Ivan's linkage of tsarist greatness with tsarist terror. This Nikola is an odd looking Holy Fool, and almost totally out of place even in Eisenstein's idiosyncratic depiction of the sixteenth-century Kremlin. With his naked torso wrapped in heavy chains, this Holy Fool may also be seen as the stock image of a heroic Revolutionary-era proletarian: you have nothing to lose but your chains. He is subdued by the tsar, along with the rest of the rabble, but he goes down snarling in defiance, not laughing in complicity.

The surface narrative in this scene tells us that as Ivan asserts his authority over the people, he begins to win their allegiance. The way he accomplishes this, however, shows the origins of his demagoguery. Ivan asserts his authority by combining deceptive humor, capriciousness and threats of violence. First he wins the people over by pretending to join them in a joke at the expense of their comrade, mocking and scapegoating Maliuta, which traps the crowd in a kind of complicitous unity. Then, just when he has them in his grasp, Ivan shifts tactics without warning to make it clear that if they do not voluntarily support him, he will use whatever force is necessary to maintain power. It is an infantilizing gesture along with a masterful display of demagogic tactics, and it works: individual young men admire the tsar's cunning in humorously scapegoating Maliuta, even before he turns to threaten the boyars. It is easy to miss the full force of the tsar's threats of violence, because as he utters the words we are distracted by images of a different kind of boyar betrayal: Kurbskii's unsuccessful seduction of Anastasiia. This is neither the first, nor the last, time Eisenstein will follow sinister humor with real threat.

The scene at Anastasiia's coffin is the climax of Part I and a turning point in Ivan's evolving use of power. The surface narrative here tells us that Ivan's grief over the death of his wife and lone supporter leaves him in despair; that despair leads him to doubt the validity of his cause, the Great Russian State. But, just as despair threatens to destroy him, he finds the strength to continue. He chooses to seek support among the Russian people in order to continue the pursuit of the Great Russian State. Ivan's isolation in leading the

Great Cause is personally tragic and his willingness to overcome obstacles is heroic. His final gesture at the head of his wife's coffin, arms flung in the air, is one of determination and triumph.

Ivan's determination is depicted in politically positive or personally tragic terms, but what is the actual outcome of his resurrection from demobilizing grief? On the advice of Aleksei Basmanov, he throws in his lot with the Russian people and vows to unify Russia in their name. The key transition here, from the boyars to the people, has a positive ring to it, but only until we look below the surface at the consequences of Ivan's decision. The instrument of Ivan's resolve is none other than the oprichniki. Synonymous with terror, mayhem and destruction, the historical oprichniki were responsible for widespread cruelty and violence, a fact well known to Russian audiences. In his notes Eisenstein describes the atmosphere among the oprichniki as one of profound cruelty and disloyalty, where "man is wolf to man."[8] The satanic symbolism, first seen in Ivan's resurrection from illness and death earlier in Part I is reiterated in this second resurrection. That Eisenstein intended us to link this resurrection from grief with Ivan's earlier resurrection from death is cued by the repetition of an image of his head in the same position, horizontal, as in the deathbed scene. Ivan lays his head back on his wife's coffin, echoing the Christ-like pose, and his beard forms a crucifix with the black candle behind it. At precisely this moment, when he reaches the nadir of grief and despair, he experiences a sudden surge of life-giving force: his grief becomes fury and his terrible vengeance is born.

But the oprichniki are not only the devil's army, they are the devil's family. When Basmanov recommends forming the oprichniki, he tells Ivan to "choose men who will renounce everything, who will deny father and mother to serve only the tsar and the dictates of his will." In other words, Ivan creates the oprichniki in his own image: alienated from all human and kinship ties, dedicated only to the political father, the tsar, and an abstraction, the Great Russian State. Basmanov goes so far as to *give up* his own son, Fedor, to Ivan.

---

8   RGALI, 1923/2/125/2.

In this embrace of the abstract and renunciation of the familial, Ivan intimately and tragically entwines the personal and the political, the individual and the national.

This act, the founding moment of the oprichniki, is one of both supreme patriotism and cold sacrifice: Alexei's offering of his son is a double deception. His main goal, it turns out, is not to support the state for its own good, but to elevate his own family and guarantee its continuity through his son. He abdicates his role as father in order to increase the power of his family. Alexei gives Fedor to Ivan as the first son of the oprichniki, but he also enhances his clan's power by offering Fedor to Ivan as a replacement for Anastasiia: he marries the Basmanov clan into the dynasty. And the next time Ivan seeks support for his cause, he will turn away from the dead Anastasiia to ask Fedor what he should do. When Fedor offers him the same simple loyalty that Anastasiia had, Ivan kisses his wife good-bye and welcomes his new children into the world.

Ivan caps the scene by discarding the idealism of the first enunciation of his Great Cause. The first time around, at the Coronation, he claimed the need to centralize power for the worthy goals of protecting the independence of the Russian lands and making a Great State. Now, in what Ivan tells us will be "a new Coronation," the tsar seeks "limitless power,…enabling him to relentlessly consummate the great task." What justifies this "limitless power" and "relentless" dedication? If it was Anastasiia's murder, then the motive is merely vengeance rather than a great historical mission. Eisenstein goes out of his way to emphasize not only Ivan's renewed commitment to his glorious cause, but a transition to pushing the cause beyond its original (and politically reasonable) limits.

The finale of Part I shows the entirety of society (peasants, clergy and boyars are clearly identifiable) coming to the tsar in supplication, falling into his trap. Ivan tested the Russian people by abdicating the throne; they have come to beg him to return and rule over them. With this act, the people abdicate their own authority in order to submit to the tsar for the purpose of supporting an abstraction, the Great Russian State. At the end of Part I, the dream of a unified, independent state (*samoderzhavie* in Russian) for the good of Russia and its people has been replaced with the reality of one-

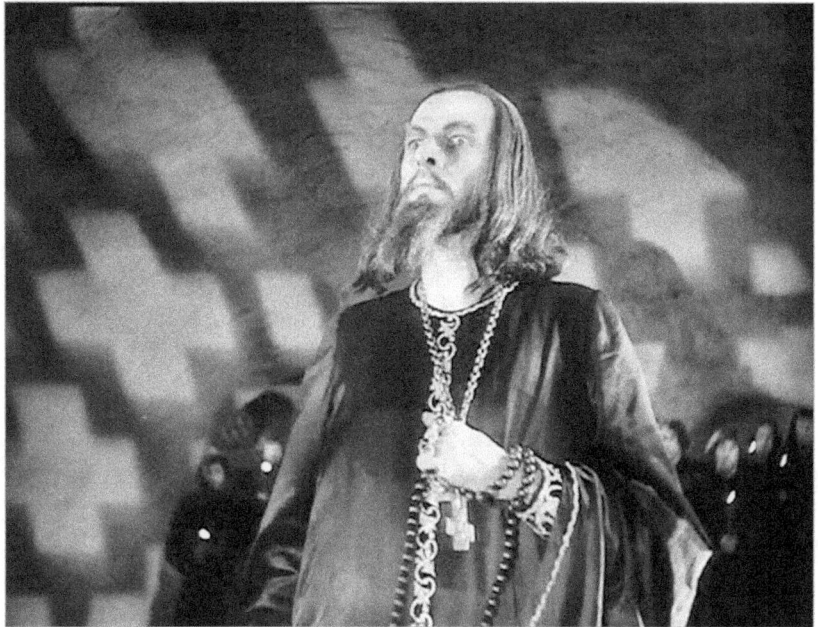

Fig. 72. Ivan Prepares to Meet the Russian People at Aleksandrova Sloboda

man rule, in which the ruler is isolated and his power centralized and unlimited (*edinoderzhavie*). He rules in the name of the people but he has created an instrument to secure and protect the tsar's power in case of opposition, the dark, wolfish and terrifying iron brotherhood of oprichniki.

The magnificent shot compositions of the finale emphasize the enormous power of the tsar and the miniscule insignificance of the people. Ivan has been speaking warmly with Maliuta about his fears and hopes as they wait impatiently together for the people to arrive, but when the people appear, Ivan drops his familiar persona and adopts a regal mask (Fig. 72). He becomes a detached, impersonal, symbolic figure, an abstraction: the embodiment of the Great Russian State. The positive valence here is political: Ivan *is* the state, he embodies the people and the nation. However, in human terms, he is inhuman, set apart, dehumanized and superhuman. Eisenstein used repetition in the finale to powerful effect. In twenty-one separate shots Ivan is viewed from a variety of different positions, with the tiny figures of the people snaking across the snow, obeying his every gesture. Ivan is truly awe-inspiring, an abstract, ritualized image of magnificence.

Ivan the Terrible. Part II: The Boyar's Plot

In Part II, the orthodox surface narrative is increasingly challenged by the ominous elements coming to the fore by the end of Part I. On the surface, Part II consists of the tsar's successful struggle against his boyar and clerical opponents, now actively seeking to dethrone him. By the end, the boyars are utterly defeated and Ivan can turn, in Part III, to Russia's external enemies in the West and the glorious expansion of the empire. Tragically, the tsar feels compelled to act against his last friend, Fedor Kolychev, now known as the priest Filipp, and to destroy his relatives, the Staritskiis, Efrosin'ia and Vladimir. In eliminating his disloyal friends and kin, Ivan sacrifices his own well-being for the good of the cause. He sacrifices his conscience and his humanity but the State remains. By the end of Part II Ivan has moved forward with his state-building project, but the structure he erects is increasingly hollow.

By the end of Part II, deviousness is intensified by repetitions and reversals that multiply, usually in more sinister form, to expose the dangers underlying specific images of state power depicted in Part I or drawing more people into the vortex of disorder and murder. To list only the most obvious examples, the Coronation is duplicated in Kurbskii's entrance to the Polish court, in Ivan's return to Moscow, and in his "farcical" crowning of Vladimir Staritskii. The tsar's marriage to Anastasiia has already been mirrored in his "marriage" to Fedor Basmanov in the coffin scene and is repeated in Part II, in Kurbskii's "marriage" pledge of fealty to Sigismund, (which itself is mirrored in Ivan's caressing Maliuta before agreeing to execute the Kolychevs), and in the Feast of the Oprichniki in the black swans, the drunken oprichnik leaders, and most obviously in Fedor's female mask and dress. The poisoning of Anastasiia will reappear in the poisoning of Ivan's mother, in Fedor Basmanov's reenactment of the poisoning which forces Ivan to recognize that his own kin is against him and that he is both guilty and not guilty of poisoning Anastasiia, and in Ivan's offer of the same chalice first

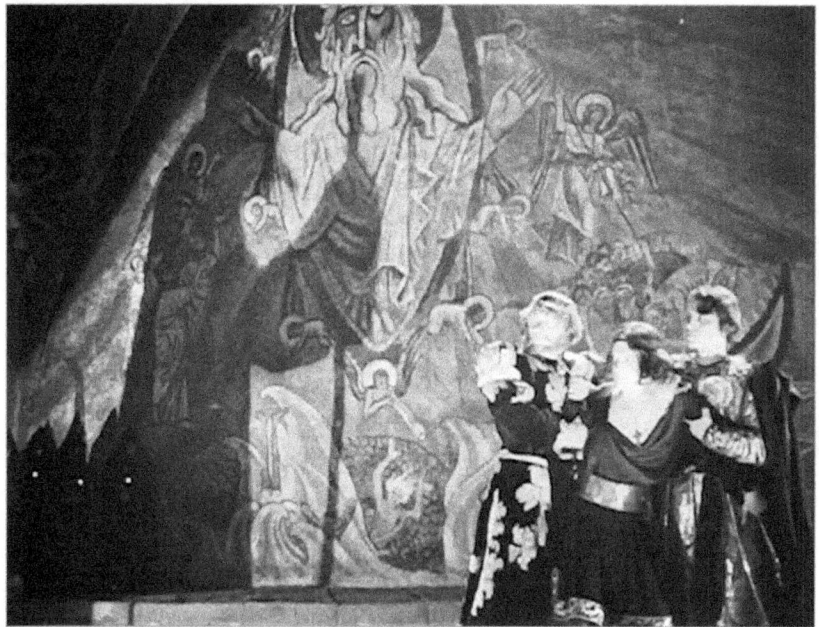

Fig. 73. After the Murder

(empty) to Efrosin'ia and then (full) to Vladimir, filled with the drink that will be his undoing.

Dual close-ups, cheek to cheek and nose to nose will reiterate the mother/child image of Ivan clinging to his dying mother: Ivan and Filipp, Ivan and Fedor, Ivan and Maliuta, Ivan and Vladimir, and Efrosin'ia and Vladimir. Finally, the finale of Part II, the snaking procession of ersatz-monk oprichniki filing through the cathedral, rhymes with the snaking line of the whole population at the end of Part I.

In Part II Ivan's strategies for protecting himself and his state, and for punishing his enemies, become more convoluted, immoral and cruel. In the final episodes, Ivan does not just protect himself from assassination, he manipulates a drunken, vulnerable child into taking the knife meant for him. He destroys the mother of that child, recalling (and avenging?) the murder of his own mother. He rewards rather than punishes the assassin Petr Volynets (Fig. 73), and though Ivan is now the unchallenged master of his domain, he bows down to the lowly novice (echoing his bow to the people

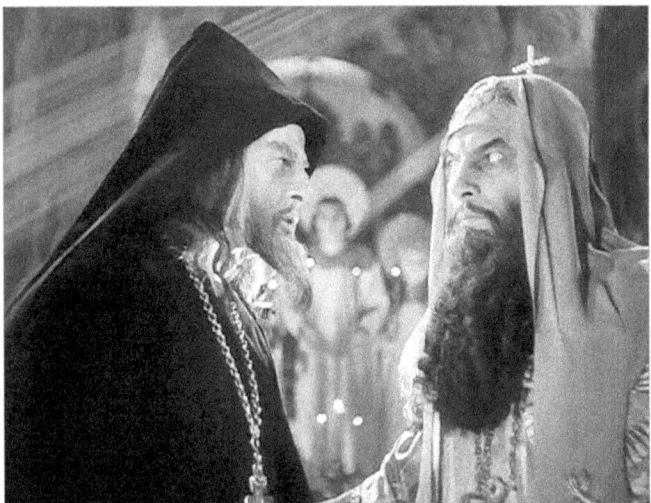

Fig. 74.
Ivan and Filipp

at the end of Part I and to Vladimir in the parody of Coronation), pretending to ignore the fact that the terrified Petr had come to murder him. Escalating deviousness and cruelty are mirrored by escalating remorse. Fits of repentance and doubt are followed by renewed commitment to the Great Cause, but each time that doubt is abandoned for determination, the cost of the Great Cause and the number of its victims grows.

In other words, Part II is less about subversive elements breaking through the surface narrative than about open combat between conflicting uses of power. Ivan can no longer pretend, despite extraordinary efforts at self-delusion, that his friends and family support him. The first half of Part II revolves around Filipp's opposition (Fig. 74) and Ivan's devious retaliation against Filipp's family, the Kolychevs. The rest of Part II is taken up with an even more convoluted action against his aunt Efrosin'ia and his intricate reversal of her plot to assassinate him. While removing old enemies (friend and kin), Ivan develops new relationships with oprichniki, his new friends and family, who will also ultimately betray and isolate him. The only progress Ivan makes towards the Great Russian State in Part II is the increasingly cruel and dehumanizing removal of obstacles.

Ivan establishes the major themes of Part II when he appears in the flesh on his return to Moscow from his abdication ploy. He divides

Russia, in the name of uniting it (into *zemshchina* and *oprichnina*) and announces that he will stamp out treason. Just as he set out his policies at the beginning of Part I, Ivan's speech at the beginning of Part II can be seen as a new Coronation speech following the new Coronation he announced at the end of Part I. We see shots of his young servitors, the oprichniki, threateningly ranged along one wall with the old boyars in their cumbersome brocade caftans lined up along the opposite wall of the throne room. Finally, in a double blasphemous reversal, Ivan forces the boyars to their knees while raising his oprichniki to their feet, and claims God-like powers. "…as God created man in his own image, so I have created men in mine." As if on cue, Filipp sweeps into the hall like an avenging angel, shouting, "These plans come not from God…but from the Devil!" In the surface narrative, Filipp's accusation can seem to be not much more than a religious cliché from the representative of Ivan's clerical opposition. However, the prevalence of demonic imagery already associated with Ivan, including the sacrilegious statement he has just uttered, give credence to Filipp's accusation. Throughout Part II and culminating in the Feast of the Oprichniki, Ivan will increasingly be associated with Satan and the oprichniki with little devils.

Ivan defends himself against Filipp's accusation with flashbacks to his childhood, in scenes originally intended to go at the very beginning of Part I and reinserted here in Part II. The Prologue, as it was called, offers a key explanation for Ivan's behavior and a justification for his desire for revenge against the boyars. The first childhood scene opens with a shot of Ivan, age seven, alone in an empty, darkened antechamber: fearful, watchful and vulnerable. Suspense turns to nightmare when he hears a chilling (though stagy, melodramatic) scream and discovers that his mother, Elena Glinskaia, has been poisoned by boyars. She warns him against trusting the boyars, clutches him to her cheek, and moments later is taken away, arms dragging limply across the floor.

After establishing Ivan's inability to save his mother from the boyars, Eisenstein shows him unable to protect his country from mercenary foreigners and boyars who are in cahoots with them. A slightly older Ivan appears in the throne room during trade negotiations. He timidly mounts the throne and listens in, unable to intercede as Shuiskii and Bel'skii, two powerful boyars (opposite in appearance, twins in self-interest), argue over which group of foreigners will control Russian trade. Political debate is a mockery, Ivan's power as ruler is a farce, and Russian leadership is a joke. Both Ivan and the country over which he rules are powerless and victimized by powerful forces around them.

Back in the tsar's chamber, Ivan leaps out of his victimhood. He emerges from silence, interrupts the boyars' pointless bickering and asserts Russia's need for independence. Shuiskii and Bel'skii just laugh at him. Ivan reasserts his intention to make Russia independent of foreign control. The boyars just laugh harder. Here is another, slightly altered example of alternating humor and threat. Shuiskii and Bel'skii are clownish in their arguing; their opposite appearance adding to the vaudeville comedy. But Shuiskii lacks Ivan's cunning. He quits joking to challenge Ivan's legitimacy, his father's identity, and his mother's fidelity before attacking Ivan physically. The young tsar lashes back, making the final leap from victim to victimizer by ordering Shuiskii's arrest. This first taste of power scares Ivan: in a brilliant bit of direction, Eisenstein has him bark out the order, "Seize him!" while stepping backward and protectively covering his face. Ivan straightens his clothes and, addressing the camera, says for the first time, "I will reign alone... I will be Tsar." When Ivan shouts "Seize him!" the innocent boy casts off his innocence, gets a taste of blood and experiences power all for the first time. Individual power and Russia's independence are closely identified with, and only possible through, violence and retaliation. Ivan comes into his own as tsar by ordering a man arrested and executed.

Eisenstein invested the Prologue with both autobiographical experience and with his understanding of human and cultural evolution. As a theorist, Eisenstein had a long-standing interest in the creative process and the way ancient myths and legends offered explanations for origins and transitions. He came to believe that transitions of all kinds—in individual development, between generations and in national histories—were traumatic and accompanied by violence. He believed that myths about such

transitions represented actual, not metaphorical, experiences in human evolution and that individuals replicated those stages in their personal development. Eisenstein found confirmation for these hypotheses in his reading about Ivan and in own his life with his father.[9] He believed that adult tyranny and cruelty were defenses developed in reaction to childhood vulnerability and fears and that a profound shift occurs in the transition to adulthood, when individuals discover their own authority. Frightened or victimized children will mimic those they feared in order to displace them. If the passage to adulthood requires the ouster of a difficult or tyrannical parent, the transition can be traumatic and violent. And that violence will bear within it the seeds of more violence. For Ivan, the first act of defiance and the first taste of power are intoxicating and addictive. According to Eisenstein's notes, Ivan tastes "first blood" in ordering Shuiskii's arrest and again on viewing the corpses of the Kolychevs, the first executions that he orders as tsar. In both cases, "first blood" intensifies his desire for vengeance and his willingness to shed blood to achieve it.[10]

Close observation of Erik Pyr'ev's subtle characterization of the young tsar, however, brings out both sides of the future tsar's character. Pyr'ev conveys the watchful exterior and placid mask the young Ivan wore to disguise his fear and hatred of the boyars, and in the last shot, he captures the fires of hatred and ambition within. A shadow of the young tsar's innocence and appeal remains throughout, but his emergence as tsar is the emergence of a beast, the prey becoming the predator. His commitment to predation is restated in one of the strangest scenes in this strange film. After allowing Maliuta to execute innocent members of Filipp's family as a lesson to all who might consider treason, Ivan shuffles into the scene, as if in a trance. He bows, starts to cross himself, stops and then glares at the corpses. Pointing off-screen to the bodies, he flings himself backwards, arching his back but straining and pointing

---

9   RGALI, 1923/2/1172/8-9 [7 January 1944]. The autobiographical and psycho-analytical will be discussed in more detail below.

10   RGALI, 1923/2/1172/9 [7 January 1944].

forward, head up but eyes down, as if to embody contradiction literally. It is a moment of excruciating suspense and one of the central transitions in his life: will his first real taste of blood propel him further or end here? "Too few," he whispers, calling for more death. From this point forward, Ivan's animal instinct for vengeance will give him no rest.

The remainder of Part II will consist of his victory over two attempts to restrain him. First, Filipp tries to shame Ivan into repentance with a performance of "The Fiery Furnace," an allegory about a tyrant and three innocent victims. But looking into this mirror and seeing himself as the wicked Babylonian King Nebuchadnezzar, Ivan not only does not repent, he embraces terror, and echoing the Prologue, asserts himself yet again: "I will be what you call me: I *will* be Terrible."

Then, the final scenes of Part II, The Feast of the Oprichniki and the assassination of Vladimir Staritskii, show Ivan (and Eisenstein) at the height of their powers. Ivan towers over everyone around him, controlling each moment like a master puppeteer. The oprichniki dance, laugh and swirl about the room as if they were mere extensions of the tsar's demonic energy. He overcomes the most serious challenge to his rule without breaking a sweat. And he makes sure that his powerful new lieutenants, Aleksei Basmanov and Maliuta Skuratov know their place as his "slaves." Ivan is all "greatness and shrewdness" here, but in reaching so high he isolates himself still further from people and defies the human being within. These final episodes are thickly layered with repeated motifs, mirror images, substitutions and reversals, yet while they allude to and even articulate contradictions, they point to Ivan's undiluted power and the clear-eyed, cold-bloodedness with which he uses power here at the end of Part II. In the face of all this evidence of Ivan's demonic tyranny, it takes an effort to remember that Stalin found the Ivan of Part II to be insufficiently ruthless, indecisive and weak.[11]

Eisenstein's method reaches its apex here in the final episodes of Part II. All of his themes—political, aesthetic, psychological,

---

11   Eisenstein, "Stalin, Molotov and Zhdanov," in *Writings*, vol. 3, 299-300.

philosophical—are represented by each character's multiple shifting representations, which come together as overlapping motifs rather than in some more realistic way. Fedor's multiple roles as Ivan's agent, wife, son, and eyes surround the tsar as a reflection of his great and terrible, seductive and disturbing authority. The absence of the mother, Efrosin'ia, subjects her defenseless son Vladimir to that predatory power.

Meanwhile the cat ensnares the mouse. In total control, Ivan feigns weakness and ignorance. Vladimir responds to Ivan's supplication, his drunken head on Ivan's knee, mimicking the previous scene in which Efrosin'ia persuaded him to participate in the plot. Just as Fedor is the son to two fathers (Ivan and his natural father Alexei), Vladimir is forced to choose between Ivan and his natural mother, Efrosin'ia. He makes a poor choice.

Ivan's seduction of Vladimir is interrupted by Aleksei Basmanov, whose usefulness is about to run out. Sweating and drunk, Aleksei chastises Ivan for consorting with boyars, especially with a Staritskii. Here a number of interesting reversals take place, all of which bear striking resemblance to Communist Party politics of the preceding decades. Ivan has the power to utter statements that diverge significantly from reality, challenging our ability to distinguish truth from lies and implicating anyone who believes either one. Agreeing with the tsar's lie makes one a lackey and a fool, but defending the truth against the tsar's word makes one another kind of fool.

Ivan tells Basmanov that it is not his job to advise the tsar, when in fact that had been his job: Ivan had taken his advice to create the oprichniki.

Ivan tells Basmanov that it is not for him to raise his hand against the tsar's relatives, when in fact that was exactly the job Basmanov was hired to do.

When Basmanov reminds him of this, Ivan denies it, saying that his own relatives are more precious than allies not related by blood, "I don't hack down oaks to make room for wretched aspens," though the destruction of the boyars and the elevation of the low-rank and commoner oprichniki is exactly what Ivan had done.

Ivan tells Basmanov that "the ties of blood are sacred," when in fact, Ivan has finally opened his eyes to his relatives' betrayal and is in the process of engineering their punishment for it.

When Basmanov guardedly suggests that the ties of spilt blood bind them more closely than the blood of kinship, Ivan pushes him aside and says, "You are not my kin. You are my slaves," deflecting responsibility for the blood spilled and repudiating the oath.

This almost endless maze of reversals and contradictions is a repudiation of the politics that allowed Ivan to gain absolute, "Terrible" power. Now at the pinnacle of his power, Ivan renounces the policies that put him there and destroy the individuals who helped him get there. Ivan realizes that to hold power alone, his goal since the Coronation in Part I, he needs not only to destroy his original enemies, the boyars, but also to protect himself from his new allies, the oprichniki.

By now Ivan has realized that his new allies have turned out to be as bad as the old enemies. Aleksei Basmanov wants power and wealth for his family more than he wants glory for the Russian State. Here, two political principles come into conflict. The old kin-based power of the boyar families is challenged by the new mass-based power of the oprichniki, who renounced kinship ties and place their loyalty in the tsar himself. The boyars are ruthless in pursuit of power for themselves and their families. The oprichniki are ruthless in their protection of the tsar, but it turns out that they seek the same kind of power the old elite enjoyed. In successfully supporting the tsar and his ideology, they undermine his cause. This repudiation of the sacred oath marks Aleksei as an Enemy of the State, but it also shows his essential humanity: he cares more for his natural son than for the abstract ideal of the state. Aleksei is as divided as Ivan. Ivan's counterfeit concern for his "son" Vladimir is reversed in Basmanov's genuine concern for his son's future. Both contradict stated vows to achieve their ends: Ivan's vow to destroy the greedy boyars and Basmanov's vow to place political loyalty above loyalty to his family. In both "fathers," the Oath and its repudiation prove a tragic flaw. Both reveal the corrosive morality of striving for power and the tragedy of autocratic, one-man rule.

These failings of the oprichniki were to be developed in Part III, when Ivan's revolution would begin to devour its own children, but they are prefigured here. In addition to the dialogue, the visual display of the episode with its intensely sensual elements brings a raw physicality into play. The explosion of color, music and motion draws attention to the instinctive, animal nature of vengeance, clan loyalties and the desire for power, which Eisenstein believed to be fundamental to human nature.

The repetitions and contradictions continue to multiply as the plot to kill Ivan unfolds and is thwarted. Vladimir, drunk now, "blabs out" the plot and then a parody of the Prologue, with its enthroned, powerless child, and the Coronation, with its transforming crowning, ensues. The duality Eisenstein strives for is never more clear than in this scene. Ivan is both victim (lonely child, lonely tsar, target of assassination) and victimizer (exploiting the child's helplessness, powerful tsar, engineer of assassination). A refiguring of the Coronation is apparent as Vladimir is crowned and discovers the thrill of power. Ivan's birth as tsar is reconfigured as Vladimir's death. The triangle formed by Kurbskii and Kolychev flanking Ivan at the Coronation is repeated here with Ivan and Fedor (at his most crocodilian and seductive) standing behind Vladimir's throne. Ivan (now the all-powerful tsar he forecast at the Coronation) bows down to the false tsar that he is sending to his death. Ivan is father to his people, but kills his son. He exchanges his tsar's garments for a monk's robe when he is at his most demonic. He covers both eyes when he has finally opened them.

Ivan lets Vladimir orchestrate his own demise. Actually this ploy is twice removed: Vladimir echoes Efrosin'ia saying "Take the crown, take the collar." Ivan answers Efrosin'ia through Vladimir (just as Efrosin'ia killed Anastasiia through Ivan) and dresses Vladimir in the royal garments. Recalling both the ill-fitting garments the young Ivan wore on the throne and his undressing by his servants, Vladimir drunkenly allows himself to be dressed and crowned. The masquerade makes Vladimir both assassin and martyr, both powerless and tasting power. When Ivan bows down to Vladimir, he is genuinely surprised to discover that the boy who refused to understand why anyone would want the crown, now finds it irresistible. "He wants it!"

At precisely that point, the real tsar puts an end to the game: "The farce is over," he shouts, but the farce is not over, it is becoming deadly serious. "Brothers, let us address ourselves to the Almighty," Ivan urges, as he turns away from the sacred bond of blood, luring his young cousin to the death planned for himself. The oprichniki, now dressed in black monks' robes, with black candles, accompany Vladimir to his death. They slowly proceed into the cathedral, where color gives way to black and white. Vladimir sees death awaiting him (and momentarily turns blue with mortal fear), the monks push him forward through the passages and doorways, into the shadowy cathedral where finally Volynets stabs him. Ivan's last rival is finished off when Efrosin'ia reveals herself and discovers her tragic mistake.

Part II has three endings. First, the oprichniki drag Vladimir away and remove the crown from Efrosin'ia's paralyzed hands, while Ivan and the oprichniki masquerading as monks file past her grief-stricken form. Second, in a parody of Christian ritual, the oprichnik-monks file behind Ivan through the cathedral to the altar, reciting their "dreadful oath" in the place of liturgy. Ivan sinks down, the oprichniki behind him drop to their knees revealing, on the fresco behind them, the devil being thrown into the flames of hell. The camera cuts back to Ivan, then to a close-up of Ivan, who looks up, covers both his eyes and mournfully answers the question he asked at the beginning of Part II, "By what right do you set yourself up as judge, Tsar Ivan?" unambiguously intoning his answer, "For the sake of the Great Russian State." And third (in color), Ivan almost addresses the camera directly, and tells us that a tsar must punish the guilty. Now that he has defeated Russia's internal enemies he can to take on the foreign forces who block Russia's power abroad.

In Part II Ivan achieves political supremacy, one-man rule, by allowing his enemies to kill each other off in a power struggle to dethrone him. "My hands are free," Ivan exults at the end of Part II, and that is exactly the problem.

Ivan the Terrible: Part III

Eisenstein never finished Part III, but no discussion of *Ivan* is complete without at least a brief reference to the ending that he wrote. The surface narrative is stretched thin in Part III. Little is left of the progressive aims announced at the Coronation, or at least little credible. The themes of betrayal, remorse, revenge, political manipulation, destruction and death are far more prevalent and powerful in the narrative than the establishment of Russian state power either at home or abroad. The stated goal of Part III is to reach the sea, but as Eisenstein's audience might have known, the actual war against Livonia was not a victory but a national disaster and what takes place on screen is not so much a battle against foreign enemies as against internal Russian traitors and defectors: Kurbskii, Pimen and the Basmanovs. At the end, Ivan's goal is achieved, but the country he rules over is devoid of all life and meaning. He not only embodies the state figuratively, he is the only thing left of the Great Russian State. Independent "self-rule" (*samoderzhavie*), which has become "one-man rule" (*edinoderzhavie*), has come to mean individual isolation and tragedy.

The extravagant, unjustifiable violence raises questions that have been lurking throughout the film that have acute contemporary significance. Is extreme, preemptive destruction brutally rational or is it an act of irrational paranoia? Does Ivan's Greatness justify Terror or does Terror undo Greatness? As in earlier actions that have sometimes been seen as signs of Ivan's "madness," there is no indication here of Ivan's being irrational or delusional. Incomprehensible cruelty is often labeled insane, but Eisenstein rejected such an understanding of Ivan. Extreme mass violence is terrifying and may be beyond our understanding, but it can be intentional and calculated. And this was no war against a foreign invader; the violence of Part III is a campaign of domestic terror.

Here in Part III, Ivan's vacillation between his superhuman persona and his fully human one becomes tragic conflict. Ivan can only create the Great Russian State because he has superhuman qualities and a cast of characters ready to act as his eyes, his hands, and his executioners. But his conscience draws him back down to human stature again and again. Destruction and salvation are mirror opposites that collapse into one inseparable whole. Ultimately, Ivan can only be a "tragic" figure because his motives were selfless and his goal was worthy one, and because he suffers remorse. Eisenstein throws even this justification into doubt with God's refusal to grant Ivan absolution.

Eisenstein sketched a large number of drawings for the final victorious scene of *Ivan the Terrible*. Several depict the waves breaking at Ivan's command and represent, as one is labeled, the "Apotheosis of Ivan." Another shows a disconsolate Ivan walking dejectedly down the beach, battle-smoke wafting up to the sky behind him, with an inscription that reads: "Alone?" Ivan has never been so alone, so why the question mark? Throughout the film, the surface narrative states that "he who is with the people is never alone." But the people are all dead or hiding. God is not speaking to Ivan. His dog, his brothers and his sons are all gone.

As we think back on the entire film, we have to wonder what did Ivan accomplish? What was the fate of the Great Russian State? Eisenstein's notes repeatedly testify to his belief in Ivan's "greatness" and the importance of his task for Russian history, but in the film, Ivan accomplishes the task in name only. Ivan's success and his glory never again match the height he attained in the light-filled cathedral under the Golden Rain at his Coronation. When he grasped the crown and placed it on his own head, he claimed power for the Russian State and embodied that power himself. That moment of dramatic transformation was his crowning achievement, his successful revolution. Everything afterwards was degeneration and survival. To succeed, to overcome the obstacles and enemies of Russian statehood, Ivan had to become ruthless, inhuman, and ultimately alone.

The Visual Universe of *Ivan the Terrible*

Ivan the Terrible is an extraordinary *looking* film. It contains such a wealth of images, motifs, symbols, musical cues, shot compositions and editing rhythms that one might be tempted to see the visual universe of the film as an end in itself. But nothing in *Ivan*

the Terrible is *only* artistically motivated. No gestures, images, objects or melodies are arbitrary or accidental. Repetition is neither ornamental nor neurotically compulsive, and images are not free-floating. The images in *Ivan* are designed to suggest connections and to hint at significance, but the repetitions and linkages are always slightly skewed or altered. This "almost, but not quite" set of connections makes discontinuity, distortion and disruption part of a system (rather than simply disrupting the system); a typical, paradoxical "unity of opposites" in Eisenstein. But while this structure complicates the process of deriving meaning from the film, it does not make meaning irrelevant or unattainable. *Ivan the Terrible* is an extraordinary film because of the dense ways in which Eisenstein has layered structure and narrative to draw viewers into his world, to awaken our curiosity, to engage us at our most primitive and intellectual, together, at our most contradictory.[12]

Eisenstein believed that a great work of art contains a tension between highly intellectual, conscious processes and emotional or "pre-logical" responses. Everything that makes *Ivan the Terrible* a haunting film (repetition, contradiction, acting, camerawork and so on) provides a tool for intensifying the poles of that tension and ultimately collapsing them in dialectical synthesis. The ever-increasing volume of formal elements can seem overwhelming, but whether or not we can nail down the significance of every single gesture and object, we can appreciate the feeling of being plunged into a strange universe of mysterious objects and behaviors, which Eisenstein used to draw the viewer into a dialectical process of thought and feeling. The thicket of associations seduces us into reading *Ivan the Terrible* at multiple levels, into marrying the logical with the pre-logical, into embracing the contradictory, into experiencing increasingly intense feelings and thoughts, and this

---

12   I do not have space here to discuss the many different aspects of formal experimentation that Eisenstein used in *Ivan*, such as the music, camerawork, lighting, frescos, architecture and set design, costumes, and eyes and beards, among many others. For those interested in reading more about the visual universe of the film, see works listed in Further Reading by Bordwell (2005), Neuberger (2003), Nesbet (2003), Thompson (1981), and Tsivian (2002).

process is intended to lead to an experience of *ekstasis*—a moment of ecstatic absorption that produces a leap out of our own everyday lives into seeing the world anew.

The primacy of the visual in *Ivan* draws attention to the unique ways films can tell stories, but the difficulty and elusiveness of the film's visual cues also remind us of the historical context in which *Ivan the Terrible* was made. The Soviet Union in the 1930s and '40s was a society where public speech had become a tissue of elaborate lies and where public masks were worn to protect murderers as well as their victims. Soviet culture had become a combination of crude, simplistic narratives with unambiguous messages and surrealistic discourses that made little rational sense. Eisenstein's visual universe conveys the difficulties of making meaning in a world where ordinary markers of meaning are no longer reliable.

Ivan the Terrible is not a "realistic" film. Its décor, costumes, sets, music and props thoroughly violate verisimilitude. Using a style known as "expressionism," the physical setting does more than convey the real world of the sixteenth century or provide simple background to the action. Instead, the details of setting and structure take on importance of their own by insinuating themselves into the construction of character, event and meaning. In realistic films, personality traits can be expressed by speech and action; in *Ivan the Terrible*, they are also signified by rhyming with symbols in wall frescos, objects on tables, shapes in the scenery, or cues in the music, which surround characters and actions and identify traits. Unconventional speech and exaggerated body movements join unconventional architecture and exaggerated decoration and costumes to create *Ivan*'s characters and comment on their actions. Repetition and musical accompaniment create a network of associations that link characters and events and allow us to analyze or judge them. At a deeper level, such structural elements create an environment from which we can derive the filmmaker's aesthetic and philosophic principles.

In *Ivan the Terrible* one of these central visual principles is strangeness itself. Strangeness serves a variety of purposes in the film. Eisenstein was one of many artists who called attention to the artificiality of art's representation of the world, by making the familiar seem strange. By "making it strange" the artist invites us to look at the world with fresh eyes.[13] Obvious stylization also served the narrative strategy of "hiding in plain sight." Among other things, these strategies keep the viewer from imagining that *Ivan the Terrible* was purely about the past, or purely about any one thing. *Ivan's* visual strangeness immediately challenges us to look beyond the surface of the film for meaning lurking behind and beneath.

Images without obvious associations function like contradictory motivations did in shaping narrative: they raise questions that remain in the viewer's mind. Why does the camera linger on Ivan's discarded fur coat? Why does Vladimir grow a beard? Why are men dressed like women and women like men? Why do so many characters draw attention to the act of dressing and undressing? Why do hands, feet, necks stretch out of their clothes? Why do people keep placing their faces unnaturally close to one another? Similar questions are raised by editing, shot composition, the musical accompaniment, and the acting. Distortion, disorientation, exaggeration and repetition force the viewer to make connections that might otherwise seem arbitrary or contradictory. They taunt us with their difficulty, begging for meaning and resolution, but remaining at least partially unresolved. Nothing is what it seems, but if Eisenstein has piqued our curiosity at all, we want to solve the puzzles he poses and look behind his masks.

Analysis of visual effects is further complicated by nature of the expressionistic style Eisenstein employs. Analysis of the acting, for example, cannot be entirely separated from a discussion of symbolic objects because certain gestures, like the stretching out of limbs or the movement of eyes function much like repeated symbolic objects, like candles or cloaks or icons of resurrection. Eisenstein's use of space, for example, needs to be analyzed as a symbolic object *and* a formal device of shot composition and camerawork.

---

13   The concept of *ostranenie,* or "making it strange," was introduced by the Russian formalist critic, Viktor Shklovskii. See "Art as Technique," in *Russian Formalist Criticism: Four Essays,* ed. and trans. L. T. Lemon and M. J. Rice (Lincoln, NE: University of Nebraska Press, 1965).

Ivan the Terrible looks so different from Eisenstein's previous films that many viewers took it to be a repudiation of his earlier revolutionary film practice, known as "montage." Eisenstein, however, saw *Ivan* as a continuation of the "montage" methods he had developed in *Battleship Potemkin*. Put simply, the purpose of montage had been to juxtapose images through dynamic, jarring editing in order to produce a strong, evocative effect on the viewer. While working on *Ivan*, Eisenstein was surprised to discover that he had constructed it along similar, though much more complex, lines. In both films, what he called "polyphony," or multiple voices and images, are brought together to produce a single heightened apprehensive experience for the viewer.

In silent film, the absence of sound and color limited the possibilities for dynamic filmmaking and drawing in the viewer. Eisenstein developed dynamic, rhythmic editing and the startling juxtaposition of individual shots in order to maximize the impact of cinema's purely visual effects. The addition of sound and color offered the filmmaker new dimensions for affecting the viewer. In *Ivan the Terrible*, Eisenstein uses the same techniques of dynamic editing and jarring visual juxtapositions, but now he expands the field to include combinations of images with sound, *within the shot*. He also juxtaposes startling images, not only from shot to shot as in earlier montage practice, but from episode to episode. Among his earliest notes are ideas about using "jagged rhythms" between shots and episodes to replicate the indistinct memories of childhood.[14]

He also developed two practices used extensively in *Ivan*, known as "vertical montage," and the "montage image." In vertical montage, music and image functioned the way single shots had functioned in earlier montage. Music and image are synchronized, but without coinciding perfectly, to achieve a more complex fusion of disjunctured elements. The "montage-image" refers to the way Eisenstein constructed complex characters and ideas through the juxtaposition of visual and conceptual fragments. As Yuri Tsivian puts it,

---

14   RGALI, 1923/1/554/62 [21 January 1941].

Ivan's true identity cannot be taken in at a glance. What matters is not so much what we see at any given time but our response to contradictory clues; a dynamic effect that Eisenstein used to call *montazhnyi obraz*, or montage image, in order to distinguish it from imagery that is merely visual.[15]

Eisenstein's later writings show how every single element in a film plays a role in the montage effect. When all these components come together, when "the unity of method penetrates the work as a whole," the result is not just a "unity of opposites" but a "new, higher unity," that could draw on all the senses.[16]

The aesthetic theories and formal devices used in *Ivan the Terrible* produced a high degree of correspondence between the narrative, the psychological underpinnings, and the formal structures of the film. This sort of coordination allows us to decipher Eisenstein's purposes and appreciate the film's extraordinary power, without diminishing the complexity at its heart. Interpenetrable layers of meaning and method, forms and identities that change shape, motifs that indicate similarities as well as differences criss-cross in ways that prevent any single idea or controlling argument to dominate our perception. Just the opposite: *Ivan the Terrible* offers alternatives, slippages and a mousehole to another universe to people living in a world of restrictive institutions, suffocating surveillance and compulsory conformity. Motifs with more associations than we can track, interruptions and resurrections deep in the layers of narrative, an independent side-story of shadow paths not taken, forms that change shape and merge into their opposites, all underscore the fact that in *Ivan the Terrible* nothing is what it seems, everything contains its antipode, and change is possible. Infinite associations, collapsed binary oppositions, shapes that constrain and expand, all suggest the very possibility of possibility for people forced to live underground or behind public masks and rigid public identities.

---

15   Yuri Tsivian, "Eisenstein's Visual Vocabulary" (DVD audiovisual essay), *Eisenstein: The Sound Years*, Criterion, 2001.

16   Eisenstein, *Nonindifferent Nature*, 302, 305, 327, in Further Reading.

Eisenstein's independent shadows and fluid musicality of forms present an alternative to mere binary exchanges that are rigid and doomed. The freedom from form offers a route out of the body—and out of the present—to *ekstasis* and transcendence.

Immersed in the sensually stimulating universe of *Ivan the Terrible*, it is possible to forget that Eisenstein operated in a world where movement and creativity were constrained, where state surveillance was invasive and often deadly, where the necessity of wearing public masks deformed private identity. In *Ivan*, Eisenstein invented a visual universe replete with escape routes. Through the collapse and inversion of restrictive social roles, through the possibility of eluding preordained forms, and through a refusal to accept rigid restrictions on identity and biography, he created in *Ivan* the possibility of possibility. Formal density and visual abundance emphasize the essential contradictions of life and show us ways in which history repeats itself in tragic cycles. But contradiction is not a dead-end. Forms offering collapse, multiplicity and diversity provide an escape from the pre-ordained and a model for discovering new ideas and feelings in well worn stories.

Joan Neuberger

Further Reading

Aumont, Jacques. *Montage Eisenstein*. Bloomington, IN: Indiana University Press, 1987.

Bordwell, David. *The Cinema of Eisenstein*. New York: Routledge, 2005.

Bulgakowa, Oksana. *Sergei Eisenstein: A Biography*. San Francisco: Potemkin Press, 1998

Eisenstein, S.M. *Nonindifferent Nature*. Translated by Herbert Marshall. Cambridge: Cambridge University Press, 1987.

------. *Writings*. 4 vols. Edited by Richard Taylor. London: BFI, 1988-96.

Goodwin, James. *Eisenstein, Cinema, and History*. Urbana: University of Illinois Press, 1993.

Kleiman, Naum. *Formula Finala*. Moscow: Eisenstein Center, 2004.

Kozlov, Leonid. "The Artist and the Shadow of Ivan." In *Stalinism and Soviet Cinema*. Edited by Derek Spring and Richard Taylor. London: Routledge, 1993.

Nesbet, Anne. *Savage Junctures: Sergei Eisenstein and the Shape of his Thinking*. London: I.B. Taurus, 2003.

Neuberger, Joan. *Ivan the Terrible*. London: I.B. Tauris, 2003.

------. "The Politics of Bewilderment: Eisenstein's *Ivan the Terrible* in 1945." In *Eisenstein at 100: A Reconsideration,* edited by Al LaValley and Barry Scherr, 227-52. New Brunswick, NJ: Rutgers University Press, 2001.

------. "Eisenstein's Angel." *The Russian Review* 63, no. 3 (July 2004): 374-406.

------. "Visual Dialectics: Murderous Laughter in Eisenstein's *Ivan the Terrible*." In *Picturing Russia: Essays on Visual Culture*, edited by Valerie Kivelson and Joan Neuberger, 201-06. New Haven: Yale University Press, 2008.

------. "Eisenstein's Cosmopolitan Kremlin: Drag Queens, Circus Clowns, Slugs, and Foreigners in *Ivan the Terrible*." In *Ours and Theirs: Outsiders, Insiders, and Otherness in Russian Cinema*, edited by Stephen Norris and Zara Torlone, 81-95. Bloomington, IN: Indiana University Press, 2008.

------. "Sergei Eisenstein's *Ivan the Terrible* as History." *Journal of Modern History* (forthcoming).

O'Mahony, Mike. *Sergei Eisenstein*. London: Reaktion Books, 2008.

Thompson, Kristin. *Eisenstein's Ivan the Terrible: A Neoformalist Analysis*. Princeton: Princeton University Press, 1981.

Tsivian, Yuri. *Ivan the Terrible. Ivan Groznyi*. London: BFI Publishing, 2002.